Anatole Litvak

ALSO BY MICHELANGELO CAPUA

Janet Leigh: A Biography (2013)
William Holden: A Biography (2010)
Deborah Kerr: A Biography (2010)
Yul Brynner: A Biography (2006)
Vivien Leigh: A Biography (2003)
Montgomery Clift: A Biography (2002)

AND FROM MCFARLAND

Anatole Litvak
The Life and Films

Michelangelo Capua

McFarland & Company, Inc., Publishers
Jefferson, North Carolina

LIBRARY OF CONGRESS CATALOGUING-IN-PUBLICATION DATA

Capua, Michelangelo, 1966–
 Anatole Litvak : the life and films / Michelangelo Capua.
     p.   cm.
 Includes bibliographical references and index.

 ISBN 978-0-7864-9413-2 (softcover : acid free paper) ∞
 ISBN 978-1-4766-1870-8 (ebook)

 1. Litvak, Anatole, 1902–1974. 2. Motion picture producers and directors—Ukraine—Biography. I. Title.
 PN1998.3.L57C37   2015
 791.4302'33092—dc23
 [B]   2015000074

BRITISH LIBRARY CATALOGUING DATA ARE AVAILABLE

© 2015 Michelangelo Capua. All rights reserved

No part of this book may be reproduced or transmitted in any form or by any means, electronic or mechanical, including photocopying or recording, or by any information storage and retrieval system, without permission in writing from the publisher.

Front cover: Anatole Litvak, 1937 (Photofest)

Printed in the United States of America

McFarland & Company, Inc., Publishers
 Box 611, Jefferson, North Carolina 28640
 www.mcfarlandpub.com

Table of Contents

Preface   1

1. From Russia with Love   3
2. Vive la France!   9
3. Hollywood Romance   23
4. Early Warner Years   34
5. Ann, Bette and Paulette   45
6. Late Warner Years   54
7. First-Class Cinema   64
8. Mixed Reviews   78
9. Far from Hollywood   93
10. Fading Away   106

Filmography   119
As Director 119 • Television Films 178 • Documentaries 180 • Other Works as Screenwriter 185 • Other Works as Producer 185 • Other Works as Director 186 • Projects with Litvak's Name Attached 186 • As Assistant Director 187 • As Co-Author 192

Radio Programs and Personal Appearances   194

Chapter Notes   197

Selected Bibliography   202

Index   205

Preface

While researching the lives of Vivien Leigh, Anthony Perkins, Yul Brynner and Deborah Kerr, I came across director-producer Anatole Litvak.* His mysterious origins and life intrigued me. In the pantheon of the popular American directors, Litvak kept a low profile—so low that, remarkably, nothing has been ever written about him apart from reviews of his films and short references to his wartime service as a combat documentarian making pictures in the field. Litvak has never discussed his life in print, giving only brief interviews exclusively related to his work.

Litvak's forty-year career took place in several European countries and in the United States. He achieved his greatest successes while working in Hollywood with Warner Brothers and Twentieth Century–Fox.

He received two Best Director Oscar nominations, for *The Snake Pit* (1948) and *Decision Before Dawn* (1951). Those two films along with *Mayerling* (1936), *Sorry, Wrong Number* (1948) and *Anastasia* (1956) are now widely considered classics.

Tola—as his friends and everybody in the industry called him—was a multi-lingual, cosmopolitan director, born in Russia into a Jewish family. He was capable of instructing his polyglot crews and casts in five different languages without pause, as many of his films were, in fact, international co-productions.

A real *réalisateur de films* chameleon, Litvak made films of all genres in several countries: Russia, Germany, England, France and the United States. One of his talents was the capacity to adapt with ease to the various cinematic cultures in each country where he worked. He proved his mastery at capturing with his camera faithful portraits of local atmospheres and all their subtleties. Litvak's rootless background is perhaps one of the reasons his works were too often criticized for lacking a consistent style, and somehow intensified the

---

*Anatole Litvak's name was often misspelled, especially in his early years in Europe. The spelling changes are explained in Chapter 1. In the filmography, the author has used different spellings of the name according to the original film credit. He consistently became Anatole Litvak at the end of 1933.

mystery around his persona since none of his pictures provide clues about Litvak the man.

Nonetheless, even a superficial look at his films would suggest that he has been unjustly overlooked or dismissed by film historians and critics. Litvak's works were star-studded pictures that successfully incorporated authentic location shooting. His main characters were often defeated by life. In his movies, women frequently played central roles as victims, captured in a spiral of events not of their own making, sacrificing themselves usually for love. Melodrama, comedy, noir, musical, documentary, and even a television period drama are all genres in which Litvak worked.

A charmer, a handsome man, a playboy, a Hollywood socialite, and a dashing figure, Tola is as fascinating as characters in his films. In his autobiography, Jean Negulesco (another underrated director) described Tola as "a good friend—complicated but devoted, considerate but selfish, primitive and sophisticated. It all depended on how you fitted into his ways and interests."

Probably the right definition of Anatole Litvak was provided by critic—film historian Richard Schickel who described him as "an adept, adaptable and prolific man; the kind of director that Hollywood likes best."

In writing this book, I have benefited from the help of many individuals and institutions, and from the assistance and support of friends, without whom the completion of this project would have been impossible. I would like to thank Yaakov Perry, Beatrice Nadalutti, the helpful staff of the British Film Institute Library in London, in particular Anastasia Kerameos and Adrienne Rasbrook-Cooper for their kind help; the staff of the Performing Arts Library at Lincoln Center, New York; the Museum of Television and Radio, New York; Christine Kruger from the Margaret Herrick Library of the Academy of Motion Picture Arts and Sciences, Beverly Hills; the staff of the British Library's Humanity Reading Room, St. Pancreas, London; Dollie R. Banner from Jerry Ohlinger's Movie Material, New York; Bibliothèque du Cinéma François Truffaut, Paris; Bibliothèque Nationale de France, Collections du spectacle, site Richelieu, Paris; Biblioteca Renzo Renzi–Cineteca di Bologna, Bologna; and Misako Ikuta. Most of all, my great gratitude goes to my editor Stuart Williams for his precious help and immeasurable generosity.

1

From Russia with Love

"I would have stayed at the little theater, had it not been transformed into an immense place absolutely unsuited for being an experimental theater. It was at that time that I chose cinema."
—Anatole Litvak

Place of birth: Kiev, Russia.
Date of birth: May 1902.
Beyond these facts, little information remains consistent among the available resources on Anatole Litvak's origins. The day of his birth—either the 10th or 21st—and even his birth name were shrouded in mystery after all official documents were destroyed during the Russian revolution shortly after his birth.

Mikhail Anatol Litvak. Or is it Mijali Anatoli Litvak? Anatolij? Anatole? Litwak or Litvak? Translating names from the Cyrillic alphabet is difficult enough without the added confusion of Litvak's own indecision on its translation. In his German films, he asked to be credited as Anatol Litwak. When working in England and France, he switched to Anatole Litvak, which was the same first and last name he used in 1939 when he was naturalized as an American citizen and the definitive name used afterwards.

In Kiev, the Litvak family was part of one of the Ukraine's largest Jewish communities. At that time, the Ukraine was still a territory of the Russian Empire. After the Ukrainian National Republic declared independency in 1917, Kiev became the capital of the new nation.

When Anatole was still a child, his father, a bank manager, moved with his family to St. Petersburg. Young Tola, as everybody would call him, spent his formative years in Russia's most cosmopolitan and sophisticated city.

In 1916, at the age of fourteen, a bright young Tola was admitted to the University of St. Petersburg as a student of philosophy. Neither the unstable political situation nor the violent Bolshevik Revolution and subsequent civil war disrupted Tola's studies. He completed them in five years, graduating with a doctorate in philosophy.

While attending the University of St. Petersburg, Tola became involved in the emerging avant-garde theater, making his debut on a local stage. He often travelled to Moscow, where he attended a few acting classes with Vsevolod Meyerhold and Yevgeny Vakhtangov (Stanislavski's pupil). Meyerhold and Vakhtangov were two great teachers and innovators of the new, experimental Soviet Theatre.

In 1922, after his graduation, Tola joined a small avant-garde theatrical company in St. Petersburg, now renamed Petrograd, while gaining admission into the State School of Theatre. By 1923 he had learned every phase of stage experience from acting and directing the productions, to operating the lights and helping to write the plays. During his time at Petrograd, he reportedly lived in a brothel, where apparently he was so well-known that the girls sheltered and mothered him (and more) until he left the country in 1924.[1]

Litvak explained years later the reason he decided to abandon the stage for cinema: "I would have stayed at the little theater, had it not been transformed into an immense place absolutely unsuited for being an experimental theatre. It was at that time that I chose cinema."[2] Under the new regime, the Soviet theater, like many other institutions, was expanding so quickly and out of control that Tola lost interest and joined the Soviet branch of the Danish film company Nordisk at the Nordkino Studios in Leningrad. According to *Sovetskie Hudožestvennye Fil'my*, Litvak's first cinematic work was *Le Chant de l'amour triomphant* on which he worked as assistant director to Vyacheslav "Viktor" Tourjansky. The picture, a Russian-French co-production set in 16th-century Italy, was based on a short story by Ivan Tourgenev. Due to Tola's reticence to discuss his life in Soviet Russia, there are no other sources confirming his participation to the production.

Tola became fascinated with the experimental work of young directors, who were now the energetic lifeblood of the Soviet cinema. Overcoming stylistic errors, the new generation of directors attempted to elaborate the expressive media of the film, paying particular attention to the importance of editing, photography and the progression of continuous action.

Immersed in this exciting atmosphere, Tola directed 1924's *Tatiana*, his first short feature; "a film about kids," as he later recalled. It starred Nikolai Petrov, a popular Russian actor with whom he co-directed his second film *Hearts and Dollars* in the same year. Produced by Kino Server and shot at the Lens Film Studio in Leningrad, *Hearts and Dollars* was a bittersweet story with an anti–American subtext: Two Russians bearing the same name but living in different economic conditions are both visited by a distant relative from the United States. The picture was released in France in 1925 as *Le Coeur*. In a 1953 interview with the French magazine *Cinémonde,* Litvak dismissed *Tatiana* and *Hearts and Dollars* as "atrocious."[3]

At Nordisk, Tola worked as assistant director and scenarist in at least ten other silent, very low-budget productions "without Kliegs or anything like that," as he stated in an interview.[4] The only record of his works as co-screenwriter appears in the credits of *Samiy Yuniy Pioner* (*The Youngest Pioneer* aka *A Very Young Pioneer*), a 27-minute short directed by Konstantin Derzhavin and released in January 1925. A young Russian actress, Galochka Levina, played the lead. The story centered on the adventures of an anti–West activist teenager at the wall behind the White Army's front lines in the days of the Civil War.

It is not known why Tola left Soviet Union in the end of 1924 for Germany via Paris. Litvak's biographical notes, included in several 1950s press releases for some of his Hollywood films, concisely stated: "The important UFA (Universum Film AG) studios in Berlin lured him from Russia." It seems that Tola's intentions were to study filmmaking techniques at Germany's most prestigious studio. His first recorded German film experience was working as editing assistant on *The Joyless Street* aka *The Street of Sorrow* (*Die Freudlose Gasse*), a silent melodrama set in Vienna and directed by G.W. Pabst. It starred Greta Garbo in her third film and featured Marlene Dietrich in a minor role. The picture was shot in 34 days with the crew working 16 hours a day. Its final cut had trouble with censorship in several countries for political reasons. After a year's run in Germany, an attempt was made to prohibit it. In America the part played by Asta Nielsen, a popular Danish star, was completely omitted, while in Russia the character of an American lieutenant, played by Einar Esterhazy, was turned into a doctor. In Britain, *Joyless Street* was given only one screening by the London Film Society on January 16, 1927. In 1937, when Garbo was an established star, a butchered dubbed version was released in the U.S. under the title *The Street of Sorrow.* In spite of horrible reviews, Garbo's presence in the picture was enough for the film to be remembered.

For a short period, Tola returned to Paris to work as one of the many assistant directors on the set of the epic silent production *Napoleon,* masterfully shot by French director Abel Gance. On location, Litvak became acquainted with Nikolai Alexander Volkoff, a Soviet émigré *cineaste* who had managed to escape his country during the Revolution. The director subsequently hired him as a gofer and later as a director's assistant on three of his productions, *Casanova* (1927), *Geheimnisse des Orients* (1927) and *Der Weisse Teufel* (1930).

Partially shot in France, *Casanova* starred Russian actor Ivan Mosjoukin. It was one of the most expensive projects made at UFA, the most technically advanced studio in Europe at that time. Like the other two pictures with which Litvak was involved, the film was produced by Noé Bloch (an uncle of Tola) and Gregor Rabinovitch.

Geheimnisse des Orients (aka *Sheherezade* and released in the U.S. as *The Secrets of the Orient*) was an Orientalist fantasy, a parody of the *Arabian Nights* with boldly exotic sets and costumes by Ivan Lochakoff and Boris Bilinsky. The silent French-German co-production was shot in 1927 at the Berlin studios. Volkoff cast Russian émigré actor Nikolai Kolin (aka Nicolas Koline) as the lead in this expensive, elaborate and visually stunning production that blended Eastern and Western motifs throughout visionary designs. Its "look" was partly inspired by the elaborately decorated productions of Alexander Benois and Leon Bask for Sergei Diaghilev's *Ballets Russes*.

Der Weisse Teufel, released in North America as *The White Devil,* was Tola's first experience with a sound film. He worked as assistant director and unit manager, and later as supervisor of the soundtrack that the producers decided to add once the silent film was completed. "Talkies," just introduced in Europe, attained enormous popularity, so the production was updated to follow the new successful trend. Music, static, noises and singing—but no dialogue—was added to the final print. *The White Devil* was based on Leo Tolstoy's final work, the short novel *Hadji Murat*, about an Avar rebel commander who, motivated by a desire for revenge, forges an uneasy alliance with the Russians he had been fighting. Once again Ivan Mosjoukin, Volkoff's *actor fetiche* (cast in nine of the director's films), was the leading male opposite the beautiful Lil Dagover.

After four years working with Volkoff, Tola was asked by UFA to direct his own picture. His fluent knowledge of Russian, German, French and basic English was an invaluable asset, since many European films, in those early days of sound, were made in different language versions. *Dolly Macht Karriere* (*Dolly Gets Ahead* aka *Dolly's Way to Stardom*) was a backstage musical showcasing singer-entertainer Dolly Haas, a popular international artist and later the wife of director John Brahm and caricaturist Al Hirschfeld. Regarding her first film experience, Haas explained in an interview that Tola saw her performing in the revue *Wie werde ich reich und glucklich?* (*How Do I Become Rich and Happy?*) written by Felix Joachimson and Marcellus Schiffer. "[Litvak] shot with me *Dolly Macht Karriere:* the traditional story of the little girl, who jumps ahead and become famous. In it I sang and performed in acrobatic numbers.... At that time there were no unions, I had to be at the studios at impossible early hours and then we would work from eight in the morning until nine at night. I was so exhausted that during the shooting I lived in a sanatorium in Potsdam or Neubabelsberg."[5]

1. From Russia with Love

In an article, a *New York Times* film editor from Berlin complained about the sound of the picture. "The singing sounds pretty diabolical, and the conversation is usually 100 percent tin. This is hard lines [sic] on Anatol Litwak, whose clever direction is thus badly handicapped."[6] Eight months later, in July 1931 when *Dolly Macht Karriere* opened in New York, the *Times* said its plot was of "stereotyped nature" but rated its acting and photography as "excellent."[7] In Germany, Haas won rave reviews and *Dolly Macht Karriere* was a box office hit.

It was Haas' breakthrough role. She instantly became one of the most beloved German actresses of the 1930s. Ultimately she acted in many productions, including the Hitchcock film *I Confess* (1953) opposite Montgomery Clift and Anne Baxter.

The great success of *Dolly Macht Karriere* guaranteed Tola the direction of his second film, *Nie wieder Liebe!*, which he co-wrote with Irma von Cube, a young talented German screenwriter. Their association lasted many years with von Cube involved as screenwriter in almost all of Litvak's early European productions.

UFA planned to shoot *Nie wieder Liebe!* simultaneously in German and in French, a popular trend followed by the studios before the introduction of dubbing. The French version *Calais-Douvres* was co-directed by Tola and Jean Boyer. The film was shot on the same sets with a shared cast but different distributors.

The *Nie wieder Liebe!* script was based on a play called *Dover-Calais* written by Julius Berstl in 1926. The shooting began on March 12, 1931, on the French Riviera. The female lead was twenty-five-year-old Lilian Harvey, English-born but long-based in Germany. She plays a young

Dolly Haas in *Dolly Macht Karriere* (1930).

woman who uses the excuse of trying to swim across the Channel to get aboard the yacht of a quirky millionaire. The young tycoon has made a $500,000 bet that he can keep away from women for five years. The woman has been hired by the man who is at the other end of the wager to check on him. In order to protect the tycoon and get him rid of the girl, the tycoon's valet breaks into his master's desk and arranges the evidence so that it will look as if the girl is the thief. Eventually she saves the rich man from losing his bet and marries him.

Along with Lilian Harvey, the large cast included eight other German film stars, all bilingual. *Nie wieder Liebe!* was essentially a musical comedy or an "operetta picture," as an article in the *New York Times* defined it.

On the set, Tola's assistant director was twenty-eight-year-old Max Ophüls, whose career as a filmmaker took off in the 1950s. He became one of the most celebrated directors of the time. In his autobiography Ophüls recalled how he was hired as assistant translator and later as first assistant director on the set of *Nie wieder Liebe!* "I fell in love with [Ina, a young actress working with him in a play] and quite by chance, while I was trying to find ways to stay near her after the completion of that play, I met a man who said to me: 'I've engaged a young director who speaks appalling German, and I need another young director to take care of the dialogues.' I took up his offer while in between times I was lucky enough to be able to put on three or four other plays in Berlin. And that's how I become assistant director to Anatole Litvak."[8]

Ophüls' son Marcel cast doubt on his father's story, recalling how Tola spoke several languages fluently and saying that it was very unlikely that he needed a dialogue coach for any of the film versions. "I am almost sure," commented Marcel, "that even without the pretty blond and the cafeteria, Tola would have hired my dad with his crew, just for pure friendship. *Les Ophulsiens* still wonder what Max Ophüls could have done during that shooting. By the reminiscence of the two main parts involved, I think I can answer: not that much!"[9]

In Germany *Nie wieder Liebe!* was a box office hit, especially among women because of the romantic tone of the story. In France, *Calais-Douvres* was distributed by L'Alliance Cinématographique Européenne (ACE). In spite of mixed reviews, it was well received by the public. In January 1932, the picture had a limited New York City release as *Never Love Again,* but with scarce attention from the public.

2

Vive la France!

> "Tola was a wonderful friend, very Russian. But I didn't like him very much as a director.... [He] made actors do the same thing six, eight, nine times but he was always using the first take in the film."
> —Annabella

Tola's huge success convinced French production company *Société des films Osso* that he was a solid name. The company offered him a contract to work in Paris, yet lent him to the small production company Fifra on his first assignment. Fifra was promoted by American screenwriter Dorothy Farnum and her husband, producer Maurice Barber, who had just bought the screen rights to Tristan Bernard and Charles Henry Hirsch's stage play *Coeur de Lilas*. Tola had lived in Paris while working as Abel Gance's assistant on the set of *Napoleon,* and now spoke fairly fluent (yet heavily accented) French, giving Tola a leg up on their first choice, director Maurice de Canonge.

Coeur de Lilas was filmed during the third quarter of 1931 with a $120,000 budget; it was the most costly picture made in France that year. Over a third of it was financed by the head of Fifra, young Dutchman Jean Hulswit, while the remainder was put up by its North American distributor United Artists.

Litvak's first crime picture is named after a prostitute whose glove is found near the body of Novion, a murdered industrialist. One of the businessman's employees is arrested but the unconvinced Inspector André Lucot conducts his own investigation while posing as an unemployed mechanic. He gets to know Lilas and falls in love with her. After a series of tragic events, Lilas admits she is Novion's murderer

Coeur de Lilas starred Marcelle Romée and André Luguet and introduced Jean Gabin and Fernandel, two rising international stars who would reign over French cinema for more than forty years. The film was not a musical but Gabin and Fernandel sang two of the three songs that played a key role in the story.

Although most of the production took place at Natan studios in Paris, assistant producer (later director) René Lucot recalls in his memoir Tola's extensive and meticulous search to find authentic Parisian locations prior to shooting. Even in the scenes filmed at the studio, Litvak used numerous non-professional faces to provide a more realistic background.

Lucot recalls that on the set, he met Dimitri Dragomir, Tola's assistant, whom he described as an ambitious young guy with a thick Eastern European accent who behaved more as Litvak's servant than a real assistant. On the first day of shooting, on a sound stage set as a judge's office, Litvak showed up two hours late. Barber nervously welcomed him and asked the reason for his delay. After greeting the crew with a gesture and a smile, Tola replied: "So what! I have been working since eight o'clock this morning. I came here directly from the courthouse. To direct my actors it's important that I know how a real questioning is conducted." Lucot wrote,

> Such professional conscience could only arouse respect. The producer did not dare remark that a visit to the courthouse could have been made in pre-production, avoiding to waste two hours of time to thirty people among actors, technicians and workers … without consulting others, [Litvak] decided to keep shooting overtime throughout the night and to start again early on the following morning. His demands are revealed by the interest he has in his work, justified by his talent, sometimes they are whims masked by lack of preparation, deep thinking or imagination.[1]

During and after the making of the picture, two awful events occurred. The explosion of an arc lamp on the set almost blinded Fernandel, then shortly after the film was completed, twenty-nine-year-old Marcelle Romée, who played Lilas, drowned herself in the Seine.

According to Lucot's memoirs, the atmosphere on the set always seemed very relaxed:

> Everybody gathered by the river La Marne to shoot the exteriors of a tavern visited on Sunday by young Parisian workers…. [I]t feels like being on holiday, the producer orders lunch for everybody inside the dive. After the meal, Litvak relaxes on a boat tied under the shade of a grove. He falls asleep. The sky is cloudless, the set is ready, the crew is ready, Barber is impatient but he doesn't dare to come close to the river bank where Dimitri, the faithful assistant, watches over his master's rest, looking out for his awakening.
>
> "René," says the producer, "would you be so kind to call Mister Litvak and tell him we are waiting for him?"
>
> I discuss in a low voice with my friend Dimitri. We are annoyed with each other. He is under the director's orders, but he wishes not to upset the producer; I am under the producer's orders, but I do not want to make the director angry. Have we spoken too loud? … Litvak opens his eyes, he stretches, stands up while the boat rocks, and he takes Dimitri's hand. He addresses with authority to the gathered crew, ready to start.

2. Vive la France!

"Everything ready? Good! All set! I have carefully pondered. That's the way we'll do it..."

We thought he took a siesta; mistake, his eyes were closed but he meditated! *Voilà* by the end of the day Mister Barber looks reassured, without needing a whiskey, Litvak is in perfect shape leading smoothly the production until dusk, furiously regretting not being able to delay it.[2]

Lucot said that watching Livak directing was an extraordinary learning experience. The image of the director apparently sleeping, watched over by his pupil, was impressed in his mind forever.

In *Coeur de Lilas*, Gabin appears only in a small supporting role, but by the time the picture was released in France on February 2, 1932, the actor was already a rising star. To capitalize on his popularity, the producers decided to bill him first on the film's poster and third in the opening credits, deceivingly marketing the picture as "a Jean Gabin film."[3]

French reviewers praised Litvak's poetic realism, particularly in representing the working class. What later film critics would call "real cinema" became Tola's signature in his first picture. When the film opened in France, Litvak clearly explained that "real cinema" should circumvent the pull of "filmed theater" through its attention to light, rhythm and images. "In *Coeur de Lilas* my cast only speaks when the situation demands," he commented. "I simply want to make cinema, nothing more, nothing less."

The film was his first major hit. At the time it opened in France, Litvak unpretentiously stated: "It may seem reckless of me to try to direct grim and cruel subjects which unfold at the lower depths of life when such subjects have already been treated with great technique by directors of great talents. My cast speaks only when it's necessary for the drama, and words are not the only sound effects. We use street noises and the sounds of motor cars.... It is necessary nowadays to remember that sounds are another support for a film's images, heightening their pictorial values, underscoring their visual beauty."[4]

A couple years later, in a brief interview with a French magazine, Tola proudly admitted that *Coeur de Lilas* was the best work he ever made since the final result was exactly what he wanted.

In the States, United Artists released it as *Lilac*. *Variety* described Litvak's direction as "very good," adding, "Film is a likely bet outside France for any theater where French original versions can be played, with every chance of drawing an audience really interested in a true picturization of a 100 percent French locale."[5]

Tola's reputation as a skilled filmmaker was enhanced by the financial and critical success of *Coeur de Lilas*. He returned to Berlin after UFA offered him the chance to direct another musical comedy, this time in a triple version, titled *Das Lied einer Nacht* in German, *La Chanson d'une nuit* in French and *Tell Me Tonight* in English. All three versions starred Polish-born Viennese tenor Jan Kiepura and German singer-actress Magda Schneider (the mother of actress Romy Schneider).

Originally the picture was going to be filmed only in German and French, but once it was shown to the Gaumont-British officials, it was decided to recall Tola to make an English edition with the same stars and a couple of English players: Edmund Gwenn (best remembered for his role as Kris Kringle in the 1947 film *Miracle on 34th Street*) and Sonnie Hale, who were sent over to Berlin. Hale starred as Koretsky, the second main male character, played in the French version by Pierre Brasseur and in the German by Fritz Schulz. The use of different editors, who also chose a different selection of songs, made the three versions slightly dissimilar with different running times.

The production *of Das Lied einer Nacht* began in early 1932. Cine-Alliance-Film was partnered with UFA. Irma von Cube and Albrecht Joseph wrote the screenplay. On the French version they collaborated with twenty-five-year-old Henri-Georges Clouzot, who was also Tola's assistant director on the French set and later became one of the most celebrated Gallic directors, making films such as *Les corbeau* (1943) and *Les diaboliques* (1954). John Orton was the co-writer of the English version. This romantic musical (Kiepura sings a few popular arias from famous operas) is the amusing story of an identity switch as a famous tenor decides to escape to Switzerland from his bossy female manager and changes places with a crook who could pass as his twin.

The picture was mostly filmed at UFA in Neubabelsberg, outside Berlin. Some scenes were shot on location in Vienna and in a small Swiss village by a picturesque lake. The charming scenery with snowy peaks and green valleys was used as scenic background for all three films and skillfully photographed by Tola's close friend, cinematographer Fritz Arno Wagner.

Kiepura, at the time one of the world's most popular tenors, had previously starred on the screen in two successful musicals. The picture became an instant winner at the box office and received excellent reviews in all the countries where it was released. In 1932, *Das Lied einer Nacht* was shown at the first Venice Film Festival; Kiepura and Tola introduced the film there.

In the United States, *Tell Me Tonight* opened in 1933 as *Be Mine Tonight*. *The Hollywood Reporter* praised Tola's work with enthusiasm: "Rather than photographing close-ups of the singer, Director Anatol Litwak has devised business for supplementary characters or directed attention to the beauty of natural scenic backgrounds. The result is a neat blending of entertainment for eye and ear."[6] (In the summer of 1956, the American press announced that

2. Vive la France!

MGM was to produce a remake of *Be Mine Tonight*, to be shot in Rome with American tenor Mario Lanza. The project was later abandoned.)

The international success of Tola's first films made him one of the hottest young filmmakers in Europe. He agreed to direct *Sleeping Car* in England after signing a one-picture deal with the producer and distributor of *Tell Me Tonight,* Gaumont-British.

Shot in English at the Shepherd's Bush Studios in London, *Sleeping Car* is a romantic comedy starring British matinee idol Ivor Novello and glamourous actress Madeleine Carroll. The picture tells the story of a handsome, flirtatious sleeping-car attendant on the train from London to Bucharest via Paris. The attendant embarks on an arranged marriage with an English heiress who is threatened with deportation from France after being convicted of driving her car recklessly. The cast also included Stanley Holloway, Claude Allister, Laddie Cliff and a young up-and-coming comedienne, Kay Hammond.

An Ivor Novello biographer states that *Sleeping Car* was made in an atmosphere of relaxed hilarity since Tola and his two stars thoroughly enjoyed

Madeleine Carroll and Kay Hammond in *Sleeping Car* (1933).

making this farce. Madeleine Carroll described the film as "an unhappy attempt at farce. I was completely lost among a lot of comics like Laddie Cliff. The only laugh I got was over a face-slapping scene. Ivor Novello hated his face slapped. I got the giggles, and we had seventeen takes."[7]

Tola seemed rather more interested in Carroll personally than in the outcome of the film.[8] At the time, the British actress was happily married to Captain Philip Astley of the King's Guards and was not interested in Tola's advances.

Despite mixed reviews, *Sleeping Car* was ultimately very popular with filmgoers. Many fans wrote Gaumont-British demanding that Novello and Carroll be teamed in future pictures. Producer Michael Balcon tried to persuade Novello to stay at Shepherd's Bush and star in a series of films, but the actor was determined to act in the theater. In fact, during the making of *Sleeping Car* he had been appearing every night in the stage play *I Live with You*.

Although the film was commercially successful, Tola despised it. After its original release in the summer of 1933, it disappeared from theaters until a version restored by the National Film Archive was presented at the London Film Festival in 1992.

In the summer of 1933, after a brief holiday on the French Riviera, Tola returned to Paris where he decided to settle permanently, since Hitler had come to power in Germany in early January. He was eager to start pre-production of his next picture *Cette Vielle Canaille* according to Nino Frank, editor of the French film magazine *Pour Vous*. In Frank's article, the director is described as "a young and happy man, with blue eyes and blond hair, who just arrived from Beauvallon, burned by the sun and with the storyboard of *Cette Vielle Canaille* in his pocket." Frank called Litvak "the ultimate polyglot director" and "the most Parisian of foreign directors." In the interview Tola claimed that, even though he had worked in various European cities, it was Paris where he worked best:

> Perhaps there is something in the air, in the way that the spontaneous spirit of all the collaborators suits my temperament perfectly. The French do the work in an instant that the English, who are nonetheless charming, take two hours to do with solemn slowness; or the Germans can only carry out with the most precise orders. The French may grumble but they do it so well! This is why I love Paris and its studios. In fifteen days I am going to start *Cette Vielle Canaille*. I have made a lot of changes to Fernand Nozièr's original play, of which I have retained only the central part of the story.... Afterward I'll direct another film in France that probably will be shot at the studios in Joinville, a "talkie" adaptation of a popular novel on aviation. I love to work on the most different subjects: someone should not restrict himself to a single genre. I made comedy, drama: honestly a dramatic story is more difficult to succeed than a comic one. But altogether I do no have any preference.[9]

2. Vive la France!

Tola adapted the original play in collaboration with Serge Veber, who had previously written the dialogue of *Coeur de Lilas*. *Cette Vielle Canaille*'s principal photography began at the end of July. Litvak originally wanted Charles Boyer in a major role. He was a great admirer of Boyer, especially after watching his performance on stage in *Le Bonheur* by Marcel L'Herbier. André Benim, a mutual friend, introduced them when Tola wished to have Boyer starring in his film. The French actor read the script and, although initially not particularly interested in the part of a young acrobat, suddenly changed his mind when he heard that Harry Baur had been cast as the other leading man. The idea of co-starring opposite one of the most popular and respected stars in France at the time moved Boyer to immediately accept the role. At the screen test, Boyer showed up accompanied by his latest conquest, actress Alice Field, who coincidentally was part of the original cast of the play and chosen by Litvak as the female lead. An unexpected offer to work in Hollywood in 20th Century–Fox's *Caravan*, directed by German director Erik Charell, made Boyer change his mind again. He bowed out of *Cette Vielle Canaille* at the very last moment. Boyer attempted to apologize to the enraged Tola, who ultimately cast Pierre Blanchar.[10] Despite Boyer's unprofessional gesture, the star would later become Litvak's go-to actor, starring in three of his pictures.

In *Cette Vielle Canaille,* Harry Baur played the role of Guillaume Vautier, a famous Parisian surgeon, who falls for Hélène (Alice Field), a pretty carnival vendor in Neuilly. After a physical quarrel with another woman, jealous of her love for young acrobat Jean (Pierre Blancar), Hélène ends up in jail. The surgeon bails her out and tries to seduce her. At first, Hélène accepts the old man's advances but later leaves him for the acrobat. When Jean is injured in a fall from the trapeze, Vautier puts aside his pride and performs a delicate operation, nobly saving the acrobat's life.

Off the set, Litvak was often seen in the company of Field. The two dated for a while but this suddenly ended when Tola became involved in his new project. *Cette Vielle Canaille*'s engaging plot, fast-paced tragic events represented without sentimentalism, and spellbinding photography pleased reviewers and the public. A classic, it was re-released in France in the '50s.

Cette Vielle Canaille opened in France in November of 1933 and premiered in New York at the Fifth Avenue Playhouse fourteen months later. On the billboards, the original French name was kept along with the translation, *The Old Rogue*—a slightly different title than *That Old Bum*, as it appeared in a positive review printed by *Variety* a year earlier.

Tola was now free to choose his scripts. A small article in the French magazine *Pour Vous* announced that his next project was titled *Mademoiselle Doc-*

teur. Once again Litvak teamed up with *Cette Vielle Canaille* producer Simon Schiffrin,[11] this time for a musical (based on a script by Irma von Cube and playwright Marcel Achard) about a doctor who falls in love with one of her patients who turns out to be a German spy. She ends up working for German intelligence during World War I. Georges Van Parys, who had written the score for *Cette Vielle Canaille,* was supposed to compose the music and the cast for the upcoming film included Jean Gabin, Alice Field, Pierre Renoir and Pauline Dubost. Then in the spring of 1934, the script was sold to Romain-Pines Films; Maurice Tourneur took over the direction. Eventually, G.W. Pabst shot the film two years later with a different cast and a new musical score.

The loss of *Mademoiselle Docteur* did not discourage Tola. In May he was already at on with a new production based on Joseph Kessel's bestselling novel *L'Équipage*. Maurice Tourneau had filmed the picture as a silent in 1928; it was released in North America as *The Crew* in June 1929. Tola, who loved the book, decided to re-write the script in collaboration with Kessel.

Kessel was a well-known novelist and a reporter famous for his legendary reportage from all over the world. During World War I he enlisted in the air force, and was later discharged with military honors. His war experiences were the source of his successful novel *L'Équipage*, published in France in 1923. Thanks to Charitonoff, the Russian owner of the trendy Parisian restaurant Poisson d'or, Kessel met several Russian producers, among them Noé Bloch. Bloch introduced Kessel to his nephew Tola and to producer Simon Schiffrin. Tola proposed that he and Kessel adapt and write the dialogue for a remake of *L'Équipage*. The author accepted, excited to embark on this film adventure, since he was not involved in the making of the silent version.

Every day Tola would meet with Kessel in a Parisian apartment located on 26 Quai de Passy along with young Jeanne Witta, whom the director had hired as a script supervisor. Her main task was to type Tola's description of each scene and Kessel's dialogue; both were indecipherably handwritten. In her memoir Witta described in detail her fruitful collaboration with Tola, who later asked her to work on his next feature, *Mayerling*:

> Litvak spoke his mother tongue [Russian] as good as French, German and English. In addition, he was a refined gentleman. He loved beautiful cars, especially fast Torpedo, he dressed himself with great consideration; this finesse was found again in the way that he very rarely mishandled performers and technicians. He presented a familiar, solid impression whilst on set but this did not prevent him from being demanding. All his films were meticulously prepared. Most of the scriptwriters he worked with had been formed in the German school—they worked with extraordinary care, leaving nothing to chance, checking the script for the smallest detail. Among all the writers, Litvak was particularly fond of Madame Von Cube, who had such a heightened professional consciousness that before writing a scene she would

rehearse it herself.... Once the script was done, he checked it and modified it depending on the kinds of lens he wished to use.[12]

Working on a daily basis together made Tola and Jef (Kessel's nickname) very close friends. They both had unruly private lives: Tola was a hardcore card player while Kessel was a heavy drinker, and they both exercised their craft with absolute rigor. In an interview with Kessel's biographer, Simon Schiffrin described the difference between the two friends. "Jef was a gentleman, he could give you everything. He had a big heart, 'a heart of a horse,' as Volodia Poliakoff used to say at the Poisson d'or. He knew he was 'important' but did not care, whereas Litvak, more rational, more reserved in everything, wanted to become *the* filmmaker after being a minor assistant director of Tourjanski [sic]."[13]

While the script of *L'Équipage* was still being shaped, Litvak made his first casting choices. Jean-Pierre Aumont was cast as Jean Herbillon, a young flyboy befriended by Lt. Maury, played by Charles Vanel. It is therefore a great source of consternation for Herbillon when he discovers that the woman with whom he's fallen in love is none other than Maury's wife, played by Annabella. The sexy French star was not Litvak's first choice; he wanted Marie Falconetti, whose amazing performance in Dreyer's *The Passion of Joan of Arc* (1927) was still fresh in his memory, but she was unavailable. Last to be cast as Captain Thélis, a daring aviator, ostracized by the other pilots because of his recklessness and standoffishness, was Annabella's husband, handsome Jean Murat.

Witta recalls that once the screenplay was completed, Litvak took her to an airfield in Mourmelon-le-Petit, where he had planned to shoot most of the exteriors. It was a large bare field surrounded by some hangars and semi-abandoned barracks. In the center, Fokkers and Berliets, old planes still in use for aerial acrobatic shows, were parked in line. "Within a few days, the aviation field was transformed into a movie set," wrote Witta. "At that time the necessary material was very heavy and bulky. To switch from a long shot to a close shot or to follow a conversation of two characters walking, the cameras had to be installed on a cart pushed by some stagehands. The two three zooms available in the world belonged to Paramount. Those carts moved on adjustable rails, a bump in the terrain or a stone would cause a change in the horizontality of the device. Consequently, the frame had to be changed as well and they had to start all over again."[14] Filming at Pathé studios in Joinville was not an easy task either. Several large screens representing the aviation field had to be installed along with some fake plane fuselages in order to look exactly like the ones used on location. Litvak strived for perfection, having each small detail checked multiple times. He also consulted with a military expert and got the support of the French Air Ministry. He boarded a Berliet biplane, together with the cameramen, to personally supervise the aerial combat scenes. Assistant director André Cerf remembered that Tola wanted those flight scenes to look as real as possible. In particular he demanded that visible flames would come out of the machine-guns. With the help of a technician, Cerf ripped some rockets from some old combat airplanes and filled them with powdered sugar, but for the final effect some kind of blowtorches also had to be used. "Litvak was a great filmmaker, who has not yet received the recognition he deserves." Cerf said. "Very meticulous, he knew what he wanted, especially with his actors."[15]

Among the crew members, the shooting of the scene with Charles Vanel became legendary when Vanel questioned Jean-Pierre Aumont: "Tell me, Herbillon, what's going on between you and my wife?" Tola asked for so many takes that the repeated sentence became hilarious. Aumont could not stop laughing each time Vanel delivered that line, forcing Litvak to ask for a new take. Taking vengeance on the director, Vanel played a small prank on him. He covertly attached some herrings to Tola's car radiator, which forced him to stop the vehicle several times on his way home because of the unbearable smell coming from the engine.

Annabella did not appreciate Litvak's meticulousness. "Tola was a wonderful friend, very Russian," she said in an interview. "But I didn't like him very much as a director.... [He] made actors do the same thing six, eight, nine times but he was always using the first take in the film. It was very funny."[16] On a different occasion she stated that even though she loved the film, she disliked her role as the unfaithful woman. In spite of all the problems, Cerf described the atmosphere as "pleasant" for everybody on the set, except that the producer was always looking morose because, according to him, the film and money were used too easily. Every day after shooting, the crew and the cast would meet at the Hotel de la Haute Mère in Châlons where they were all lodged, spending the long nights in an atmosphere of pleasant camaraderie.

L'Équipage was a real triumph. The story of the aviator torn between his love for a married woman and his friendship for her husband moved French audiences and thrilled the critics. Reviewer André Lang had the most flattering words for Tola: "[*L'Équipage*] is a very good movie.... Litvak is doubtless one of the rare foreign filmmakers, working in France, who belongs to us: because he respects our authors, because he has made his own our way of understanding and feeling and he has a taste for quality."[17]

But not everyone shared Lang's enthusiasm. In the picture Litvak used 200 meters of generic footage from Raymond Bernard's 1932 film *Les croix de bois* (*Wooden Crosses*) since both films were produced by Pathé-Natan. Dis-

2. *Vive la France!* 19

gruntled Bernard, with the help of Société des auteurs de Films, sued Litvak for breaching author rights.

In the States, *L'Équipage* was released in 1938 as *Flight into Darkness*, opening one year after Litvak had made RKO's *The Woman I Love*, the American version of the film.

Despite the incredible success of *L'Équipage*, Litvak was still considered a loner, outside the mainstream Paris production scene. The situation radically changed when he decided to direct *Mayerling*, the true and tragic story of doomed imperial love between Archduke Rudolph of Austria and his mistress Baroness Marie Vetsera. The script, based on the novel *La Fin d'une idylle* by Claude Anet, was a collaboration between Irma von Cube and Joseph Kessel. This moving story had already been filmed in Russia in 1915, in Germany as *Tragödie im House Habsburg* in 1924, and as *Das Schicksal derer von Habsburg* aka *Die Vetsera* in 1928.

Litvak began *Mayerling*'s pre-production while *L'Équipage* was being edited. He split his working day in two: First he would supervise the work in the cutting room with editor Henri Rust and his assistant Marthe Gauthier, a young woman from Alsace. (She happened to be a talented pastry cook, spoiling him by bringing him all his favorite cakes.) Later, Tola would go to his office on 26 Quai de Passy to discuss the progress of *Mayerling*'s script. Kessel and Tola were now bound by a fraternal friendship. Joseph appreciated Tola's compulsion for details while Tola was touched by the author's modesty, which was demonstrated by his willingness to cut or add to his dialogue as Tola deemed appropriate.

Unlike *L'Équipage*, *Mayerling* was almost entirely shot at the Pathé-Natan studios in Joiville. Litvak spent a fortune on constructing an exact replica of a grand Austrian imperial palace, claiming that this was the only way he knew to make a historical melodrama. The picture required the use of an incredible number of actors and extras dressed in lavish costumes, which Litvak personally selected. For the leading roles, he was able to have his first-choice artists. According to him, a half dozen top actors were anxious to play the role of the Archduke Rudolph of Austria, "including [Pierre] Blanchar," he was reported to say. "Except now he is much too old and never handsome enough to be matched against [Danielle] Darrieux." From the beginning Tola had in mind only Charles Boyer, who was doubtful about accepting the role. Boyer even suggested to Litvak that the renowned French actor Pierre Fresnay play Rudolph. Tola's reply was: "Why not Charles Boyer?—Fresnay could play Rudolf [sic] if there were no Charles Boyer. But for Charles Boyer there can be no substitute. I will not make the picture without you."[18] After a little cat and mouse game, Boyer agreed to wear a toupee and be transformed into the handsome Hapsburg archduke.

Danielle Darrieux, a rising star in French cinema, was cast as Baroness Marie Vetsera. She received a call from her agent who told her that Litvak wanted her in his next film opposite Charles Boyer, who had become an international film star and a romantic idol. Darrieux, who was working in another film, *Mademoiselle Mozart,* was slightly hesitant, intimidated by Boyer's celebrity status. Advised by her husband and her agent not to miss the incredible opportunity, she finally accepted. In order to appear in *Mayerling*, she had to abandon *Mademoiselle Mozart*. "All my salary from *Mayerling*," she recalled, "was barely able to cover the penalties I had to pay for *Mademoiselle Mozart,* which I was unable to complete before being Marie Vetsera. Charles Boyer was adorable and helped me a lot."[19]

As Jean Witta stated in her memoir, "The atmosphere on *Mayerling*'s set was more peaceful than *L'Équipage*. We did not have the same producers: Noé Bloch, Litvak's uncle, and Pathé were substituted by Émile Natan and Nébenzahl.... As a production manager Nébenzahl chose a man called Loewenberg. In order to save his boss money, Loewenberg made all his decisions without consulting Litvak—who, it goes without saying, did not agree. One night

Danielle Darrieux and Charles Boyer in *Mayerling* (1936).

when the production ordered all the extras who formed the audience at the opera to take off their costumes, Litvak demanded their immediate return as a condition to resume the shooting."[20]

The picture was made in five weeks with the crew working often overtime because many cast members had to respect previous engagements, some with theatrical productions, others (like Boyer and Darrieux) expected to resume work on other movies' sets. Throughout the shooting Tola and Boyer got along famously. On weekends they would often travel together to Deauville to gamble at the casino, where Tola particularly loved to show off beautiful women, mostly fashion models. He slowly acquired the status of playboy even though he always remained evasive when discussing his personal life.

On the set, Tola proved to have a funny sense of humor. Witta noticed that actor Vladimir Sokoloff, who played the part of the chief of police, would remain seated for hours every day waiting for the director to call him. She questioned Litvak; the reason he made the artist wait for so long, the director explained, was that Sokoloff needed to work in order to pay him back some money he had borrowed in the past and never returned.

Mayerling turned out to be a delicate film, tastefully directed and acted with subtlety and intelligence. Tola's masterful direction stressed the love interest rather than the political implications of the events, making the picture one of the most powerful tragic love stories ever filmed. Highly praised by critics of all countries, it became an international success and in 1937 received the New York Film Critics Award for Best Foreign Film.

Tola often pointed out that his film could not have been as strong without Boyer because "it is sublime tragedy and Charles Boyer is, in essence, a tragic artist."[21] The North American distribution rights were acquired by Pax Films, Inc., who originally had intended to dub the picture. Litvak and Boyer categorically opposed the idea and the film appeared on American screens in French with English subtitles. The presence of an established Hollywood star such as Boyer certainly contributed to the film's success, especially in the States where it was released in New York on September 13, 1937. *Mayerling* opened with great fanfare at the Filmarte Theater with a special gala premiere for the benefit of the League of Women Shoppers. First Lady Eleanor Roosevelt topped the list of influential patronesses. The language barrier did not stop the critics from writing rave reviews, which made *Mayerling* a box office success. The *Daily News,* at that time one of the largest New York City newspapers, alerted its readers, "Don't let the fact that the film *Mayerling* was made in France and the dialogue used in the great human drama is French keep you away from the Filmarte Theatre.... A knowledge of French is not essential to a complete enjoyment of the film. The English subtitles are concise translations of the dialogue, conveying satisfactorily the essence of French conversation and fully interpreting the action of the tense drama. So I repeat, don't let the language barrier prevent you from seeing one the finest dramatic films of the year."[22] Following a very long run at the Filmarte, Pax managed to get the picture into some small, artsy theaters all over the country. After breaking the house record in a movie theater in Pittsburgh, Warner Brothers acquired the distributor rights and released it in its own circuit theaters in Pennsylvania. Through 1938 *Mayerling* was shown in nearly 1500 American cinemas, grossing $250,000, a modest amount for Hollywood standards, but an extraordinary sum for a French import. *Mayerling* introduced quality French cinema to American audiences and the number of French films imported to the States tripled the following year.

3

Hollywood Romance

"Mr. Litvak is a charming and distinguished man, and the type who makes friendship such a delightful experience."
—Miriam Hopkins

Once *Mayerling* was completed, Charles Boyer hurried back to Hollywood. After the film was released in France he was sent a copy, which he privately screened for some of the biggest names in the industry. Suddenly the French picture became the talk of the town. It did not take long for Tola to receive a ticket to Hollywood, which came by compliments of Irving Thalberg, head of production of Metro-Goldwyn-Mayer. The producer was so impressed by the film that wanted to meet Kessel and Tola and offer them the opportunity to write and direct Boyer's next picture. The two friends were thrilled when, a few weeks later, they received tickets from Paris to Hollywood, via Le Havre, New York, Chicago, and Los Angeles, including six weeks in hotels with all expenses paid for them and two companions.

As a travel companion, Tola invited his close friend Roland Toutain, a French actor and songwriter who gained fame starring in *Le mystère de la chamber jaune* (1930) and its sequel *Le parfum de la dame en noir* (1931). Kessel asked his brother George to travel with him. At the end of January 1936, the quartet met at Saint-Lazare station in Paris to board a train to Le Havre. Tola and Kessel arrived very early, afraid to miss the train, while their travel companions showed up at the very last moment.

The crossing on the *Champlain* was uneventful except for a strong storm that hit the boat on the second day. Kessel and Toutain spent most of the time getting drunk at the bar, while Tola played cards at the casino.

New York was the first stop on the way to California. "Two unforgettable weeks," as Tola would tell his friends once he returned to France. He was particularly impressed with the quality of the shows on Broadway. Among the many plays he saw in those two weeks were *Dead End* and Bella Spewack's comedy *Boy Meets Girl*, a sharp satire on Hollywood, where making movies

Anatole Litvak, left, and best friend writer Joseph Kessel circa 1945.

was "the way Ford is doing automobiles." Tola stated in an interview, "I would say that at the time it was pretty much like that. It wasn't really very much a question of what we were doing or how well you do it—It was a question of making movies. The subjects were very superficial, to say mildly, and the people working in pictures were earning enormous salaries at that time."[1]

When they finally arrived to Hollywood, Tola and Kessel were immediately escorted to the studios to meet with producer Walter Wanger and a pair of screenwriters. Wanger was eager to discuss a film called *Sahara,* to star Charles Boyer and Madeleine Carroll. The producer handed Tola and Kessel an outline of the story, a desert melodrama involving the French Foreign

Legion. "I will try to make the picture as authentic as I can," Tola told the *New York Times*.[2] However, it was not as easy as it seemed. Once they began to work on the script, the triviality of the subject quickly turned them off.

Among many film industry moguls Litvak met during his stay in Hollywood, Harry Cohn, president of Columbia Pictures, stood out for his bluntness. Cohn told Tola that he liked *Mayerling* but objected to the director's choice of having almost all the scenes dissolve into the next. Asking him the reason for that choice, Tola's annoyed reply was, "Because I wanted it. That's all—there was no other reason for them. I dissolve once from a medium shot to a close-up because there was a certain rhythm to it."[3]

While Tola and Kessel continued struggling to write the *Sahara* script, producer David O. Selznick asked to borrow Boyer from Wanger for *The Garden of Allah* with Marlene Dietrich. Suddenly the *Sahara* project aborted and Tola and Kessel returned to France. Upon his return, Kessel published *Hollywood, Ville Mirage*, a memoir about the incredible experiences he had during the stay in Hollywood. The book was dedicated to Tola with the inscription: "To ANATOLE LITVAK, who taught me everything about a new job."[4]

While working in Hollywood, Litvak contacted every major film operation in town to inform them of his availability. The most interesting offer came from Jack Warner. Two months later Tola was once again preparing to cross the Atlantic to try his luck again in Hollywood. Jeanne Witta, Jean-Pierre Aumont and Blanche Montel accompanied him to Le Havre to say goodbye before he boarded on the ocean liner *Normandie* bound for New York.

"After descending the accommodation ladder," recalled Witta, "when I found myself on a bumpy tugboat that was taking us back to the port, I was rather upset: with Litvak leaving, I was losing 'my rock.' I felt as a stage curtain was dropping in a theater where I was all alone."[5] The screenwriter would meet Tola again in 1953 when she worked for him one last time on the set of *Act of Love*.

On the *Normandie*, Tola met thirty-four-year-old American movie star Miriam Hopkins, whose first screen success was in the 1931 horror drama *Dr. Jekyll and Mr. Hyde*, followed by her breakthrough in Ernst Lubitsch's *Trouble in Paradise*. Hopkins was at the height of her career, after being nominated for an Academy Award as Best Actress in the historical drama *Becky Sharp* (1935). She was returning from an eight-month holiday tour of Europe. One evening after dinner, she was introduced to Litvak in the first class lounge of the *Normandie*. For Tola it was love at first sight. He fell so madly in love that, on the last day of the crossing, he proposed to her. Hopkins, who had already divorced twice, laughed at him. She enjoyed the temporary interlude of shared fun aboard, but she was not interested in any serious relationship.

While in New York, they kept seeing each other, prowling around the city for hours. Miriam, who had a very distinct personality, independent but also very moody, did not give any false hopes to Tola. Her parting words before he left New York were, "Tola, darling, you're sweet. When we arrive in Hollywood, try to meet a young man, Jean Negulesco. He knows me well. He can help you." Tola was furious. When friends finally introduced him to Negulesco, he was very sarcastic. "So you're Jean Negulesco?"

"Well, yes I am," answered the baffled filmmaker, as he related in his autobiography. "Why?"

> "I crossed the ocean with Miriam Hopkins," Tola continued.
> "Lucky you."
> "I asked her to marry me."
> "Good God, why?" asked Negulesco.
> "Because I love her."
> "I still ask you why."
> "Haven't you ever been in love?" Tola said, still ironic.
> "Sure, many times. But not to marry," responded Negulesco.
> "Never been married?"
> "That's another story."
> "Miriam suggested that I meet you. That you can show me ways."
> "Ways?"
> "How to change her mind—to marry me."
> "That's kind of Miriam. I loved her for years, and I don't pretend to know one thing about her. She's one of the most exciting ladies I ever loved. She was kind to choose me—temporarily among so many admirers. But to know her, never."
> "Miriam talks too much—and talks, and talks. As a matter of fact, you have to wait until she takes a breath through her ramblings before you jump in to say yes or no. You don't get another chance for a long time."
> "I still don't know why she asked me to meet you. And I still love her," Tola insisted, puzzled.
> "Tola," I began kindly, "one phase I am sure about. Miriam loves life, and people, and knowledge. You have every asset she likes in a man, but do not ask her. Don't tell her what you want or how you feel. One night after much champagne and caviar and laughter and you're absolutely sure you've really had a good time together, order more magnum of champagne and one pound of caviar. Put 'em in your car and put Miriam in your car too. Carry her if you have to. She is petite. And stop at the first marriage place (of course you got the marriage license days ago). Open the magnum and ask the mayor and the witnesses to drink to your happiness. And get *married*. She'll love it. Not much of a script, but it usually works—particularly with Miriam."
>
> Indignant, Tola followed Negulesco's advice bit by bit and married her.
> And it was a *disaster*.⁶

The buzzing rumors of romance between Tola and Hopkins reached Hollywood from the minute he arrived in New York. Tola had searched constantly for his ideal woman, but while he went through periods of momentary infatuation, he had never settled down for long. His feelings for Miriam were completely different. When she was asked to comment about the romantic whisperings, her diplomatic reply was, "Mr. Litvak is a charming and distinguished man, and the type who makes friendship such a delightful experience."[7]

In Hollywood, Litvak struggled to find the right project. His ideas often did not match the interests of the studio executives he met. *The Hollywood Reporter* announced that he had been chosen to direct a new version of *The Phantom of the Opera* for Universal. In August, another article reported that Walter Wanger had hired him for an adaptation of the novel *Wuthering Heights* starring Charles Boyer and Sylvia Sidney. Neither project materialized.

Finally he signed a contract with Warner Brothers to make six films in three years. First in line was a Joan of Arc picture starring Claudette Colbert, based on Tola's own ideas. The script was written by Kessel and the music was composed by Arthur Honegger, who had composed the original soundtrack for *L'Équipage* and *Mayerling*. Seven months later, the press reported that the studio had abandoned the project and that Litvak would direct Colbert in *Tovarich*. Before beginning work for Jack Warner, Tola convinced RKO to produce the American version of *L'Équipage,* with the intention of casting Katharine Hepburn in the role originally played by Annabella. The picture was scheduled to begin filming at the beginning of 1937.

In June, happy with the outcome of his second visit in Hollywood, Tola returned to France with the idea of making a film in Paris before returning to America to begin filming the RKO version of *L'Équipage*. He told *Pour Vous* that, although he had received many offers on his return to Paris, none of them were serious. "So after four months spent in long discussions," he said, "I go back to Hollywood without making any film, without planning anything. I am disappointed, a little sick and in a really bad mood.... I just asked my French producers the easiest thing: to guarantee me that a film would be made. For this I was ready to make some sacrifices. I even offered to give up my salary, but they reassured me that I could have made the picture without any risk."[8] Since no serious producer could promise to find the necessary funds to make a movie on such short notice, Litvak gave up the idea altogether. He explained that he was ready to go back to work in Hollywood where upon completion of the RKO version of *L'Équipage,* four other movies were already lined up: the Joan of Arc bio, *Wuthering Heights*, an untitled project for Alexander Korda to be made in London, and a screen adaptation of the play *Tovarich* starring, once again, his favorite actor Charles Boyer. Of those four projects, only *Tovarich* would come to fruition for Tola.

Before working for Jack Warner, Litvak directed *The Woman I Love* for RKO—a film he later described as "an enormous mistake." Tola was very reluctant to shoot this remake of *L'Équipage*, but RKO executives convinced him that it was a perfect story for the American audience. Tola believed that the plot had to be re-adapted completely, but the producers insisted on leaving it the way it was, asking for very minor alterations. Not yet aware of what the American public really liked, Tola trusted the judgment of RKO and eventually directed the remake.

The working title of the film was *Escadrille*. It was later changed to *The Woman I Love,* apparently inspired by King Edward VIII's famous 1936 abdication speech, in which he referred to Wallis Simpson as "the woman I love." According to *The Hollywood Reporter,* Republic Pictures, a small movie studio, considered suing RKO over the use of the title because they had advertised a claim on it immediately after the abdication speech., The proceedings were dropped when the U.S. Copyright Office confirmed RKO's contention that they had acquired the title when they purchased the FBO Picture Corporation studios in 1928.[9] Even though the title *The Woman I Love* had nothing to do with the picture, RKO thought it would incite audience interest.

RKO wanted Boyer to play the role of Lieutenant Claude Maury. The French actor had a commitment with the studio for one more picture, but producer Albert Lewis held out for Paul Muni, a close friend and a popular star. Lewis was able to get Muni on loan-out from Warners after the actor saw *L'Équipage*. Muni thought the part would a be a nice change of pace; he dreaded being typecast into historical roles as in his last two films

Lewis opposed RKO's casting choice of the female lead, as he explained in an interview:

> Miriam Hopkins, with whom I had an unfortunate experience at Paramount when she defected from a Gable picture, was suggested by the studio to play the wife. She was now under contract to RKO, and over my objections, she was set. The studio had reason to regret this decision when Miss Hopkins again proved herself a disturbing element during the shooting. Muni refused to tolerate her behavior on the set. I threatened to remove her. The director offered to resign in protest. It was a miracle that the picture was finished at all. Miss Hopkins was not given another picture to do at RKO, but she gained a husband. She "won" Mr. Litvak![10]

I do not know what Tola's involvement was in the campaign for Hopkins to get the role played by Annabella in the French version. The actress was under contract to Samuel Goldwyn's company, which agreed to loan her out to RKO. Louis Hayward, the third lead, was borrowed from Universal.

Just a few days after principal photography began, Hopkins was injured in a car crash near her Beverly Hills residence, receiving facial bruises and a dislocated shoulder. Also in the car were her maid Yvonne Miller, who suffered two broken ribs, while Phyllis Livingston Potter, Fred Astaire's wife, was only badly shaken. Hopkins was away from the set for a while, delaying the shooting for several days.

It was while filming *The Woman I Love* that Miriam finally fell in love with Tola. When he had to go on location to Point Magu, California, sixty miles away from the studios, for scenes in which Hopkins did not appear, she would drive to the site each day to spend time with him. During the shooting of the picture, famous aviatrix Amelia Earhart visited the set. A fan of Paul Muni, the two posed together for a photograph. The actor remarked later, "It was the only time during the making of the film that I really felt like an aviator—by association."[11]

The three-month production of *The Woman I Love* did not run smoothly. Screenwriter Anthony Veiller, listed as a co-writer in the production charts, suddenly withdrew his credit from contributing writers after a quarrel with his colleagues. In addition, Tola had to deal with the personalities of temperamental Muni and mercurial Hopkins, who constantly clashed. There were many moments when it seems almost inevitable that shooting would have to be abandoned. Nevertheless, with great effort and thanks to his resilient personality, Litvak was able to complete the film. The picture finally opened in April 1937 to generally unkind reviews, mostly because of the uninspired screenplay and the lethargic performances of the three stars; RKO lost $266,000 on the film. Less than three months after its release, Colin Clive, one of the supporting actors, tragically drank himself to death. When *The Woman I Love* was screened in Rome two years later, students staged a riot because they felt that the film exalted French aviation.

On May 21, just a few weeks after the film was released, Miriam Hopkins opened her newly redecorated Bel Air home to her friends throwing a Russian-style dinner to celebrate Tola's thirty-fifth birthday. The magnificent villa once belonged to the late actor John Gilbert, Hopkins' former lover, who allegedly wanted his ashes scattered around the house. Tola joked with his friends that on moving in, he vacuumed them up.

On September 4, 1937, after spending most of the summer together (and appearing constantly in the gossip columns), Tola and Miriam secretly boarded a plane at Clover Field, Santa Monica, for Arizona. Their plane landed in Yuma, where the two were married in a small private ceremony. The following morning the newly wedded pair left for Coronado, California, where they spent a four-day honeymoon. Once they came back to Los Angeles, Miriam returned to her Bel Air home while Tola lived in a beachfront house on the Pacific Coast Highway north of Santa Monica. The Santa Monica house, designed by architect Douglas Hannold and with interiors by Harold Grive, had a stunning ocean view. The couple's excuse for living separately was Tola's allergy to the foliage at the Bel Air home, but the truth was that their two personalities could not dwell too long under the same roof.

In his biography of Hopkins, George Eells states that Litvak's attitude that the man of the house made decisions "went against the strong egocentric streak in her personality. In the beginning she submerged her distaste for nightclubs and accompanied him on his rounds of the Clover Club, the Trocadero and Ciro's. Her parties, which had customarily been small and composed of personalities who enjoyed exchanging ideas, were abandoned for spectacular affairs where conversation was all but impossible. Cost was no deterrent to the showmanly director, and Miriam helped pay for things she didn't enjoy." If she and Litvak were a mismatched, she could take comfort in the fact that her husband was excellent with Michael [Hopkin's adopted child]."[12] From the very beginning Tola treated Michael like a son, giving him the attention Miriam's other suitors didn't. It was more of a father-son relationship, with genuine affection that continued after the couple split in 1939. Tola and Hopkins' two-year roller coaster marriage instantly became Hollywood's stormiest union.

While shooting *The Woman I Love,* Tola thought that a remake of *Cette Vielle Canaille* would be perfect as his next project. He notified Charles Boyer that he could finally play the role of the acrobat he had regrettably refused. But Warner Brothers' producer Robert Lord forbade a remake of another French film, considering it too risky. Instead, he gave Tola the option to choose from among several stories owned by the studio.

Tola selected *Tovarich* (a Russian word meaning comrade), based on a successful comedy written by Jacques Deval and translated into English by playwright Robert E. Sherwood. Warner bought the screen rights in 1936 for $185,000. *Tovarich* was the amusing story of a couple of aristocratic Russian émigrés in Paris, in economical dire straits and forced to work as servants in the house of a wealthy man. Tola knew the play had been seen with different casts in Paris, Vienna and New York. He preferred the Austrian version starring Hungarian actress Lili Darvas.

In making the picture, Warner gave Tola *carte blanche.* The film's preproduction (especially casting) and the shooting were very troubled. The female lead was given to Claudette Colbert, who was the fourth choice for the role of the Grand Duchess Tatiana. Miriam Hopkins was Tola's preference but she was no longer attached to any studios and too expensive. Kay Francis was considered, being under contract to Warner, but was quickly ruled out since her box-office value had dwindled. Bette Davis was the third possibility,

3. Hollywood Romance

but Warner instead cast her in *Jezebel*. Eventually Colbert was borrowed from Paramount for the hefty amount of $150,000. In the beginning, the actress was quite hesitant to play a Russian, but the idea of working for the third time with Charles Boyer made her reconsider. Boyer, dubious about playing the part of Prince Mikail, resisted Tola's offer. Although Boyer enjoyed working with Tola, he felt, as a Frenchman, that he would look ridiculous attempting a Russian accent. Eventually he accepted, feeling that playing in a light comedy after portraying Napoleon in *Conquest* (1937) opposite Garbo could be an interesting change of pace. Behind the casting of Colbert and Boyer was the astute agent Charles Feldman, who also represented Tola.

Litvak asked to work once again with editor Henri Rust and insisted on the use of expensive camera setups even for minor scenes. Colbert requested Travis Banton as her costume designer and Charles Lang as the cinematographer. Even though she had never worked with the cameraman before, she admired his amazing use of soft lighting, which won him an Oscar for *A Farewell to Arms* (1932), and thought he could photograph her at her best.

Charles Boyer and Claudette Colbert in *Tovarich* (1937).

Lang was borrowed from Paramount, but a few days into the production a Warner cameraman suddenly replaced him. Colbert was greatly disturbed and stormed into the front office to talk with the executives. The producers explained that Lang had the habit of taking too long to set up a scene and they blamed him for further production delays. Colbert was persuaded to allow the new cinematographer to photograph her and to look at the rushes. If she did not like his work, Lang would be recalled. Ultimately, Lang *was* recalled with the agreement that Colbert would work two weeks without pay.

From the first day, things did not go too well on the set. Afraid he had to prove himself with his first film at Warner, Tola became extremely demanding with crew members and cast. His relationship with producer Robert Lord did not improve when the director insisted on using three cameras even for trivial sequences. As a *New York Times* article claimed: "[Litvak's] demands have the technicians in a high state of excitement, for just as shooting is to start some new inspiration usually causes him to order the set altered. A minor crisis was reached when, just as the cameras were to turn, he decided that the stovepipe which led to the ceiling in orthodox fashion ought to be carried twenty-five feet through the room and out of a window of the poverty-stricken apartment in the Hotel du Quercy. George Hopkins, who was once Ziegfeld's art director, attempted to argue, saying that the pipe would never draw in such a position and that there was no reason for it anyway, but the order had been given. Shooting was delayed for a long period while enough pipe was found."[13]

Four weeks after shooting began, Colbert fell ill, putting the picture several weeks behind schedule. Then another technical problem arose when the opening Paris street scene, complete with 300 extras engaged in a Bastille Day celebration, was about to be shot. Before the cameras could be transferred from street level to the rooftops to film the scene, a thick fog rolled in and made shooting impossible. Instead of calling the extras back for another night, it was decided to use a process screen, and the rooftop set was moved onto the stage. There it was found that the confines of the stage made it difficult for Tola to shoot at the angle he desired, with the principals on the eaves and the crowd below as a background. Special effect designer Byron Haskin solved the problem with a huge mirror borrowed from the set of the musical *Wonder Bar*. Together with Tola, Haskin set up a 75-foot cloth tunnel. At one end a regulation rear projection machine was placed, focused on the glass on the other end. The glass was tilted so that it reflected the image upward to a transparent screen erected on the edge of the roof set. Then the cameras were mounted on the roof ridge and photographed the action of the players against the reflection of the surging crowd in the street.

During shooting, the picture was called *Tonight's Our Night*; exhibitors and salesmen believed that the word "Tovarich" was too difficult for the customers (and for themselves) to pronounce. They said that the title didn't mean anything, despite the fact the play had been a success worldwide. In a meeting with Jack Warner, Colbert said that in 1933 she had made a Paramount film called *Tonight Is Ours* and that audiences could recall that picture and confused it with *Tonight's Our Night*. If Paramount reissued that film, a theater marquee could read: "Claudette Colbert in *Tonight's Our Night* and *Tonight Is Ours*." After that conversation, Warner decided to go back to *Tovarich*.

While Colbert and Boyer got along perfectly, the actress and Tola did not. Basil Rathbone, who played the villain Gorotchenko, revealed in an interview:

> There was some tension between her and Litvak. Litvak was not the right director for her, or for the picture itself, in my opinion. He tended to be arrogant and peremptory after his recent successes and Claudette was not accustomed to this kind of style. He was married to Miriam Hopkins at that time, and Miriam, who appeared some years before with Claudette in a film, and was always catty and gossipy about her costars, may have stirred him up about her, but they didn't like each other. Claudette tried to be civilized about it.... Claudette had a personality just as strong and determined, but she had her own way of handling boorish arrogance and Litvak soon began to get frustrated. Also I think he favored Charles over her in the camera angles—or anyway, he tried to. He was very opinionated and officious and would overrule the cameraman. I believe that was the way he operated in Europe. Claudette was sensitive to her camera angles and how her face was lighted, and she did not get the personal consideration on the picture that she felt she was entitled to. But she gave a very fine performance, I thought.[14]

Asked to comment about *Tovarich* years later, Colbert stated diplomatically, "I've done better and I have certainly done worse, a lot worse."[15]

On September 18, 1937, *Tovarich* was completed after sixty-three days of shooting, reaching a budget of $1.4 million. It was a box office hit and a critical success. Reviewers praised Colbert, Boyer and Rathbone's performances along with Tola's direction. Many years later, reminiscing about his career, Tola admitted that the play was far superior to his film. He felt that the picture could have been better if he did not stay too close to the original play, using instead all the possibilities the motion picture afforded him instead of using stage technique. He felt it would have made the film less static and claustrophobic.

4

Early Warner Years

"Directing was Anatole Litvak, surely one of the most urbane, sophisticated, gourmet, haut monde, anti–Nazis ever known and one of the most talented."

—Edward G. Robinson

About the same time that *Tovarich* opened nationwide, Tola was assigned to direct another play-based film: *The Amazing Dr. Clitterhouse*. "When he first heard that Warner had selected him for this task he was delighted," wrote a New York Times columnist, "because there was no love story in the play, so Warners made him put one in."[1]

The stage version of *The Amazing Dr. Clitterhouse* debuted on the London stage and later had a three-month Broadway run with Ralph Richardson and Cedric Hardwicke. After the New York production, Warner had some difficulty obtaining the movie rights because playwright Barré Lyndon retained control of the movie rights and placed them on the open market. The rights were first bought by Carl Laemmle, Jr., Universal Pictures' head of production, for a sum in excess of $50,000 and then given to Warner Bros. in exchange for the loan of Paul Muni, whom Laemmle wanted for *The Hunchback of Notre Dame*—a project that never got made.

The film's first treatment was called *Fog Over London*. William Faulkner worked on the screenplay, but Warner found his script too gloomy. New York playwright John Wexley and screenwriter John Huston were assigned to the adaptation, which they completed at the end of 1937. When Tola was offered the film, casting choices were already made. Although actor Roger Colman was producer Robert Lord's first choice as Dr. Clitterhouse, the part went to Edward G. Robinson. Dr. Clitterhouse is a psychiatrist who, in trying to understand the criminal mind, turns into a criminal himself. He becomes involved with a gang of thieves run by glamorous gang leader Jo Keller and mobster "Rocks" Valentine. Despite his character being written by John Huston, who two years later directed one of Bogart's best films *The Maltese Falcon* (1941),

4. Early Warner Years

Humphrey Bogart, Edward G. Robinson, Claire Trevor, Maxie Rosenbloom and Ward Bond in *The Amazing Dr. Clitterhouse* **(1938).**

Bogart loathed his part, finding it ludicrous. He would boorishly referred to the film as "The Amazing Dr. Clitoris."

The shooting began in late February 1938. Editor Warren Low visited the set daily, becoming well acquainted with Tola and the script. "Anatole Litvak," remembered Low, "would pan his camera with the people, dollying in and out, trying to save shooting close-ups. I would say to Mr. Litvak ... that I felt we needed a close-up because Edward G. Robinson, for example, is saying a very important line and this must be played in the close-up so the audience gets to see it. And the idea of cutting is to make a cut when there's a reason to have that cut which makes a much smoother picture. So, I was always standing by for any questions the director might ask from the editorial standpoint of a picture."[2]

Litvak became so fond of Low's work that they collaborated on four other films. Tola, who always loved to use the same crews, would always ask for Low before starting a new movie. "He would go to Jack Warner and to Hal Wallis and say he'd like to have Warren because 'He understands me,'"[3] Low recalled in an interview. "In *Dr. Clitterhouse* [Litvak] would pan Edward G.

Robinson, talking his dialogue, across the room, then cut, then pick up Humphrey Bogart and pan him to Robinson. Then the camera would slowly dolly in to a real tight two-shot, then he would protect two close-ups there through the whole sequence. But we might never use it because the camera moving in saves the cutting and we're in a nice two-shot which plays much better and much smoother. He did that a lot through the picture."[4]

The Amazing Dr. Clitterhouse was completed in early April and released at the end of July. It was generally well reviewed by the critics but did only mediocre business.

Only eight weeks after work ended on *Clitterhouse*, Tola was back to work, directing *The Sisters,* starring Bette Davis and Errol Flynn. Based on the best-selling novel by Myron Brinig, *The Sisters* was a project first assigned to director William Dieterle, who turned it down. While the search for a director continued, the script was sent to Fredric March, who did not like the part of Frank Medlin, a drunken, self-pitying reporter. "It is not a particularly interesting character," wrote March to Jack Warner, "principally because he is so frightfully weak and sorry for himself throughout."[5]

Once Tola became the designated director, John Garfield tested for the part. The actor was excited since the project seemed to be one of Warner's most ambitious films. Tola was impressed by Garfield's knowledge of the Russian theater, since he had studied with the late Richard Boleslavsky. Garfield did his screen test dressed in an Edwardian costume. After some discussions with people around him, Tola asked the actor to do the scene one more time. Irving Rapper, the dialogue director, found Garfield's inflection unmistakably New York and too modern. Tola suggested that Garfield modify his dialogue to erase the problem. This time the actor delivered his lines stiffly and awkwardly and did not get the part.

For the role of Louise, Irene Dunne was Warner's first choice but the part was eventually assigned to Bette Davis, who had just completed *Jezebel*. After reading the script, Davis was reluctant to accept it. Nonetheless, since she needed the money and the part looked better than most of the ones she had been offered, she signed on. "I was delighted with this part," commented Davis years later, "because it was a change of pace. My ambition always has been—still is—for variety in the kinds of parts I play.... I was extremely happy to be co-starred for the first time with Errol Flynn. He was a big box office star at the time, and it could only be beneficial to me to work with him. At that time I had no billing clause in my contract. I felt after *Jezebel* that my name should always appear above the title. This is star billing. Warner Bros. decided to bill Errol Flynn as the sole star—Errol Flynn in *The Sisters* with Bette Davis—my name below the title. Not only did I feel that Errol Flynn in *The*

4. Early Warner Years

Sisters had its humorous, even 'far-out' connotation, I also felt that *The Sisters* was a female star's title. After taking a very definite stand with the studio, the billing read Errol Flynn, Bette Davis in *The Sisters*."[6]

The picture went into production on June 6, 1938, and was completed in almost nine weeks. It was entirely filmed at Warner's studios in Burbank. Tola often asked Flynn for repeated takes, since the actor could not remember his lines. Bette Davis was very methodical and precise. Her acting was a profession she embraced with the highest professionalism, while for Flynn making movies was like practicing a sport, basing his skill on pure instinct. But Davis adored working with Flynn "because he never really worked," as she explained in an interview. "He was just there.... [He] was the most beautiful person we've ever had on the screen. He openly admitted he knew nothing about acting, and I admired his honesty because he was absolutely right."[7]

Regarding Litvak, Davis commented: "Tola Litvak had everything worked out on paper, and on *The Sisters* and *All This, and Heaven Too,* the camera couldn't deviate one inch from its position, ever. If something didn't go right in the blocking, we did it over and over again, trying to make it work for the camera.... Litvak was a slave to his preconceptions. All of his work took place the night before with his blueprints; he didn't do anything spontaneous on the set. That's why all of his pictures moved so slowly, and were so ponderous."[8]

Dialogue director Irving Rapper, who later became a filmmaker directing Davis in two of her biggest successes *Now, Voyager* (1942) and *The Corn Is Green*

Bette Davis and Errol Flynn in *The Sisters* (1938).

(1945), shared Davis' opinion of Tola. "[Litvak] was pretty good, but insecure—with 60 or more takes to his credit."⁹ Rapper later worked with Tola on *All This, and Heaven Too, Castle on the Hudson* (1940) and *City for Conquest* (1940).

The Sisters was the story of three daughters of a chemist living in Montana at the time of Roosevelt's presidency. Two of the sisters marry for money. The eldest, Louise (Davis), follows her heart and runs off with a newspaper reporter (Flynn), who suffers from an inability to settle down. Once they get married, he drinks and runs away, leaving Louise in the middle of the San Francisco earthquake.

Warner Bros. built $200,000 worth of special sets to be wrecked and burned for the San Francisco earthquake-fire scene. Three weeks were required to film that sequence, which also featured some stock footage from Warner's film *Old San Francisco* (1927). To make the catastrophic sequence as realistic as possible, Tola ordered Davis to stand in the middle of the room on set marks, while everything on the set fell to pieces. Without blinking an eye, Bette went ahead and did as she was told. Tola was impressed by the star's determination. He had so perfectly rigged the set that if she been a few steps off her mark, she could have been badly injured. He told her to stay precisely on the position agreed. Everything went well except for a splinter from a crystal chandelier that almost hit Davis' eye.

That day Davis' sister, Bobby, was also on the set. After Litvak called "cut," she ran to Bette and screamed, "Tola Litvak! You are a son of a bitch!" Bette wrote in her autobiography, "[Litvak] went on relentlessly in what seemed to be a subconscious desire to eradicate me once and for all. He probably saved the studio thirty-five dollars a day for a double. I was much too proud to show my terror and give him the satisfaction of calling me a coward."¹⁰

Tola shot two endings for the picture. In the one which was true to the novel, Louise marries her employer William Benson (Ian Hunter); in the other, she reconciles with her estranged husband Frank. Preview audiences preferred the second ending and it was added in the final cut. When the film opened in October, the most flattering critical comments were about Davis' performance. Unexpectedly, this pairing of Warner's biggest star Errol Flynn with Bette Davis sank at the box office.

One day, the set of *The Sisters* was visited by a beautiful young girl accompanied by her mother, brother and cousin. This stunning seventeen-year-old girl was future Hollywood star Gene Tierney. In her autobiography she described Tola as "stocky, white-haired, distinguished. A Russian immigrant, he was part of that wave of European directors and actors who had fled to

America into the 1930s to escape the growing repression of their own homelands."[11] Tierney mesmerized Tola, who was a great admirer of female beauty. "Young girl, you ought to be in the pictures!"[12] he exclaimed—a line that even in 1938 sounded like a mere pick-up line. But in this case he was right. Tierney's brother Butch thought it was a joke; her mother wanted to encourage Gene's interest but feared her husband's reaction. Tierney was flattered and curious: "The next step was up to my cousin Gordon [producer Gordon Hollingshead], who did not take Litvak's opinions lightly. He swept off to the casting director; a decision was made to test me."[13]

Tierney was immediately offered a contract with Warner. Her father forbade her to accept, later allowing her only to study "serious" acting to be in "legitimate" theater. Tierney debuted on Broadway later that year and in 1940 she signed a contract with 20th Century–Fox. She became an overnight sensation, working with the most prestigious directors, but never with Litvak.

At a picnic, Tola was introduced to a young, aspiring Canadian actor named Raymond Burr. During a long conversation, Tola agreed to connect him with a repertory group of players and a few weeks later he arranged for Burr to act in a summer theater in Toronto. The engagement led the actor to tour England in a series of plays. It was the start of a long-lasting professional career for Burr, who later appeared in several Hollywood hits and on popular TV series including *Perry Mason* and *Ironside*.

It was Tola's next film for Warner, the controversial *Confessions of a Nazi Spy*, that finally made American critics sing his praises again.

"[It] was entirely my idea," Tola said in an interview.[14] A more believable version is that Tola came aboard the project at a much later stage. "I must say that very few studios at that time would dare to make a picture of this kind," Tola explained in 1959. "Jack and Harry Warner let me do it. I had trouble in inducing them to do it. They got scared many times ... they got scared even practically before we started the picture—but they finally let me do it, which is the most important thing."[15]

Confessions of a Nazi Spy was based on actual events. In early 1938, FBI chief J. Edgar Hoover announced that the bureau had cracked a Nazi spy ring working in American territory and that involved several members of the German-American Bund. Hoover suggested that producer Hal Wallis do a picture based on the story. Warner quickly acquired a $25,000 unpublished book written by G-man Leon G. Turrou and employed him as technical adviser on the project. Yet the studio was required to provide guarantees to the federal government that it would not release the film until the trials ended. Were it to be prematurely released, it could prejudice the jury and undermine the Nazi spies' right to a fair trial. In his autobiography, Wallis revealed,

President Roosevelt was extremely enthusiastic about the project, and he and Hoover promised extraordinary cooperation.... In August 1938 I instructed [writer Milton] Krims to go to New York, disguise himself as a Nazi, and attend meetings of the notorious German-American Bund, the organization devoted to subversion in our country.... With Krims assisting him, Turrou prepared a series of articles that ran in the *New York Post,* infuriating J. Edgar Hoover. He had forbidden Turrou to use classified information, but Turrou felt privileged to do so because of his position. When Hoover dismissed him, Turrou proceeded to write [the] bestselling book *Nazi Spies in America* (1939) about his experiences.[16]

Under the working title *Storm Over America,* preproduction began in December 1938 under absolute secrecy for fear of repercussions from the German-American Bund or the Federal government. Tola was chosen as director, while Edward G. Robinson was to play a fictional Turrou counterpart Hungarian actor Francis Lederer, Czech Paul Lukas and Brit George Sanders all played Nazis. Marlene Dietrich, who was German and opposed to Hitler's regime, was supposed to play a spy-hairdresser, but Paramount refused to lend her to Warner.

Robinson was eager to do the picture. "Directing was Anatole Litvak," the actor wrote in his autobiography, "surely one of the most urbane, sophisticated, gourmet, haut monde, anti–Nazis ever known—and one of the most talented. He approached the film with zeal and commitment; that it was less than an artistic triumph was due to the fact that the participating actors, including myself, were too familiar to be taken seriously."[17]

Many Hollywood actors reportedly refused parts in the picture because they feared that their participation would result in reprisals by the Nazis against their relatives in Germany. Tola had to travel to the East Coast to cast many of the parts, and several of the actors were credited under pseudonyms to avoid future retaliations.

The film focused on the activities of a German doctor who leads the American Nazi movement, and a naïve German-American who offers his services to the Nazi intelligence service, hoping to become rich and popular inside the party. This man's spy activity brings him to the attention of the FBI. A competent agent is able to round up the German spies trying to undermine American democracy.

Krims' script was reportedly polished aboard a Hollywood-bound train by the screenwriters and producers Warner and Wallis. The first draft was submitted to the Production Code Administration by late December 1938, at which time the PCA informed Warner Bros. that although the screenplay appeared to be "technically" within the provisions of the Production Code, because of its controversial nature it could be rejected by censor boards who feared that the exhibition of the film would result in public disorder or incite a riot.

4. Early Warner Years

Construction began simultaneously on eighty-three sets. Even Miriam Hopkins was asked to wait for Tola outside the sound stage. The pages of the script were given out to the cast on a daily basis to prevent their being leaked to unfriendly third parties. One day, Tola received a threatening note written on Warner Bros. letterhead and delivered by a studio messenger. It was speculated that a visitor had infiltrated Warner Bros. offices and stolen letterhead paper. Tola announced to all the extras and doubles involved in the production that if they wanted to quit, fearing any sort of retaliation, they were free to do it. Everybody stayed on, including one actor cast in a bit part as a crew member of a German transatlantic ship and required to do the Nazi salute screaming "Heil Hitler!"

Future director Don Siegel, who at the time was part of the editorial department, recalled in his memoir an episode that describes the tense atmosphere:

> An excellent stuntman, Sal Gorss, refused to put on a Nazi uniform. In any of the sequences we had to shoot, we needed uniformed Nazi soldiers. Sol was trembling with rage. I told him this was an anti–Nazi film we were making. I pointed out to

Wolfgang Zizler, Edward G. Robinson and Fred Tozere in *Confessions of a Nazi Spy* **(1939).**

him that Warner Brothers, for whom we were shooting, were Jewish. I was born a Jew and realized the importance of being American making an anti–Nazi picture. I said what he was doing by refusing to wear a Nazi uniform was sick, stupid and un-American. Then he abruptly left the set, I felt sorry for what I had said to him and felt damn lucky he hadn't punched me out.[18]

As soon as the shooting commenced, trouble began for all involved. Jack and Ann Warner were the first to receive threatening mail. The studio head claimed that making *Confessions of a Nazi Spy* made some powerful Hollywood executives furious and also placed him on Hitler's personal death list. Edward G. Robinson received obscene letters and phone calls threatening him and his family with death, forcing Warner to hire armed bodyguards to protect him. In addition, German officials kept storming into Warner's office to protest.

According to Wallis, Tola, who was famous for being late on the set and for shooting many takes and printing them all, respected the instructions to film as little as possible to comply with the schedule and budget constrictions. To give the most authentic look to the picture, Tola used a semi-documentary style. He originally wanted Westbrook Van Voorhis, the voice of the *March of Time* newsreels, as the narrator, but the commentator was unavailable and so Litvak opted for voice actor John Deering. To emphasize the drama, he added footage from Goebbels' speeches and clips from the German-American Bund's rally in New York along with scenes from Leni Riefenstahl's *Triumph of the Will*.

The film was completed with a $1.5 million budget on a 55-day shooting schedule. Warner considered releasing it without any credits to give extra security to everyone involved in the production, but eventually they appeared at the end of the film. The picture was released two years before the United States officially entered the Second World War. It was the first mainstream Hollywood attack on Hitler's regime and the earliest to show Nazi espionage in America.

On the morning of *Confessions of a Nazi Spy*'s world premiere in Beverly Hills (April 27, 1939), Ann Warner received a letter with a detailed floor plan of their home and all the roads around it. "If the picture opens," the letter read, "the whole Warner family will be wiped out, and the theatre will be bombed."[19] For the three days before the premiere, policemen were stationed on the theater roof to prevent a bomb from being planted in the chimneys or the air vents. That same night there was almost as many security people in attendance as there were members of the audience. Fortunately nothing happened.

The German-American Bund tried to sue Warner Bros. for $500,000. The action was later withdrawn when the man who filed the suit was jailed for misappropriation of his own finances.[20] The German ambassador sent a message to the Secretary of State denouncing the film as propaganda poisoning German-American relations. The State Department ignored the protest.

When the film opened nationwide, Nazi sympathizers burned down a Milwaukee theater where it was playing. In Germany, a Warner representative was murdered when he opposed Nazi policy, while two of the film's distributors were killed in Poland. It was banned in many countries including Germany, Italy, Yugoslavia, Holland, Norway, Sweden, Japan and several Latin American countries.

Tola's direction was highly praised by reviewers along with the film itself. The National Board of Review selected it as one of the best films of 1939. In spite of the critical success, the picture failed to make money. Warner tried to re-release it in June 1940 with additional documentary footage of Nazi military aggression, but once again it proved to be a commercial flop.

In September 1941, the American Senate held a hearing on propaganda in Hollywood films. Tola and Harry Warner were subpoenaed as offenders in this regard because they had made *Confessions*.[21] However, the attack on Pearl Harbor two months later put an end to the inquiry.

Tola's professional life was now on the fast track. Working for Warner was giving him the opportunity to direct big-budget productions. After only one year, however, his marriage with Miriam was on the rocks. Tensions were running very high between the Litvaks, whose personalities were frequently clashing. When Miriam started making a picture, Tola would visit her sets and comment on how the director *should* have handled the scene he had just seen filmed. He would not share in the expenses they would have for the several parties they co-hosted, leading to furious arguments. Miriam had never completely forgotten Tola's brief affair with Bette Davis during the shooting of *The Sisters*. The lovers would spend weekends at Tola's beach house in Malibu and were spotted several times having dinner at Ciro's, Tola's favorite restaurant. "They really couldn't call what Tola and I had a 'romance,'" Davis commented years later. "We both needed someone at that time."[22] Adding, "Loneliness—pure and simple loneliness—drove me into that."

Litvak allegedly commented, "Marriage with Miriam—an affair with Bette—I've had enough of crazy, temperamental women to last me for years. Now I need a rest, no?"[23] According to one of Davis' biographers, Hopkins was so enraged when she learned about the fling that she called Davis and threatened to name her in her divorce action against Tola. She never forgave Davis, and the feud between the two stars continued when they were both cast in *The Old Maid* (1939).[24]

The inevitable happened and Miriam decided to take residence for six weeks in Nevada for a quick divorce. Hopkins' drastic decision first amazed and then devastated Tola, who learned of the separation after Miriam had already left with her son Michael. Despite the fights, Tola was still profoundly in love with his wife and made several unsuccessful overtures for a reconciliation. Jean Negulesco recalled that difficult period:

> We walked on the beach, long exhausting walks. He talked constantly and cried and hoped for reconciliation.
> "I'll give anything to have Miriam back: ten thousand dollars, twenty, twenty-five, my Picasso, my contract. I must not lose her."
> ... I had one suggestion: "Tola, you want Miriam back? We engage a helicopter and fly over her villa in Reno, each of us carrying a magnum, and we will parachute into her garden. 'Miriam, this is stupid, let's go back home,' you tell her."
> "No, she will never do it," Tola whispered, shaking his head.
> "What can we lose? Maybe a broken neck if the parachute doesn't open in time," I said. Of course we didn't do it and the divorce was final; they remained good friends for a long time.[25]

On October 11, 1939, after almost two years of a roller coaster marriage, Miriam won an uncontested divorce on the grounds of cruelty—and without naming Bette Davis as an accomplice only because her pride could not have handled it. Tola, who had sent his attorney to a private hearing, had filed a cross-complaint charging desertion, but without offering any evidence. Judge William McKnight permitted Miriam to drop the name of Litvak and assume her stage name of Miriam Hopkins. (Her real name was Ellen Miriam Hopkins.)

During those turbulent times, Litvak was asked by Hal Wallis, to work on a gangster film called *The Roaring Twenties* starring James Cagney. Tola disliked the story but agreed to help the producer, provided than the script was revised. He hired a pair of screenwriters who were soon fired by Jack Warner. Tola felt his promise to Wallis was no longer valid and quit. "Warner couldn't fire me," he added, "because I had a contract."[26] Raoul Walsh replaced him.

5

Ann, Bette and Paulette

"If I shoot one take of a scene, I am Eason! If I shoot 100 takes of a scene, I am Litvak!"
—Anatole Litvak

Tola's fifth picture from Warner was the penitentiary drama *Castle on the Hudson*. The press first announced the project in June 1939: "Litvak would put shortly into production *20,000 Years in Sing Sing*, in which George Raft will probably be starred."[1] The film was based on the novel *20,000 Years in Sing Sing* by Lewis E. Lawes and was a remake of Warner's Spencer Tracy–starring hit of the same title. Tola began filming on July 10. Background footage from the 1933 original was used and many of the sets were designed to match the originals so that stock footage could be used.

Contrary to what was originally announced, John Garfield and not George Raft played the leading role of jewel thief Tommy Gordon, serving a 25-year-minimum sentence but expecting his political pals on the outside to help spring him. The film reunited Garfield and Ann Sheridan, who had previously appeared together in *They Made Me a Criminal* (1939). Although Tola was very eager to work with Garfield, whom he had tried to cast in *The Sisters*, the actor did not like the script. But director-screenwriter-producer Robert Rossen, an old friend of Garfield, had persuaded him to take the role that brought Tracy to stardom. According to one of Garfield's biographers, the actor agreed to do the picture under two conditions: first, that Warner had to agree to keep the original ending, wherein his character goes to the electric chair for a murder he did not commit; second, to receive a bonus of $10,000.[2]

Sheridan portrayed Kay Manners, a tough and vulnerable singer madly in love with her criminal beau. Sheridan was a young, sexy blonde, known to be straightforward, and often used coarse language. She had previously appeared in Warner's box-office hits *Black Legion* (1937) and *Angels with Dirty Faces* (1938).

Tola had a soft spot for his leading lady. A few months later, the two were romantically linked after being photographed together on several occasions: at the 1939 premiere of the film *When Tomorrow Comes* and while dancing tenderly at the Hollywood nightclub Trocadero. Sheridan fell madly in love with Tola. However, after a few weeks he started to be late for dates, behaving inconsiderately and abusively, sometimes even forgetting to show up at all. His behavior drove Ann crazy. John Negulesco recalled a night when Tola's butler Sammy, concerned by Sheridan's violent behavior, called him asking for help. The actress was drunk and cursing like a sailor. She had been waiting for Litvak for over three hours, throwing Tola's best china off the terrace. The director tried to calm her down. But, she would relax only when he agreed to drink with her. Negulesco wrote:

> It was past midnight when Tola arrived wearing a pure-rose-angel look and offering no excuses.
> "And how's everybody? Did you have any dinner?" [Litvak] hiccupped.
> "So where were you?" Ann bellowed. "We had a date at eight, remember?"
> "Busy, Annie, busy. Sorry I couldn't make it. I apologize."
> "See Annie, he apologized," I shouted with relief, getting ready to go home.
> "I don't buy it, Buster."
> Annie stopped me and turned a steely glance at Tola.

Burgess Meredith, Ann Sheridan and John Garfield in *Castle on the Hudson* (1940).

"Lover, I'm not going to tell it to you tonight, but sometime. I'll tell you to go and fuck yourself. Not tonight, but sometime."

"You're vulgar, Annie. I'm tired. Good night."

He started from the room but turned to me at the stairway.

"Close the door quietly Johnny, when you take her home."

A sullen silence, then Ann burst out laughing, her raucous, earthy laugh.

"What a ham! And what a stinking, lousy performance!—Imitating his voice:—Close the door quietly Johnny, when you take her home. Ha! Can you believe it? I hate the creep."

"No you don't Annie. You love him and admire him. We all do. But he's peculiar." I put my arms around her. "Now go upstairs and make up? Be the clever one." She didn't give me much of an argument after that. She was lonely. They made up. And fell in love all over again. But this reconciliation didn't last long either. The Tola suffering pattern erupted with imaginary suspicions, one-way questions, and fanciful pains. Ann Sheridan finally told him one day "to go and...." Sheridan later married George Brent, the polished, handsome star."[3]

Despite Tola's lean and forceful directing style, *Castle on the Hudson* (released in England as *Years Without Days*) was essentially a verbatim remake of the earlier version. The picture opened at the Globe Theatre in New York on March 3, 1940, to strong box-office but to mixed reviews. Tola did not really care about the critics dismissing the film since his mind was already on his next project.

For a week in September, Litvak took over the direction of the melodrama *'Til We Meet Again*, starring Merle Oberon and George Brent, after the director Edmund Goulding was felled by a respiratory infection. Then it was announced that Tola would direct *Saturday's Children*, adapted by Philip and Julius Epstein from Maxwell Anderson's Pulitzer Prize play. It was to star James Stewart and Olivia de Havilland but neither of them liked the script and turned it down, feeling that although the story was nice it did not have enough to be a big hit. Tola subsequently withdrew as well. His name was then attached to a film called *Villa on the Hill* based on W. Somerset Maugham's novella *Up at the Villa*, but the production never materialized.

On February 8, 1940, Tola was back behind the camera shooting *All This, and Heaven Too* with Bette Davis and Charles Boyer, a melodrama based on a bestselling novel by Rachel Field. The producer David Lewis had Greta Garbo in mind for the female lead; Helen Hayes was also considered for the part. Eventually it was given to Davis, who was at the peak of her stardom. In the second female lead, Tola wanted to cast his former wife Miriam Hopkins.

"The Duchess de Praslin is a heartless and venomous bitch," said Tola. "Miriam will be perfect."[4] Hopkins recalled when Tola discussed the film with her for the first time: "I knew the marriage was over when he came home from the studio one night and said he had found a marvelous property. 'It's going to make a wonderful movie for Bette Davis, and a radio play for you.' Fortunately it was *All This, and Heaven Too,* which didn't make a very good movie."[5]

This romantic costume drama was budgeted at $1,400,000, including $1,000 each for the thirty-five costumes created exclusively for Davis by Orry-Kelly. Art director Carl Jules Weyl designed sixty-five exterior sets and thirty-five interiors. He gathered over 12,000 authentic items of the Louis-Philippe period, after searching several museums, to achieve a faithful reconstruction of that period. The gloomy tale dealt with the employment of Henriette Deluzy-Desportes as a governess and the murder of the Duchess de Praslin by her husband. It was a tragic story based on true events experienced by the author's great aunt. Warner had purchased the rights two years earlier for $100,000.

"I had Charles Boyer as my co-star, and Anatole Litvak again as my director," wrote Davis in her autobiography. "But there were no earthquakes, holocausts or floods this time in which he could torture me.... Boyer was a joy to work with, intelligent and professional to the core—a truly fine actor!"[6] (In a later interview, Davis described Boyer as "the most vain man I worked with. Terribly serious about his looks. A wig, a corset, lifts in his shoes, and so on."[7]) Boyer returned Davis' compliments:

> She was, in my opinion, the most gifted American actress on the scene. She had enormous reserve of emotion, a splendid disciplined technique, and could convey so much with gestures and expressions.... I heard about her temperament, and how difficult she was supposed to be. I found none of that. We worked together amicably and harmoniously from start to finish. I know she and Tola had their artistic differences, but I always felt both of them were concerned for the good of the picture, and even though their concepts were different, they were sincerely expressed.[8]

During the early filming, Boyer kept in his dressing room a radio so that he could listen to the news about the war in Europe between takes. Tola noted the star's extreme nervousness on the set and confronted him. Boyer told him the war news was destroying his capacity to concentrate, and so the radio had to be removed. The extreme unhappiness the French actor was experiencing, he later admitted, was at least appropriate for his role as the Duke de Praslin, a discontented and gloomy character. He was so stressed that twice a studio doctor was summoned to the set to find him suffering from nervous fatigue, which made him lose some weight as well. Litvak said,

> Somehow, though, Charles's performance transcended the curse of overproduction. He was easily the best actor I ever directed, although in the three pictures we made I didn't direct him once—he was his own creative artist. Possibly *All This, and Heaven Too* was the best work he ever did. It was a much more complex performance, cer-

tainly, than *Mayerling* or for *Tovarich*. It also shows that the great performances are not given by contented actors. Charles was a happy fellow in the other pictures we made, but in *All This, and Heaven Too* he was surely the least contented with whom I've worked.[9]

On the set, Davis did not find Tola's directing method any different from when they worked together in *The Sisters*. "Tola planned every move beforehand and the camera was his God.... Tola had it all on paper. His method of directing was never to my taste. There was not the spontaneity or the flexibility I found in [William] Wyler."[10] She added in a later interview, "Each morning [Litvak] arrived on the set with the complete blueprint for shooting that he had worked out the night before. Each shot was set up exactly as he had envisioned. (More times than not, not the way I had envisioned it. He was a very stubborn director.)"[11] She also called him "a slave of his preconceptions."[12] When Tola and Davis would argue, their screams could be heard all over the studio, making the other members of the cast and crew retreat discreetly. A major fight erupted when she played the courtroom scene in which she wept

Anatole Litvak and Paulette Goddard (1940).

and gesticulated passionately. Suddenly Tola stopped the take, accusing her of trying to overdo the scene after he had restrained her in the past. Davis was outraged and called Wallis and Lewis in to look at the footage in which she had played it her way. The producers overruled Tola and ordered the scene to stay as it was. In spite of all the friction between Tola and Davis, whose affair now belonged to the past, they still remained good friends off the set. They were photographed together on several occasions including at the Warner Club's Sixth Annual Dinner Dance at the Biltmore Hotel on February 17, 1940, and at a black-tie event benefiting the French and British Red Cross organized by Boyer.

Tola's methodical, slow-paced, accurate ways of filmmaking clashed with Wallis' ideas about containing costs. The producer was extremely concerned about delays in the shooting schedule, which would have inflated the costs. The night of the first day of shooting, Jack Warner saw Tola and Davis coming out of the studio café together at 2:15 a.m.; the head of production of Warner Bros. told Wallis that it would not be a bad idea to have another director ready to replace Tola because of his characteristically slow pace of working and his notorious lateness on the set in the morning.

Charles Boyer and Bette Davis in *All This, and Heaven Too* (1940).

5. Ann, Bette and Paulette

As many predicted, the production was already behind schedule on February 19, in part because the children kept forgetting their lines. Young actor Richard Nichols had a hard time forcing himself to cry in a scene. Enraged, Tola told the child that if he would not cry, he would be left alone all night long there on the stage. Little Richard finally cried but he was so terrified that he could not stop sobbing long after the scene was completed. Wallis rejected Tola's idea of using a sophisticated crane shot of Davis going up a staircase, instructing him to cut and dissolve to the second floor. But the director did not follow the orders and did it his way, justifying it on an authorization given by the associate producer David Lewis.[13] "I don't like the way things are going at all," Wallis complained in a memo in mid–March. "One and two scenes a day, doing things over and over again from many angles, etc." By mid–April the situation had not improved. The picture wrapped on April 20, 1940, twenty days behind schedule and over budget. The film had a final cost of $2,500,000.

Tola shot an incredible amount of film. His fame for shooting dozens of takes of a scene was often compared to his fellow Warner director and action specialist B. Reeves Eason, who was notorious for shooting only one take of a scene, no matter what happened. When asked why he shot so many takes, Tola replied, "If I shoot one take of a scene, I am Eason! If I shoot 100 takes of a scene, I am Litvak!"

The initial cut of *All This, and Heaven Too* ran about three hours and twenty minutes. The film was previewed again in June with only twenty minutes having been edited out. When It finally went into general release the following month, it was "only" 143 minutes long.

A happy moment on the set was Davis' celebration of her thirty-second birthday, shared by the cast gathered around an enormous birthday cake. Two weeks later after the picture was completed, Davis and associate producer David Lewis threw a Hawaiian dinner party for all the children in the film at the Beverly Tropics restaurant.

The world premiere of *All This, and Heaven Too* took place at the Carthay Circle Theatre in Los Angeles on June 13, 1940. Tola and the cast, except Boyer, attended the gala event, greeted by a cheering crowd, estimated to be 15,000 people. The reviews were mostly favorable but not enthusiastic; many argued that the film was a bit too old-fashioned. *All This, and Heaven Too* was nominated for three Academy Awards (Best Film, Best Supporting Actress and Best Cinematography in black and white). Tola was very disappointed by the final outcome and commented, "The picture was overproduced. You couldn't see the actors for the candelabra, and the whole thing became a victory for matter over mind. Bette Davis was the world's most expensively costumed governess. I'll tell you what was wrong with the picture. *Gone with the Wind* was wrong with it. If it hadn't been for the one picture, the other might have been managed nicely on a more modest scale."[14]

In his free time, Tola shared a passion for gin rummy with Europeans colleagues William Wyler and Billy Wilder and with producers Sam Spiegel and Paul Kohner. This group of European expats would usually meet once a week and play cards till dawn, drinking heavily and reminiscing about the old times in their native countries. However, what suddenly became their favorite subject was the particular hot night in the summer of 1940 that Tola spent with actress Paulette Goddard (who was unhappily married to Charlie Chaplin) at Ciro's, becoming a national scandal.

Many versions of the Tola-Paulette date at Ciro's circulated in Hollywood over the years. They all agreed that the couple was having dinner there and they were both tipsy, flirting with each other. From this point on, all the accounts diverge into different stories. In the most widely circulated version, a shoulder strap of Goddard's dress supposedly broke and the gown dropped, exposing her breast. Delicately Tola first kissed her breast and then pulled up the edge of the tablecloth to cover the actress while she was trying to fix it. On the spur of the moment Goddard slid under the table, followed by Tola few seconds later, and allegedly they engaged in various sexual activities. The restaurant management immediately put a screen around the table and later the couple was escorted out of the dining room. Tola went into a phone booth located at the restaurant entrance, followed by Paulette who also squeezed in. Both continued whatever was interrupted under the table. Another version claims that Goddard dropped an earring under the table. Tola went to retrieve it and performed oral sex on the actress. Other stories had Goddard engaging in oral sex under the table while Tola remained seated. Playwright Clifford Odets wrote in his Hollywood journal, "A. Litvak, director, and P. Goddard, actress ... they have been sleeping together, in public, for weeks. Drunk at Ciro's, sitting at a ringside table, he took out her breasts and kissed them, passionately." He described how Tola, banished by the management to the outer sanctum of the bar, "suddenly disappeared, and finally was discovered under the bouffant skirt of Miss Goddard, on his knees kissing the 'eagerly sought triangular spot' with the blissful unawareness of a baby at the bottle."[15] Quickly the story transformed into a Hollywood legend. The following day all the Hollywood columnists printed that Tola had disappeared for a while under a Ciro's table with Goddard. Perhaps the most accurate report was provided by Jean Negulesco, who was at Ciro's that night with a date seated at a table next to the couple:

Returning to the table from the dance floor, Paulette dropped one of her earrings under the table. Tola—quite drunk by now (as was Paulette), but still the perfect gentleman—disappeared under the table to find it. But how long does it take to look for an earring? The silly joke grew to be phony acting. Tola's disappearance under the table lasted beyond the time limit of a prank. Paulette began to moan convincingly. Friends, waiters, and photographers become voyeurs. They laughed and whispered encouragement to Tola. They felt they were witnessing a free and bold Hollywood scandal. When finally, fifteen minutes later Tola appeared from under the table, to the applause of the amused audience, he straightened his hair with just the right amount of embarrassment. Flashbulbs popped on and off rhythmically, and the rumor spread through the night and filled the gossip columns. For days, syndicated newspaper and cine-magazines carried the story enlarged and distorted out of proportion.[16]

Negulesco claimed that Tola later got a mouth infection at the height of the scandal. Although Tola enjoyed all the publicity built around the episode, he fervently denied the incident. Goddard's only comment was, "Isn't that silly?"[17] Nonetheless the story became a serious matter. The State Department in Washington D.C. received letters of complaint. Negulesco was summoned as a witness and had to explain that the whole matter was simply a joke and a misunderstanding. Thanks to the intercession of W. Averell Harriman, the ambassador to the Soviet Union under President Roosevelt, who was very fond of Goddard, the matter was put to rest.

6

Late Warner Years

"Anatole Litvak was an inspiring help.... I like his severity. It keeps you on your toes."
—Tyrone Power

In 1940, Warner bought the screen rights to a well-received 1936 novel by Aben Kandel, *City for Conquest*. The picture was intended as a vehicle for James Cagney, one of the studio's highest paid stars, with his brother William "Bill" Cagney as associate producer. *City for Conquest* was the story of an aspiring boxer who loses the championship and his eyesight in a fixed fight. The film was a hot property that had several directors asking to helm it. Cagney, a huge fan of the book, was delighted when he learned that his friend Raoul Walsh would direct the script adapted by John Wexley. Yet Warner, at the last moment, decided that a prestigious high-budgeted production deserved a director with more of a reputation, hence Walsh was replaced by Tola. Although most of the picture was filmed on Warner Bros. soundstages, a technical crew spent over three weeks shooting background footage on location in New York City. While the film was in preproduction, Tola spent a long time in New York getting more acquainted with the city and its people, to have a better flavor of the place where the story took place. The shooting was then scheduled for the end of May.

However, the Cagney brothers objected to the directorial substitution and dismissed Wexley's script draft as weak and untrue to the novel's spirit. The screenplay was then rewritten with the help of Robert Rossen; although not fully matching Cagney's ideal, it was now acceptable. Arthur Kennedy, in his first screen role, was chosen to play Cagney's composer brother, because he was thought by many to resemble Cagney. Anthony Quinn won the role of the sleazy dancer, beating out George Raft and Cesar Romero. For the female lead, Jack Warner wanted Ginger Rogers, but she had other commitments, so Sylvia Sidney was cast. Yet when pre-production began, the studio assigned the part to Ann Sheridan, considering her more appropriate for the role of Peggy Nash. Sheridan, thrilled to work with Cagney, later told the press, "To be in a picture with him was just the greatest."[1]

Who was *not* thrilled at all was Cagney, who without any apparent reason detested Tola from the first day they met on the set. In his autobiography Elia Kazan, who was cast by Tola in the secondary role of "Googi" (Jack Warner saw Humphrey Bogart in the part), wondered about the motive behind Cagney's strong antipathy for Tola:

> I could see that Jimmy didn't tolerate the man, but he never said a word out loud against Tola; it was more elemental than that. Was it racial? I wondered (until I knew Jimmy better). Cagney was an Irish-Catholic. Litvak a Jew. The bad feeling had an intensity beyond reason. I tried to guess what there was about the director that his star detested so. I must believe that he didn't like the way Tola was shooting the film and the kind of rehearsal this technique necessitated. Litvak's method was not straightforward, like that of Raoul Walsh or Jack Ford; it was showy and somehow European. First thing in the morning, he'd ask that the camera be put on a dolly, a small platform rolling on a track. Then he'd sit on the camera seat and try to get as much of the scene as possible in one shot by moving in and out and panning right and left. The rehearsals were longer and more complicated than the traditional long-shot, medium-shot, close-up techniques required, and those rehearsals were for the benefit of the camera crew, not the actors. The performers in each scene were required to hit the marks chalked on the floor, not just one or two but a series, one after another, so that the movie camera's frame would contain the action neatly at all times. "Hitting your marks" became the main concern of rehearsals, and Jimmy found this irksome and let us all see that he did.

"A squirrely son of a bitch," were the eloquent words used by Cagney to describe Tola. "There are some guys who are just natural-born assholes, and Tola was one of them."[2] It was obvious, as Kazan noticed, that Cagney not only did not need direction from Tola, he did not want it."[3] Moreover, the actor detested the abrupt way Tola would talk to the crew, giving orders, "always dominating and impatient with objection and error."[4] Years later Litvak confirmed the problems he encountered in directing Cagney: "Only once in my life did I ever have any difficulties and this was with Jimmy Cagney. He was playing a character he'd never played, a weaker man than he used to play, and he couldn't quite adjust to the part and I came to an impasse with him. And that's the only time in my whole career that I had any troubles with any actor."[5] Things went quiet only for a few days when Jean Negulesco assumed the direction of the film, when Tola suffered an eye injury.

Kazan, who two years later would be directed once again by Tola in *Blues in the Night* (before quitting his career as an actor and becoming one Hollywood's most celebrated and admired directors), described Litvak as a "man of culture," a man who "had several reputations, and one in particular intrigued him—that of a Don Juan." Kazan also believed that Cagney, being a prude,

Ann Sheridan, Frank McHugh, James Cagney and Anthony Quinn in *City for Conquest* (1940).

did not approve of Tola's reputation as a lady-killer. Tola's adventures were daily reported in the gossip columns and every day on the set everybody already knew what he had done and with whom the night before.[6] In spite of his deep dislike for Tola, Cagney did his best for *City for Conquest*, as he wrote in his memoir: "I played a truck driver turned fighter, and so I dieted and trained myself from 180 pounds down to 145 in order to do the fights. To get in the ring and be convincing one has to be in shape or one drops down dead. I did all my own fight scenes."[7]

When Cagney saw the final cut, he was so appalled that he vowed never to watch one of his own movies again. He later told Hollywood gossip columnist Louella Parsons, "I sat there thinking. Was that what it is about? It didn't add up to the hours and days of work that had gone into it. It was all right, but it didn't represent the effort we'd all made."[8]

Audiences liked *City for Conquest*, which was a moneymaker. Tola received from *The Hollywood Reporter* one of the most flattering reviews of his career: "The work of Anatole Litvak is the outstanding credit. He seems to have topped every other effort in his direction of each and every sequence of this picture. His fight scenes are terrific; his love scenes give you creeps of joy; his pacing of the yarn, because it told so much, was perfection.... Litvak is definitely at the top of the heap with this contribution. It was no easy task."[9]

In 1941 Litvak directed his last two films for Warner, *Out of the Fog* and *Blues in the Night*.

The former, based on Irwin Shaw's successful play *The Gentle People*, was the story of Harold Goff, a small-time crook terrorizing the tiny fishing community of Sheepshead Bay, Brooklyn. His victims include Stella Goodwin, a young telephone operator who falls for Goff, and her father Jonah. Shaw had John Garfield in mind when he wrote the story, but it was Franchot Tone who starred in the Broadway production performed by the Group Theatre. Before Warner Bros. purchased the Shaw drama, both Columbia and Paramount expressed interest in making a film of the play. Once the rights were secured, producer Henry Blanke offered Barbara Stanwyck the role of Stella, but she declined. Ann Sheridan was considered, but it was Ida Lupino who eventually got the part. The actress, who was under contract to Warner, was not particularly excited to do it, hoping instead to star in Fox's upcoming big production *How Green Was My Valley*. Once that opportunity vanished, she agreed to do *The Gentle People* (the film's original working title) on the condition that her close friend John Garfield play the lead. After George Raft and Louis Hayward turned down the role of Goff, producers asked Humphrey Bogart; Lupino opposed to that casting decision. She and Bogart had not been on good terms since they worked together for the first time in *They Drive by Night* (1940), when he accidentally kicked her script across the sound stage. Their feud continued while making *High Sierra* (1941) when they got into an animated political argument in the Warner Bros commissary. Garfield was then signed. The production began on February 14, 1941, on Stage 21, which had been transformed by art director Carl Jules Weyl into Sheepshead Bay. A huge tank was installed at the top of the sound stage to release a thick fog. Water in a large pool was dyed blue-black so the waves reflected a better light and photographed more realistically.

Screenwriters Robert Rossen (future director of *The Hustler* [1961] and *Lilith* [1964]), Jerry Wald (future producer of some of Hollywood's best-written films) and Robert Macauley remained true to the play. The Breen Office found the script unacceptable, ordering several drastic changes. Jack Warner received a five-page letter detailing all the "violations" present in the screenplay. According to the Production Code, a murder could not go unpunished; therefore the end in which the fishermen kill the racketeer had to be changed so that his death was accidental. Eventually, the script was completely revised until it looked like a pale reflection of the original play.

While filming, Tola received several angry memos from Hal Wallis telling him to "get more life" out of Garfield, whose performance he (Wallis) intensely disliked after watching the first rushes. Tola paid little attention to Wallis' suggestion and to the numerous other memos in which the producer urged him to speed up the filming. Jack Warner had also been scrutinizing the daily production reports and he was amazed by Litvak's technique of shooting many takes of the same scene. He wrote to Tola: "It is ridiculous that you, an important director, cannot understand that if you get the scene right the first time, stop and go to your next scene." Warner accused Tola of "wearing out the actors, causing a furor," which forced Warner to leave the city "to get my nerves together after going through two weeks of pressure that I have never gone through before."[10] Finally, after two months of a nerve-wracking atmosphere, the production wrapped up.

Out of the Fog opened on June 14, 1941, at the Strand Theatre in New York. Critics complained about the several changes made from stage to film. The picture did not generate the excitement that the studio had hoped for and the box office returns were disappointing. Nevertheless, the studio offered Garfield and Tola another minor film, a drama about jazz players called

Ida Lupino and John Garfield in *Out of the Fog* (1941).

Nocturnes Blues. The star turned it down, and the studio put him on suspension.

Tola was then assigned to a film called *One Foot in Heaven* (1941), but for some reason the studio decided to pull him from the project and entrust it to Irving Rapper, who had been the dialogue director of four of Litvak's pictures. A similar thing had happened when Litvak was assigned to *The Sea Wolf* (1941), which was then turned over to Michael Curtiz.

At the end of June, two months after *Out of the Fog* was completed, Tola made *Blues in the Night,* his ninth and last film with Warner over a five-year period. The picture was first announced in the press as *Hot Nocturne,* then as *New Orleans Blues,* and attached to director Curtis Bernhardt. James Cagney was slated to star after Garfield turned it down. When Tola took over, the film was downgraded to a B cast: Priscilla Lane, Betty Field, Lloyd Nolan, Jack Carson, Richard Whorf, Wallace Ford, Billy Halop and Elia Kazan plus the bands of Jimmy Lunceford and Will Osborne.

The original story was adapted by Robert Rossen from Edwin Gilbert's play *Hot Nocturne.* Some claimed that Kazan helped write the play but for unknown reasons agreed to have his name removed. In an interview years later, Tola claimed that the film was only partially based on the play but the rest was his own idea, explaining that since his arrival in America, he had been fascinated with American music, particularly jazz and its history.

Blues in the Night was indeed a musical but with the overtones of a film noir: Five musicians form a jazz group centered on a piano player who falls for a woman connected to a gangster. The picture marked Kazan's last role as an actor. ("When *Blues in the Night* comes on the late-late show," Kazan wrote in his memoir, "I advise you to skip it."[11] With those words he dismissed his experience in the picture, adding, "I sure as hell can direct better than Anatole Litvak."[12])

Warner was anxious to capitalize on one song's popularity, so the title was changed to *Blues in the Night* after saxophonist-bandleader Jimmy Lunceford's song of the same title became an instant hit. To save on the budget, the set designers used a turntable as the foundation for a cabaret where a large part of the story took place. Instead of maneuvering his camera through swinging doors on a long boom, Tola merely had the set turned. One view was the front, another the inside. Also, a special piano was built with a keyboard made of marshmallows, so when the main character struck it, desperately trying to remember the music, his fingers got stuck to the keys, giving him (and the viewers) a shocking sensation.

The editor of the picture, Don Siegel, recalled a curious episode: Both Hal Wallis and Tola wanted to watch the cut before the other one did, since they wanted to impress each other with their power to change the montage. Therefore Siegel's idea of having a screening for both was out of the question. At the suggestion of Byron Haskin, who ran Warner's special effects department, Siegel made a second print and ran the picture on the same day exactly at the same time but in two different projection rooms at opposite ends of the lot. The gimmick worked and an unnecessary conflict between producer and director was avoided.[13]

Afterwards, when Tola supervised the dubbing of the film, he expressed his concern with Siegel about the title song "Blues in the Night." As Siegel recalled:

> ME: I wouldn't worry about that. It's the best blues I've ever heard. If I were you, I'd worry about your picture, which is five percent as good as the song.
> LITVAK (annoyed): You think you're pretty good, don't you, Don?
> ME (fresh as usual): You said some pretty nice things about the montages.
> LITVAK: True, but when you dolly into the poster you could have had someone walk past the poster. And you should have started on that person and ended on the poster. You must always have a reason for your camera movement, be it a dolly or a pan.
> And you know he was right. He taught me a lesson I used for the rest of my life.[14]

When *Blues in the Night* came out, it was well reviewed but not well received by the public. It did not get the usual exposure given to most Warner films and it did not stay long in the theaters despite earning an Oscar nomination for Best Music, Original Song. Over the years it acquired the label of an art-house film, and has been remembered only because of Kazan's presence.

In August of 1941, Tola made news after he was fined $200, given a suspended ten-day jail term and ordered to surrender his driver's license for two months (he had run through a boulevard stop the previous June). In imposing the penalty, the judge pointed out that Litvak had three similar previous offenses and commented: "You are either a careless driver or a willful law violator. I caution you against any such practice in the future."[15]

Litvak was treasurer of the Russian War Relief Association, which began a campaign to relieve the distress of his homeland. The first activity was sponsoring a transcontinental benefit radio show that included the participation of stars such as Edward G. Robinson, Ronald Colman and other celebrities whose origins were Russian.

A year before his contract with Warner was about to expire, a few major studios interested in Litvak's craft started to contact him. Tola was determined not to be tied up again by a contract with any Hollywood major studios. Instead, he joined a newly incorporated company called Group Productions, formed by his agent Charles Feldman. Feldman had gathered several established artists (including Charles Boyer, Irene Dunne, Ronald Colman and Lewis Milestone) who, like Tola, preferred to produce or work in the film industry independently. In November 1941 a long-rumored production reorganization at 20th Century–Fox took in an outside, independent producing company, and an agreement of collaboration was made with Group Productions. So it was almost natural for Tola to direct his first film with Fox. The picture was *This Above All*, based on a blockbuster novel by Eric Knight, the author of *Lassie, Come Home*. *This Above All* starred Joan Fontaine and Tyrone Power. Fox had secured the rights to the book for over $100,000 after a bidding war against two others major studios. The story was a wartime drama about a love affair between a young aristocratic woman and a lower-middle-class British soldier hero-turned-deserter. In October 1941, Fontaine was approached by producer David O. Selznick about doing the film. The actress, now a star after playing in the hits *Rebecca* (1940) and *Suspicion* (1941), was very reluctant to accept it. It was not until Selznick threatened to put her on suspension that Fontaine agreed to be loaned to Fox. For the part played by Tyrone Power, Fox first considered Robert Donat, Laurence Olivier and Richard Greene. Originally the studio planned to spend a total of $6,500,000 on six films scheduled for shooting at Shepherd's Bush in London and that *This Above All* was set to receive the largest share of that money. By late September 1941, however, all the films set in England had been canceled, presumably because of the war, and producer Darryl F. Zanuck had taken over supervision of the production from Robert Kane, whose new assignment was to film background footage in England. Further delays were then caused by the change in location. Fox postponed the start of production again in mid–November to give Tyrone Power a brief rest. *This Above All* was delayed again in late November by Tola, who wanted to give Power and Fontaine more time to rehearse their love scenes. A $26,000 set, designed to match the look of the background footage shot in England, was constructed on a Fox sound stage. It was a replica of the exterior of a WAAF encampment that included seventeen buildings and dirt roads. Newsreel footage of the London blitz was skillfully intercut throughout the film along with the background footage filmed in England. On December 14, two weeks after the shooting began, Tola broke his foot in a fall over a camera dolly on the Fox lot, but a few days later he was able to resume his work from a wheelchair. To satisfy the demands of the Hays Code, screenwriter R.C. Sherriff had to eliminate from the script reference to Fontaine's character's pregnancy and tone down the illicit love affair.

On the set, the relationship between Fontaine and Tyrone Power was professional. Power was then married to Annabella, Tola's friend from the days

Tyrone Power and Joan Fontaine in *This Above All* (1942).

she had starred in *L'Équipage*. Between takes, Power and Fontaine played gin rummy in her dressing room. Fontaine described her co-star as "circumspect, fairly distant."[16] "He was a very sensitive, gentle person but he wasn't English, so the balance was thrown a bit, and Eric Knight's marvelous book had to be changed in concept quite a lot."[17]

Power loved playing his character, which he considered one of his favorites of his career. He particularly enjoyed being directed by Tola, as years later he revealed in an interview. "I had to think hard to reach an understanding of the character and I had to work harder to make sure he would be understandable to the audience…. Director Anatole Litvak was an inspiring help. Some directors, seeing the mechanical setup of a picture clearly and being interested in putting the jigsaw puzzle together, overlook the human element. Litvak knows the mechanics but he also works closely with you as an individual. I like his severity—it keeps you on your toes."[18]

In spite of all the difficulties encountered, Tola completed the film in about eight weeks with a couple of retakes shot a month later. He had a great professional relationship with executive producer Darryl Zanuck, "[who] with me always behaved wonderfully."[19]

6. Late Warner Years

This Above All was extremely profitable. Reviews were almost all favorable, yet Power's work did not convince some critics who considered him miscast since he did not make any effort to pretend to be English, as his character required. Out of the four Academy Awards nominations the film received, including Best Black-and-White Photography, Best Film Editing, Best Sound Recording, only Best Art Direction-Interior Decoration, got an Oscar.

7

First-Class Cinema

> "[Litvak is] one of the most charming men in the world."
> —Bennett Cerf

In 1940 Tola finally became a naturalized American citizen. His two-year marriage to Miriam Hopkins had certainly helped expedite the process. On December 7, 1941, Japan attacked Pearl Harbor as Litvak had just started principal photography on *This Above All*. A few months after completing the picture, despite suffering from asthma, he joined the Special Services Film Unit of the U.S. Army.

"I was a photographic officer on the staff of Gen. Patton when I was ordered to cover test maneuvers for the invasion ... so that his staff could study the film," Tola said of those early days in the Army. He continued:

> It was a rough assignment—our crew got no sleep for five days and nights—the film had to be ready for viewing forty-eight hours after the landings. This was my first job—I was more nervous than ever before in my life—the general was the critic in this case. In Hollywood, when you make a bad picture, everybody tells you it's great—you have to wait for the critics to get the truth. In this case, I knew the truth would be written all over General Patton's face. During the screening of the final film, I watched the general much more closely than the movie—there was no question about his reaction: first a frown, then a scowl! At the end, he stalked out of the projection room in a barely controlled rage!

Tola sweated it out all night, slept very little, waiting for an official verdict. The next morning he got it from his commanding officer: "Stop worrying, Litvak—the general is not mad at you ... only at your 'cast.'" The film had uncovered dozens of bonehead decisions, clumsy tactics, and glaring flaws in training and execution of orders.

"That night I had a very select audience ... and very attentive. Every staff officer hand-picked by Patton, ordered to sit there and look at the film and suffer through their mistakes all over again."[1]

Afterward, at director Frank Capra's invitation, Tola joined him in making a series of orientation films called *Why We Fight*. It was an idea conceived by General George C. Marshall, who wanted every soldier knew the reason why he must serve and may die for his own country.

Capra, a prolific and successful Hollywood filmmaker, had been put in charge of the War Department's film program and was commissioned to make films designed to detail the causes, the progress and the goals of the war. To better understand the enemy's concept of war and supremacy, the director was shown Leni Riefenstahl's *Triumph of the Will* (1935), the most prominent example of Hitler's propaganda. Capra began work in Washington in early 1942 creating the 834th Photo Signal Detachment, using the expertise of five key men: writers Anthony Veiller and Eric Knight, film editor William Hornbeck, documentarian Edgar Peterson and co-director Tola. Soon the detachment transferred to the more congenial atmosphere of the old 20th Century–Fox studio on Western Avenue in Hollywood. It had been abandoned a few years earlier; Capra asked Darryl Zanuck to let him have it for his film section. Without hesitation the producer agreed and had the space cleaned up and painted. Meanwhile, Capra, Tola, Veiller, Robert Heller and Leonard Spiegelgass began to work on the *Why We Fight* scripts, seven training films, each an hour in length. Although the whole series was made in that decrepit studio with borrowed furniture and equipment, Capra was surrounded by the industry's most skilled professionals, including Walt Disney and his animators who created animated maps and cartoons to be inserted in the documentaries. A group of translators rephrased the German and Japanese films into English, while another group later catalogued and cross-filed the film scenes. In pre-production, Tola worked with Capra's other key men on research and scripts. A team of assistant producers, writers, editors and research men was organized in order to work more or less concurrently on the preparation of each film.

In the beginning, Tola's collaboration was fraught with suspicion of his patriotism by Republican Senator Ralph O. Brewster. The politician asked the War Department about Litvak, expressing concern about his status as a "naturalized American," thinking that he owed his position in Capra's team to the influence of his wife Miriam Hopkins. Brewster urged the military to use a more "seasoned citizen" than Tola, who had become an American fairly recently and at age forty. However, in an extended memo, Julius H. Amberg, special assistant to the secretary of war, informed the Senator that Litvak and Hopkins were divorced and that Litvak had demonstrated high artistic merit in his collaboration with Capra.[2] Tola played a large role in the effort, solo-directing *The Battle of Russia* and co-directing with Capra *Prelude to War, The Nazi Strike, Divide and Conquer, The Battle of China* and *War Comes to America*.

Veiller was the screenwriter of the entire series (Tola co-wrote *The Battle of Russia*), which was narrated by Walter Huston with music by Dimitri Tiomkin. The films contained fiction footage capably combined with documentary material and animation. In his autobiography, Capra revealed that the films were

> primarily made by the Army for the Army, they were used as training films by the Navy, Marine Corps and the Coast Guard. The British, Canadians, Australians, and New Zealanders used them as training films for their armed forces. Translated into French, Spanish, Portuguese and Chinese they were shown to the armed forces of our allies in China, South America and in various parts of Europe and Africa.... By an order of Winston Churchill all were shown to the British public in theaters.[3]

Tola was also sent on a special mission to Russia, where he showed *The Battle of Russia* to the Russian General Staff. Its main theme was the heroic manner in which the Russian people as well as their armies had shattered the horrendous legend of Nazi invincibility.[4] *The Battle of Russia* showed Tola's continued deep attachment to his mother country. He said,

> Because I speak Russian, Ambassador Harriman and Major General Deane, head of our military mission in Moscow, asked me to handle the commentary of the film, explaining what had just happened on this second front, for which the Russians had been pressing so hard. Afterward, the Russian generals came up to me, very friendly, and asked me how I had learned to speak Russian so fluently.... I explained that I was born in Russia, but I had left there when I was twenty-two and now I was an American citizen. I had no chance to say anything more ... they turned, said goodbye politely, and quickly left me. No Russian spoke to me the rest of the evening. Even then, though we were allies fighting a common enemy. I was a "traitor" to them ... because I had come to live to America.[5]

While in Russia, Tola briefly reunited with his old mother, whom he had left in Leningrad almost twenty years earlier. "[Russian filmmaker Vsevolod] Pudovkin gave a party for me. My mother read about it and called the American Embassy, which called me,"[6] he recalled in an interview in the '60s.

Journalist Edgar Snow, who was in Moscow with Tola, asked him his impression of Moscow and the Russians after so many years away. He replied,

> The city is still recognizable, but I wouldn't have known the people. They aren't the same Russians. They are proud and confident and full of hope—even my old mother. The Russian I remember was humble and pessimistic. I have talked to many Russians now. They say something like this: "I've lost my son, I've lost my brother, I've lost my husband. The roof leaks and I have paper soles in my shoes." But then they look at the rockets celebrating a victory and they say: "Never mind, the worst is over. Tomorrow is another day and everything is going to be all right."[7]

In spite of the hard feelings the Russian commanders had for Tola, the film was shown in all their theaters. In the end of 1943 *The Battle of Russia* opened to excellent reviews in the States. In 1944 it was the recipient of the New York Film Critics Award as Best Documentary. In addition, Tola supervised three other Army orientations films: *Substitution and Conversion* (1943), which depicted the Pentagon's resource program and the necessity for ingenuity in dealing with the lack of critical materials, *Operation Titanic* (1944) and *D-Day: The Normandy Invasion* (1945). Capra requested that Tola be assigned as a producer for *Here Is Germany* but Major Edgar Stevenson was put in charge instead. Some sources claimed that Tola also collaborated with Capra on two other series, *Know Your Enemy* and *Know Your Ally,* neither of which was completed because of priorities eventually given to other forms of Army filmmaking. Since these documentaries did not have any credits, we cannot determine with certainty which one he was directly involved.

In May 1944, Tola was sent to France to work on a film about the retraining of American troops in Europe for the expected invasion of Japan. However, as biographer Michael Shnayerson states in his book on writer Irwin Shaw, who participated in that mission together with Tola, the shooting plan changed when they arrived in Paris:

> The French had survived their quick bout of gratitude to the American forces and wanted to know why the Americans felt obliged to make use of French railroads to mass troops and supplies for the Japanese invasion. A film, perhaps, would help them see why. To help, Litvak rounded up two other capable hands: Broadway producer, director and writer Josh Logan, and French writer Maurice Druon, whose novels would eventually earn him a place in the Académie Française.... The filmmaking mission, it devolved into a glorious junket. From Paris the crew drove east to Germany, passing through Cologne, Bonn and Munich, ending up in Berchtesgaden, Hitler's Bavarian mountain retreat. "All that while," recalls Pickney Ridgell, who went along as a cameraman, "we were filming at Litvak's direction—and a brusque direction that was. He was white-haired, short and gruff. But somehow—I guess because he was a well-known director by then—he had beautiful girls, actresses many of them, appear out of nowhere wherever we stopped." The crew finished filming just as President Truman sanctioned the bombing of Japan; with the Japanese surrender on August 15, the entire project was shelved.[8]

Once all the projects were completed, Lieutenant Colonel Anatole Litvak was left in command of the Hollywood Photo Center on Western Avenue. For his services, the British Government decorated him with the gold medal, ribbon and citation as an honorary officer of the Order of the British Empire. He was unable to attend the official ceremonies at the British Embassy in Washington because he was then shooting *The Snake Pit*; he received via mail the gold medal, ribbon and citation. The French Government awarded him the Légion d'Honneur and the Croix de Guerre. He also received the United States Legion of Merit and a Bronze Star.

During a brief stay in New York, Litvak and his friend, director Billy Wilder, decided to go to visit director William Wyler, who was in the hospital recovering from a war injury that had damaged his eardrums. Wilder recalled,

> On the way to the hospital, we were caught by a heavy thunderstorm that forced us to stop the car. Heavy rain, thunder and lightning made it impossible to keep going. Five years earlier, when we were friends and neighbors, I never asked Litvak anything about that infamous night in West Hollywood—I was too discreet to do it. Now, while we were sitting side by side in the car stuck while another lightning [bolt] was striking with typical noise that followed I said, "Tola, this could be our end. In front of a possible death, tell me the truth! What really happened at Ciro's that night?" And while another lightning tore the sky apart, Litvak raised his hand like if he was about to swear and answered, "Billy, I swear that I'm telling the truth, the whole truth and nothing but the truth! You know how crazy I was about Paulette. We were dancing. She was wearing a sensational strapless dress. While dancing, a shoulder strap fell down revealing for a split second a part of her breast. So I kissed her breast and with my mouth I put the strap back in its place. God is my witness!" Since shortly after the storm was over, I have to assume that Anatole told me the real truth.[9]

Back to Hollywood Tola was committed to direct *New Orleans Blues* for producers Herbert J. Biberman and Jules Levy at United Artists. The picture was based on a Biberman-Elliot Paul-Dick Irving Hyland screenplay about the migration of African-American jazz musicians from New Orleans to Chicago. For unknown reasons, Litvak withdrew from the project in favor of Arthur Lubin, who directed the picture in the summer of 1946 under the title *New Orleans*.

The first project which saw Litvak's name in the credits was *Meet Me at Dawn* (whose working title was *The Gay Duellist*), based on the story "Le Tueur" by Tola and Marcel Achard. This comedy of romance and adventure, set in *fin de siècle* Paris, was about a politician forced into a fight with a deadly professional fighter. *Meet Me at Dawn* was produced in the United Kingdom by 20th Century–Fox and directed by Thornton Freeland. It opened first in England in January 1947 and a year and four months later in America to disappointing reviews, quickly disappearing from screens.

While in France in 1944 making a war documentary, Tola reunited with his old friend Joseph Kessel. After the success of *L'Équipage* and their first trip together to Hollywood, they both wished to work together. Now at the end of the war, the two planned to write a script based on Kessel's 1936 best-selling novel *Coup de grâce*. An Enterprise Production, it was announced in the press in May 1946. At that time the book did not have an English translation, so Tola took a trip to New York to attend to that matter. He told the press that once the American reading public had a chance to read it, the book would be as much as a sensation as *Gone with the Wind*. Nothing came out of

Anatole Litvak, left, with Talli Tallichet Wyler and William Wyler at an event in the early '60s.

it. The picture was made five years later as *Sirocco* (1951), directed by Curtis Bernhardt and starring Humphrey Bogart.

A Time to Kill, released as *The Long Night*, marked Tola's Hollywood return. In the spring of 1945, producers Robert and Raymond Hakim purchased the rights for an American remake of *Le Jour se Lève* (Daybreak), an internationally popular French picture directed in 1939 by Marcel Carné, starring Jean Gabin, Jules Berry and Arletty. The producers thought that the perfect director to handle the project was Tola who, according to them, possessed that cosmopolitan flavor able to remake a French hit for American audiences. The proposal thrilled Tola. He had greatly admired *Le Jour se Lève,* a morality tale written by French poet Jacques Prévert, about a doomed French criminal. He accepted it immediately, demanding *carte blanche* in his casting choices. Henry Fonda seemed to him the right choice for the main role that had previously given French star Jean Gabin international popularity. Like many movie stars returning after the war, Fonda was looking for more mature material to break his previous image as the innocent or romantic hero. He was intrigued by Tola's proposal and accepted the role of ex-soldier Joe Adams, falling in love with a young girl and forced to fatally shoot a wicked nightclub magician with whom she is involved in a sort of Svengali relationship. Opposite Fonda, Tola cast Barbara Bel Geddes after seeing her on Broadway in *Deep Are the Roots.* Bel Geddes was the daughter of noted theatrical producer Norman Bel Geddes. *The Long Night* marked her screen debut. Subsequently, she signed a seven-year contract with RKO. Although the actress made a number of films, including Hitchcock's *Vertigo* (1958), she became best known for her work on the Broadway stage and for her role as Miss Ellie Ewing on the long-running television series *Dallas.* Vincent Price was borrowed from 20th Century–Fox to play the part of the magician and received equal billing with Fonda. Before the start of shooting, Tola demanded that Price take instructions from professional magician Charlie Miller, who reportedly taught the actor complicated tricks with cards, a magic floating ball, a mind-reading dog, etc. No camera tricks were used, Tola elected to "make the tricks mystifying to the extras in the audience as they would be people paying actual admission."[10] On the first day Price suffered from a swollen face caused by a repeated slapping called for in the script. Then he sprained his wrist while performing a magic trick following a dog attack that was part of the scene. The worst and final injury was a fractured rib, incurred when he was required to fall down four steps after a stuntman had tumbled two flights for him.[11]

The shooting was completed in 86 days. While it was being edited, the film's working title *A Time to Kill* was changed into *The Long Night* and the opening credits now included with the quotation "The night is long / That never finds the day ..." from Shakespeare's *Macbeth* Act IV, Scene III.

RKO planned an elaborate publicity event for the film's New England showings: William Courtney, the lawyer who prosecuted Al Capone, and Herbert L. Callahan, a prominent defense attorney, were to try a mock case, similar to the one depicted in the picture. Before *The Long Night* was released, the producers bought up copies of *Le Jour se Lève* and destroyed them, causing a great outcry in the press. Only one print was left in the National Film Library in the United Kingdom with strict instructions to never be shown unless the producers who bought the rights to the story gave permission.

In spite of all the gimmicks, *The Long Night* was a box-office disaster. The picture found little favor with the public and the critics, who unanimously compared it to the far superior French original. *The Hollywood Reporter's* review praised Tola's direction: "It is Litvak's first picture since the war, and from the standpoint of his contribution ranks with his finest."[12] However, the director elsewhere was accused of making a film lacking proper pacing, too slow, too dark and overly talkative—a product stylistically more European than American. RKO lost a million dollars and the movie was promptly forgotten.

The first mention of Tola's next project, *The Snake Pit*, appeared in an April 1946 article in the *New York Times*: "Also on Mr. Litvak's list is *The Snake Pit*, the bestselling novel by Mary Jane Ward, for which he plans to journey to England for the purpose of signing a leading player." During his Army

Henry Fonda and Vincent Price in *The Long Night* (1947).

days, Tola learned a lot about psychiatry, making several Signal Corps shorts about rehabilitation, especially of soldiers suffering of posttraumatic stress disorders and how their families should interact with them. The subject fascinated him. In May 1945, he read the galley proofs of *The Snake Pit,* Ward's semi-autobiographical novel about a young woman's harrowing experiences in a state mental hospital. The title refers to the overcrowded ward where the incurable mental patients are warehoused. Tola was so captivated that he bought the film rights, hoping to make an independent production. Bennett Cerf, president of Random House, wrote in his autobiography:

> Many producers who inquired about the movie rights to *The Snake Pit* backed away at the last minute because a couple of big scenes involved shock treatment, and they thought the whole background of an insane asylum was too gruesome. But I finally sold the rights to Anatole Litvak, a close friend of ours and one of the most charming men in the world.... I sold *The Snake Pit* to Tola one night while we were having dinner at the St. Regis Hotel. He bought it on his own, but finally had to get backing from 20th Century–Fox. He made the picture, which was a knockout and won a string of prizes. I remember the price: it was forty-five thousand dollars, which was a lot of money in those days, especially for Mary Jane Ward.[13]

Other sources claim Litvak paid seventy-five thousand dollars, paid in installments. "As I kept paying, I got broker and broker," Tola told *Time* magazine.[14]

Litvak proposed the project to many studios, but nobody seemed interested in taking a risk on a film about such a delicate subject. After a number of rejections, in the summer of 1946, Tola went to Fox's Darryl Zanuck. Litvak still owed a couple of pictures to Fox after making *This Above All.*

"Darryl," he said, "here is the story, I think it's a great story; I tried to do it independently, but I couldn't. Would you consider doing it? Because it would be a crime if this picture wouldn't be made."[15] Zanuck asked him to put on paper the story outline and promised to give him an answer in a couple of days. Tola described *The Snake Pit* in five pages and the producer called a meeting to ask the opinion of his assistants. No one liked it. They believed that the story was too downbeat and the topic—tasteless, perhaps offensive—would keep people away from the theaters. But Zanuck thought that audiences had changed with the war and were more interested in subjects about problems with current life. After several meetings with Ward, who had spent almost nine months in a state mental hospital, he decided to buy the rights from Tola for $175,000 and let him direct and co-produce.

The Fox mogul carefully supervised the scripting, the shooting and the final editing. It was agreed that the picture would be shot in black and white in an attempt to give a more accurate representation of the colorless world of the institutionalized. Tola spent nearly six months in New York with the scenarists assigned to the project—Hungarian screenwriter Frank Partos and noted novelist-poet Millen Brand. Five of the six months he spent at the Brooklyn State Hospital conducting research. Simultaneously, he spent that entire period working very closely with three of the most illustrious American psychiatrists acting as technical advisors: Dr. M. Ralph Kaufman, chief psychiatrist at Mount Sinai Hospital, and chief of all Army neuropsychiatric activities in the Pacific during the war; Dr. Carl A. Binger, associate professor of Clinical Psychiatry at Cornell University; and Dr. Sidney Loseef Tamarin, supervising psychiatrist at a New York mental institution.

For the difficult role of Virginia Cunningham, Tola wanted Ingrid Bergman, but the actress declined the offer. Olivia de Havilland was his second and final choice even though some press in 1946 announced that Gene Tierney and Joan Fontaine (de Havilland's sister) were candidates. Tola asked de Havilland to read his copy of the galleys. She did, and immediately saw the picture's possibilities. She told Tola she was interested and later signed the contract accepting that challenging part. To better understand her role, she visited a mental institution at Camarillo, California.

"I went three times to do research," she said later. "It was regarded as a model hospital but it was sadly undermanned as to doctors. There I talked to and watched inmates in varying degrees of mental illness. I steeled myself to look at these cases objectively."[16]

In pre-production, Tola asked for script help from Arthur Laurents. Originally, Tola had asked Laurents to write the script. They had met in the office of Bennett Cerf, as the screenwriter mentioned in his memoir: "To Litvak I said no politely too quickly, with not enough reverence for his Hollywood rank.... His white hair, however premature, made him seem younger than I first thought he was, his carriage made him seem taller; his blue eyes had an amused glint that belied his very gracious acceptance of my rejection. Those eyes said, It's your loss and dismissed me."[17]

A few months later, neither Tola nor Zanuck was satisfied with Parros and Brand's script. The producer and director lunched at Romanoff's together, smoked Havana cigars, played gin rummy, and agreed that changes needed to be made. The screenwriter's mistake: being too faithful to the book, making the story unfold too slowly, and the character's cure at the end looked phony. Tola stubbornly tried once again to contact Laurents. The screenwriter recalled:

> The meeting was over lunch at [Litvak's] house in Malibu. He sent his secretary, Ann Selepegno, to pick me up and drive me there.... The house she drove me to—a red door in a small stretch of gray fence—looked like a shack from the Coast highway. I was wrong there, too. It was on the beach but it wasn't a beach house; it was the

house Tola Litvak lived in and it said so eloquently once you went through the red door.... The design was so dramatic it was duplicated for *Mildred Pierce* ... quiet Calvin and Esther who took care of him and his house as long he lived there or Ann, unquiet but his whenever he was and whenever he went. The love and the devotion all three had for him was remarkable in view of what a formal, undemonstrative man he was. His clothes were never casual nor was he. Ann called him Colonel (the rank he earned making army films). He was polite always, remembered small things and appreciated small things. He could be caustic when irritated, could suddenly laugh, be intimate for a moment, open up like a window, then close down but not tightly: a breath of air remained even after.[18]

Convinced by Tola's charm, Laurents agreed to review the script. Laurents was under an MGM contract from which I could not get a release. Finally the studio loaned him to Fox. With Laurents' help, the screenplay was completed. Zanuck liked the final script, yet he wanted some twenty-odd pages cut within a week, threatening to cut them himself if the writer would not do it. The producer did not care which pages; all that mattered was that exact number be cut because the cost of shooting each page each day was budgeted with amazing accuracy. Tola, his secretary and Laurents met and removed all the unnecessary words, made the spacing smaller and extended the margins, finishing two pages short of Zanuck's request. In spite of his major involvement with the script, Laurents' name did not appear in the on-screen credits. In an interview the screenwriter explained:

> A friend of mine, Irene Selznick, said, "You ought to do something; your name's not on that script." Well, credits never meant anything to me. But I said something about it to Tola, who as I say, remained a great friend despite that incident.... He said, "Well, that's ridiculous. You wrote the script! We had to throw out what they wrote." When the picture was finished, the credit went to the Screen Writers Guild [for arbitration], and they ruled that Millen Brand and Frank Partos had written it. There was no screen credit for me. The Guild hearing was during the shooting of the picture, and Tola said he was too busy to attend to testify. So I didn't get the screen credit! ... Millen Brand apologized to me. It was wrenching for him to do this because he was a very moral man. But he had a wife whom he was insane about, and she was telling him [the screen credit] would help him get other jobs. He didn't want to write movies anyway. So he lied. And the wife left him anyway.... They did something very cleaver, but dastardly. There was a whole slew of scenes that were nothing like anything they'd written, so they typed them up and threw away the originals and kept the carbons as thought they had written them. I didn't learn about that [trick] until after on.[19]

Laurents' credit claim, refuted by the Screen Writers Guild, ignited a controversy. After the decision was announced, Tola publicly stated: "[The Writers Guild] held a hearing and decided against giving Mr. Laurents screen credit, but I want to see that his contribution doesn't go unnoticed."[20] It was the first time a producer (Tola was a co-producer of the picture) had acted contrary to the findings of the Guild. The statement outraged Sheridan Gibney, president of the Screen Writers Guild, who wrote an open letter to the *New York Times* listing the reasons for his indignation.

Zanuck was extremely pleased with the final outcome. In a memo dated September 20, 1946, he proudly told producer David O. Selznick: "Litvak and his writers have come up with a wonderful slant on *The Snake Pit*. They have devised an angle which develops the strange romance between the girl, the doctor and the husband and goes a long way toward solving the obvious problems of this spectacular novel."[21]

Tola shot the entire film on a soundstage, making a great effort to recreate the exact atmosphere he had found while visiting New York's Rockland State Hospital and other mental hospitals along with crew and cast members. He borrowed cinematographer Leo Tover from Paramount and took him to the mental institutions to absorb the atmosphere and feel of such places. Tover observed the inmates, their patterns of motion, and the effect of the light falling upon their contorted faces. Tola also demanded that the actresses in the picture look as natural as possible with very little makeup applied. The

Olivia de Havilland and Leo Genn in *The Snake Pit* (1948).

women were told not to wear any accessories (including girdles, bras, nail or toe polish) since the former were not permitted in mental hospitals. De Havilland had to go through a physically exhausting ordeal, losing weight and getting dark circles under her eyes. False eyelashes were applied because they sunk her eyes and made her face a death mask. In a scene in which she was confined in a tub of warm water prescribed to soothe her hysteria, she was drenched with water coming from a gigantic barrel placed six feet above her head. It took numerous takes before Tola achieved what he called "a perfect take."

De Havilland was confined in bed for two days to recover from the resultant cold and fever. Co-star Beulah Bondi, who had also appeared in *The Sisters,* was asked by Tola to play a difficult scene several times. After each take, he offered no criticism but simply said that he wanted her to do it again. The scene was filmed seven times. After the seventh take, a bit exasperated, she turned to him and told him that she didn't mind doing the scene again if he would offer her some sort of comment. "I just love to watch you act," was Tola's simple explanation.[22]

For the role of Dr. Kik, Richard Conte and Joseph Cotten were considered, but British actor Leo Genn got the role. At de Havilland's suggestion, Mark Stevens was cast as Virginia's husband. Studio legal records indicate that recordings of patients were made at the Camarillo hospital for use either on the soundtrack or as a "technical guide," but they were later destroyed due to fear of lawsuits. Tola avoided montage and impressionistic photography. Much of the action is seen through the eyes of the psychiatrist who treats the heroine. "The camera," according to Litvak, "will merely see the outward manifestations of the disorder from the viewpoint of realistic sanity."[23] Tola was convinced that the public was "always grateful when they get something different, not a message—perhaps, just some pure information presented in an interesting, dramatic form." He also specified that he chose to make the film to "awaken public interest in the vital matter, to reassure people that mental disorder is an illness which can be cured, and to direct attention to the facilities now available in our institutions.... This was the toughest thing I ever attempted. Everything else will have to be easier."[24]

According to Betsy Blair, who had a small role in the picture, Tola did the editing of the film in Paris. "How he managed to be doing this in Paris, I have no idea, since it was a 20th Century–Fox film, shot on a lot in Los Angeles."[25]

Zanuck was so proud of the final cut that he sent *The Snake Pit* to the 10th Venice International Film Festival, figuring that a premiere before all the critics at such a fashionable event would help blunt the film's grim edge. Blair accompanied Tola to the premiere, where the film was a success. Critics from all over the world unanimously loved the film, which was quickly sold to many foreign countries. The picture was nominated as Best Picture and de Havilland received the prestigious Coppa Volpi as Best Actress. In Venice, Tola was often seen accompanying Italian starlet Mariella Lotti, driving tabloid speculation about a love affair and an impromptu wedding, but as soon as the Festival was over, the fling faded away.

When *The Snake Pit* was released in late 1948, critical raves and strong word of mouth helped make it a hit. De Havilland could not take part in the glamorous New York premiere, so Tola had Blair and her husband Gene Kelly accompany him. At all the other events nationwide where the film was showed, de Havilland was encouraged by Zanuck to look particularly glamorous, in sharp contrast to the shabby look of her character. For his work, Tola received a quarterly Screen Directors Guild award for directorial achievement. He was also nominated for a Best Director Academy Award. The film's other nominations included Best Picture and Best Actress. Litvak lost out to John Huston for *The Treasure of the Sierra Madre*. Litvak's greatest satisfaction was the fact that *The Snake Pit* brought wide public attention to the problems related to the conditions of mental institutions in America, which resulted in a certain amount of change in the laws and their administration. Despite the initial doubts, the $2,000,000 film broke box office records in many American cities and became Fox's highest grossing picture of the year.

In the spring of 1949, *The Snake Pit* was allowed to be shown in England by the British Board of Film Censors, but with 12 minutes cut "to avoid causing apprehension and distress." Moreover an introduction was added pointing out that conditions depicted applied to American and not to British asylums. Children under 16 were not allowed to see it. The British press was divided whether those cuts were legitimate and necessary. In Birmingham the management committee controlling the city mental hospitals urged in vain that the picture not be shown. The frenzy created around the film contributed to making the film one of England's biggest hits of the year.

8

Mixed Reviews

> "I was very very lucky. Anatole Litvak was ... a very fine director and a marvelous person to work for."
>
> —Barbara Stanwyck

Months before making *The Snake Pit,* Tola had the idea of directing a film based on a 22-minute radio play called *Sorry, Wrong Number,* made popular by Agnes Moorehead in a tour-de-force performance in 1943. The play was so successful that it was rebroadcast seven times and translated into fifteen languages. Tola bought the screen rights for $15,000 after the war and brought the story to Hal B. Wallis, who loved it. Wallis had his company repurchase the rights for $100,000, commissioning the author Lucille Fletcher to expand it into a full-length screenplay. Fletcher wrote a script based on *Murder on the Telephone* (a novelization of her radio play) with Tola's supervision. "I worked as hard with the writer, as any director ever works," recalled Litvak, "but this is one of the few stories in which I had the luck to have a woman who was so deeply involved in the story: Lucille Fletcher.... I worked maybe three weeks with her on the final script."[1] The screenplay was initially rejected by the Production Code because of its focus on the main character's involvement in illegal drug traffic. After some alterations, the final draft was approved.

Tola and Wallis agreed that Agnes Moorehead was not enough of a movie name to cast her as the lead. She was later offered a secondary role, but got offended and turned it down. The top part was given to Barbara Stanwyck, who seemed the right choice to play neurotic, bedridden Leona Stevenson, who overhears a phone conversation and realizes her husband is plotting her murder. Tola was a great admirer of Stanwyck as an actress and had always hoped that one day they could work together. "But in spite of [this], not knowing her personally, and just from talk around town, I was a bit afraid of working together because of her strong personality," he confessed in an interview.

> However, from the time I met her during a lunch we had together in a small restaurant across from the Paramount Studios, any doubts I might have had about her vanished.

8. Mixed Reviews

Barbara Stanwick in a dramatic moment from *Sorry, Wrong Number* (1948).

I'm not one who pays compliments easily, but I can tell you that in all my years as a director I've seldom known an actress not only so extraordinarily talented but so unselfishly professional ... the part she played in this film was not an easy one. We didn't have a very long schedule and Barbara had to work practically every day from morning to night. There was never a word of complaint—only encouragement and enthusiasm, which certainly influenced and helped not only me in my work but everyone connected to the film.[2]

It was indeed a very difficult role for Stanwyck, as she explained: "I was very very lucky. Anatole Litvak was the director, a very fine director and a marvelous person to work for. I had twelve days of the terror in bed. And he very kindly ... asked me, did I want to do those twelve days all at once or spread them in between continuity.... I thought it would be better if I could do the twelve days at once so that I myself might have continuity, and he very graciously fixed his schedule as such. And I did twelve days—consecutively."[3]

During the production Stanwyck's hair turned completely white. "I don't know whether it was the part," she said to Bill Hahn during a 1965 interview on his WNAC radio show. "Of course, I worried every night that I went home, because all the scenes in bed were filmed sequentially—which means that at six o'clock at night if I have hit a high emotional peak, then I must come back the next morning and start up there. Well, this worries the life out of a performer, because how do you go home and eat and shower and sleep and then at nine o'clock in the morning start way up there? It's rather difficult. So, I worried quite a lot about it. Now I don't know whether that was part and parcel of [the change in hair color] but it did start on that."[4]

On the set Tola, who always strived for perfection, had Stanwyck do several scenes over and over. In a particularly emotional one, after quite a few takes, he called for a break to allow her to rest. Tola left the set for a drink and immediately the crew complained to Stanwyck about Tola's behavior. The actress was moved, but did not accept the sympathy of her co-workers, being concerned that only the director should have judged her performance and no one else. In the end, her performance was impeccable and Tola was quite satisfied. She had refused to wear any makeup to look the part, which required expressions of pure nervous tension.

The casting of the role of Henry Stevenson, the weak husband who pays a killer to murder his wealthy wife for insurance money, was not as smooth as it was for Stanwyck. During a fishing trip with Burt Lancaster, Hal Wallis, who had the actor under exclusive contract at Paramount, talked about his dilemma about who should play the male leading role in *Sorry, Wrong Number*. The producer had in mind Lee Bowman, who was not available. "I need someone who specializes in weak parts," said Wallis.

"Why don't you not let me play it?" suggested Lancaster.

Wallis said, "You can't play it. You're too strong for it."

"But that's the whole point; a strong-looking boy on the threshold of life allows a woman to buy him and then he suffers for it, and all of his character has been drained out of him. And at the beginning of the film they'll believe I'm strong, and then the contrast will make for real dramatic excitement."[5] At the time Lancaster was looking for different kinds of roles to give him new challenges. He was tired of playing gangsters as he had done in *The Killers* (1946), *Brute Force* (1947) and *I Walk Alone* (1948); he had just started to break the mold playing in *All My Sons* (1948). *Sorry, Wrong Number* seemed to be a perfect chance to keep following that path. Back at Paramount, Wallis discussed the possibility of casting Lancaster with Tola, who liked the idea. So the actor was hired.

"I really sweated bullets on that one," said Lancaster. "This was the first part with which I couldn't identify Lancaster on the screen. Usually there's some movement, some characteristics which you recognize as your own. But not this one. Ten minutes after I walked into the theater I gave up looking for Lancaster. Seemed like a different person up there. It's a good movie."[6]

On the set, Lancaster had a few arguments with Tola about how to play his character. In a moment of rage the star reportedly said, "Okay, let's leave it up to the studio: Either you leave or I leave and who the fuck do you think is gonna be out?"⁷ Nonetheless Tola described Lancaster as a "nice down-to-earth hard worker young fellow.... He knows exactly his own limits and struggles to give the best he can with uncontrollable patience and obstinate persistence."⁸

Although the entire film was shot in a studio, the opening scene of a telephone switchboard was shot on location at a telephone company office on Gower Street in Hollywood. With the help of cinematographer Sol Polito, Tola turned Leona Stevenson's luxurious apartment into a virtual no-escape cell. Sound was used to heighten the tension, giving the film a feeling of claustrophobia.

Although *Sorry, Wrong Number* was filmed right after *The Snake Pit*, it was released three months earlier. Before opening nationwide, several private screenings took place across the country, resulting in exceptional word-of-mouth publicity. According to a memo written by Darryl Zanuck to producer Spyros Skouras, "Everywhere you go you hear people talk about [it], even though they have not actually seem it [and] this word-of-mouth publicity eventually reaches the theatergoing public. No one knows exactly how or why this occurs, but the fact of its occurrence is indisputable."⁹

Reviewers were impressed by Stanwyck's sensational performance, which earned her a fourth Academy Award nomination, competing with *The Snake Pit*'s Olivia de Havilland. (Both of Tola's divas walked away from the ceremony empty-handed: The Oscar went to Jane Wyman for *Johnny Belinda*.)

In December 1949, after the acclaim heaped on Tola's last two films, 20th Century–Fox assigned him to direct a biography of Sigmund Freud. The subject had been under consideration for some time and now Fox seemed ready to do it. Screenwriter Charles Kaufman started his research while Tola planned to go through all of Freud's autobiographical notes and to meet with Anna, the psychiatrist's daughter, and as many of Freud's friends as possible to better understand his personality. The project never came to fruition. (In 1962 Universal Pictures produced *Freud*, a biography directed by John Huston and starring Montgomery Clift.) Tola was also attached to a film called *Take Care of My Little Girl*, based on a novel by Peggy Goodin and dealing with problems created by college fraternities and sororities. Litvak was replaced; dear friend Jean Negulesco made the picture two years later.

Hoping to direct and produce another hit, Tola acquired the screen rights to *Montserrat*, a play by Emmanuel Robles and adapted by Lillian Hellman, about a young Spanish officer sent to Venezuela in 1812 to help capture Simon Bolivar. Tola planned to cast Gregory Peck in the lead, but the film was never produced.

In June 1948 Tola traveled to Europe aboard the *Queen Mary* together with his close friend, director Billy Wilder. In Paris he stayed at the Hotel George V while promoting *The Snake Pit* and *Sorry, Wrong Number,* both just released in France. Zurich and Rome were his next destinations, "The purpose of my trip," he told the French press, "is to prepare the making of a film whose subject I have not chosen yet, but I plan to shoot in Paris within a couple of months."[10]

Tola's plans to make a film in Paris changed once he returned to America. He became interested in making a picture based on the war novel *Call It Treason* by George Howe, who had served as a civilian documents expert in the Office of Strategic Services. The book was a fictionalized account of a behind-enemy-lines intelligence mission undertaken by a young German prisoner of war, who agreed to spy for the Americans. Thanks to John Huston, screenwriter Peter Viertel was introduced to Tola, who was eager to discuss this project with him. Tola was impressed by the coincidence that Viertel had been involved in that same operation during the war that had inspired Howe's novel. However, the screenwriter was hesitant to work on a story with the same background (his experiences in the O.S.S.) that he had already started to write as a novel. "'You can always go back to your novel later,' Tola replied, brushing my objections aside," remembered Viertel. "Then he admitted that one reason the story intrigued him was that it offered him a chance to make a movie in Europe.... 'You wouldn't mind getting out of this place for a while, would you?' he asked."[11] The terms offered by Fox to Viertel were persuasive enough to make him agree to write the script.

According to the screenwriter, the experience was interesting but far from satisfying. Although he was better acquainted with the background of the story than Tola, the director tried to inject into the script his personal experience. "Long before principal photography began there were countless arguments about every sequence I was to write, quite a few of them acrimonious," recalled Viertel. "'I may not be talented,' Tola shouted during one of our heated discussions, 'but I'm very, very intelligent.' It was an allegation I could not dispute. He was also a generous and fatherly boss who had the unusual ability to forget the bitterness of our disagreements, although I was constantly exasperated by his attempts to write dialogue with only a tenuous grasp of the English language. As we continued working and arguing, the figure of final arbiter loomed nearer and nearer. He was none other than Darryl Zanuck, the 'big boss,' whom Tola seemed to respect and even fear."[12]

After several alterations were made to the script, a final screenplay was distributed to all the studio departments. Frank McCarthy, a retired U.S. Army colonel who had been General Marshall's secretary, was appointed by Zanuck to be associate producer on the film. He accompanied Tola to Germany to scout the locations and attempted to get the U.S. Army of Occupation to provide technical assistance. The film's pre-production represented one of the most difficult tasks ever undertaken. To recreate the background vista of war-battered Germany of five years earlier, Tola and McCarthy spent months travelling across West Germany looking for locations. As a result of their search, a 20th Century–Fox unit traveled more than 2,000 miles throughout the French and American zones of occupation to film sequences in 16 cities and small villages in 79 days. One of the most difficult problems was to procure German guns, tanks and other military vehicles, which were found eventually in an abandoned arsenal of captured German equipment. It was also hard to find authentic uniforms. The production advertised for uniforms in German newspapers. Since under occupation law the wearing but not the possessing of costumes was forbidden, more than 1500 former German officers and men who retained their uniforms, offered to sell them. The black SS uniforms had to be made up from drawings by the wardrobe department.

Production, which was to begin on September 18, 1950, was delayed first by bad weather and then by Tola's involvement in a minor car accident and a bout of pneumonia. With the exception of two Americans who played G.I.s, Richard Basehart and Gary Merrill, all the main roles were played by German and Austrian actors who spoke English with a German accent, and were later dubbed. Many of them rose to fame later, particularly Oskar Werner and Hildegard Neff, who went on to international stardom. "The German actors that knew English never seemed suited for the parts," Tola said in an interview.

> When I found the right type he could not speak English. So we had to take time to train these players in the language. Moreover I needed Americans for the G.I.s. You cannot call up a casting director in the Army and ask for your bit players as you do in Hollywood. We had to search through the various military units in Germany and even hold contests to find talent that might qualify.... Casting was not the only problem. Between the time I made my first scouting trip, and the actual filming, devastated Germany had begun to change. We had to hurry to get the proper impression of ruined vistas of buildings. This became a second major problem.... Then rumors were circulated by actors whom we didn't engage that we were making an anti–German picture. We had to negotiate with the newspapers to publish that such was not the case.... There was also no end of red tape. Add all these things together and they explain why *Decision Before Dawn* was the most difficult picture.[13]

Tola had decided to cast Hildegard Neff before he came to Germany. The actress was reluctant to test for him but when Litvak arrived in Hamburg, she agreed to meet him in a projection room to look at the first scenes of the film she was working in at that time. Tola was convinced by Neff's performance. After some negotiations, the actress signed up and a few weeks later she traveled to Munich for a second meeting. In her autobiography Neff vividly described that encounter:

> At the head of the only occupied table in the restaurant of the Four Seasons Hotel sat Anatole Litvak. He wedged a chair between his own and those of a long row of his collaborators, introduced me, and called for a waiter. "You must be hungry," he said and I suddenly knew where I had seen the face before, where I had mistaken it for someone else's, where it had confused me to such an extent that I had thought I would never forget it again but did; I hadn't recognized it at our meeting in Bendestorf.... [Once we began shooting,] Litvak's personality was ideally suited to the bedlam of mammoth production; he blossomed, shed years with each confrontation with danger, scaled walls and clambered up vertiginous chimney stacks, goaded his court to suicidal feats with his example of zealous idealism and absolute dedication to the job at hand, sparing no one, least of all himself.... In the evening he was a different man altogether: It was as though in discarding the baseball cap and the fur-lined army jacket he had discarded himself, becoming an easy host with apparently nothing on his mind but the well-being of his guests. Only the voice, racked by asthma, remained tetchy and ill-disposed, made his small talk strenuous and his humor aggressive, prompted sympathy.[14]

To prevent alarm among the population during the filming of air attack scenes, there were extensive advance warnings via the local press and radio. Still, many people in Nuremberg actually thought that a new war had started. Filming was temporarily disrupted when the mayor of Würzburg protested the depiction of the bombing of his city, but the situation was rectified when Tola submitted a synopsis of the story to German censors. Only a few scenes were shot on a sound stage at the Geisalgasteig studios in Munich; no stock shots, no miniatures, no special effects photography was used in the film. Because the Munich train station had been rebuilt since the war, a new ruined station of debris and twisted girders had to be constructed. When Tola had to shoot a scene of a river crossing, military experts were so indignant that they refused to be on the set. They stated that no man could possibly swim the river in daylight under the guns of the enemy. Tola argued with them and explained that he could not get any excitement out of the episode if the sequence was shot at night. So, even though he had listened to reason from the experts throughout the picture, whenever there was a case of losing something of value he did what he thought was best for the entertainment value of the film. That scene became one of the most exciting episodes in the picture, even though it violated every tactical rule.

The total shooting schedule in Germany was four and a half months. Filming was often done under harsh weather conditions, causing no small hardship to cast and crew. One of the worst snowstorms ever recorded hap-

8. Mixed Reviews

Richard Basehart and Corporal D. G. Devine in *Decision Before Dawn* (1951).

pened while the troupe was in Upper Bavaria. The constantly changing weather conditions (including floods and thick fog) created a cameraman's nightmare; several sequences had to be shot by technicians with mud up to their knees. For cinematographer Frank Planer, filming *Decision Before Dawn* was an assignment filled with challenges and a certain nostalgia: This was his first visit to his native country after the war. It also marked a happy reunion with Tola, with whom he had previously worked in *Nie wieder Liebe!* and *Calais Douvre*.

Although the working title of the film was *Legion of the Damned*, it had to be changed due to German protests, since it was impossible to convince the German press and public that the use of the word *Damned* in the title did not refer at all to the German people. In September 1951, a *Chicago Sunday Tribune* article reported that Tola was in Europe preparing a German-language version of the picture, scripted by Carl Zuckmeier, but the existence of another version has never been confirmed.

Decision Before Dawn was among Tola's favorite films. He called it "the important postwar film I've done." He won the 1951 Directors Guild of America award, and the film received two Academy Award nominations (for Best Picture and Best Editing). After a successful American release in January 1952, the film was shown in Germany two years later and only thanks to Oskar Werner's rising popularity in that country.

Hilde (2009), a German film by Kai Wessel on Hildegard Neff's life and career, showed a fictionalized making of *Decision Before Dawn,* with Dutch actor Jeroen Willems playing Tola. The box office and critical success of *Decision Before Dawn* was so intense that Tola was eager to direct a sort of a sequel, *The Steeper Cliff,* once again shot in Germany. From a novel by David Davidson, the story concerned the plight of a young American newspaperman who goes into the army, gets a desk job, and six weeks after V-E day is sent to Munich to start a democratic newspaper, but can't find any anti–Nazis to support him. Richard Basehart and Oskar Werner were to be part of the cast. Zanuck gave the green light to the project immediately, even though the subject seemed controversial. For budgeting reasons the project was never produced and Tola went on to make a film based on Alfred Hayes' novel *The Girl on the Via Flaminia.*

Gary Cooper originally purchased the film rights to Hayes' book in 1949 and hired the author to work on a screenplay. Later that same year, he sold the rights to agent Leland Hayward and Tola for $50,000 as well as some profits from the production. Irwin Shaw was then hired by Tola to write the screenplay, which was being scripted to star Montgomery Clift, whom Hayward represented. The actor turned down the role and Kirk Douglas was cast instead.

The novel was set in Italy, but because both Tola and Shaw were familiar with France at the time of liberation, they agreed to mold their own army experiences and first-hand knowledge into the script, moving the action to Paris. For this reason the original title that referred to a popular street in Rome was changed, first to *Somewhere in the World* and later into *Act of Love.* As Tola stated in a press release, "[Shaw and I] both believe that wars and [a] victorious army are not the timely subject they were five years ago. The drama of today is the drama of allies. Our armies are all over the world. The problem of their adjustment and that the people in whose countries they are living is an urgently needed story." *Act of Love* told the story of ex–G.I. Robert Teller, who revisits the French Riviera and, in flashback, remembers his tragic romance with Lisa, a French refugee girl he met in Paris during the war.

The production was a reunion after almost twenty years between Tola and many of his old French friends: Armand Thirard, *Mayerling*'s cinematographer, screenwriter Joseph Kessel, and Jeanne Witta, supervisor of the scripts for his last French films before moving to America. Witta was disappointed. "I did not recognize anymore Litvak, maybe captured by the American snobbery which hierarchizes excessively social conditions and certainly annoyed by my trade union activity."[15]

In early January 1953, production began at Villefranche on the French Riviera where the beginning and the end of the story were filmed in two weeks. Interiors were later shot at Victorine Studios in Nice followed by other sequences shot at the Joinville and St. Maurice Studios in Paris. It took three and a half months to complete the film, which was shot simultaneously in two versions—a French and an American—sharing the same cast and crew.

A two-year search for a girl to play Lisa ended when Dany Robin, a young French starlet, was signed. Originally the role was intended for MGM star Pier Angeli, and the studio was willing to lend her to Tola, but her mother pleaded with the studio not to let her do the movie because she disapproved of her daughter's relationship with Douglas, who was divorced with children. Dany Robin had to become fluent in English in just six weeks. For six weeks the French actress, who had not studied English since her school days, was followed everywhere by a team of four Americans coaches. At the end of this time, she was ready for give a performance. Among many French actors playing small roles, Tola cast future French screen goddess Brigitte Bardot in the tiny part of a hotel maid. In her autobiography Bardot recalled Tola with deep affection:

> Anatole Litvak, a great American filmmaker of Russian origins, an amazing man, good, generous and full of talent, who did not care about what people would say about the others, asked [Olga Horsting, Bardot's agent] if I wanted to play the part of a French maid in his film *Act of Love*.... [K]nowledge of English was required and since I spoke a bit of it, I was cast.... I had to deliver my lines to a dialogue coach. There were only two or three lines but I had to learn them perfectly.... Litvak was adorable with his crown of white hair and with those big clear eyes, he was amused by me being very nervous and fearful.[16]

Being in *Act of Love* was an amazing experience for Kirk Douglas. "Tola was a sweet man," the actor wrote in his memoir. "The picture occupied most of my time. I had to work very hard trying to keep up with everybody in French."[17] He had to take daily French lessons to improve his knowledge of the language. Tola wanted to hire someone to handle Douglas' public relations and be his personal assistant. Belgian Anne Buydens, who had been John Huston's assistant while he was making *Moulin Rouge*, was chosen. "When I heard that the star was Kirk Douglas," she recalled, "I wondered if something had happened to Litvak's good taste. While crossing the Atlantic on a boat, I had seen Kirk in a picture called *The Big Trees*. It was so terrible everybody was laughing. But Litvak was an old friend, and I decided to take the job."[18] Romance bloomed between Buydens and Douglas, who still had feelings for

Kirk Douglas and Barbara Laage in *Act of Love* (1953).

Pier Angeli. The couple then took a trip with Tola and his wife to Baden-Baden in Germany after the picture was completed. They got married sixteen months later.

Act of Love was shown at the 1953 Cannes Film Festival where Tola and the United Artists publicity department sent Kirk Douglas along with a few minor members of the cast, including Brigitte Bardot, to promote it. The picture then opened in a limited release in New York in December 1953, a few weeks after a stage version of the novel had played at the Circle in the Square Theatre. The official premiere took place on February 11 at the Astor Theatre on Broadway, with scores of entertainment world celebrities as well as government and business leaders in attendance. Tola and Dany Robin served as hosts at the event. The following May, the film was released in France. Most critics found *Act of Love* long and their reviews were lukewarm. Tola was disappointed at the overall result. "[It] was a story that didn't work out as well as I thought it would, some of which was my own fault," he later admitted.

Tola stayed only a few months in America, just long enough to promote *Act of Love*. In February 1954 he traveled once again to Europe after refusing to do *Désirée*, an adaptation of a bestselling novel for 20th Century–Fox.

8. Mixed Reviews 89

According to *Variety*, his refusal had created a conflict with Zanuck, who asked Tola to shoot the film in CinemaScope and in Hollywood, while Tola wanted to make it in Europe and in standard format. The press speculated that the divergence had brought to an end Tola's multiple-picture deal with the studio, Tola denied the allegations and cabled from Paris that he was "an enthusiastic CinemaScope partisan" and never was "officially assigned" the *Désirée* direction job. Zanuck later confirmed that Fox had okayed Litvak's postponement of his commitment to allow him time for an outside production.[19]

At the end of 1954, while in Paris, Tola received the good news that the U.S. Tax Court handed down a decision that saved him $50,000 that the Internal Revenue Service was trying to collect in additional income taxes from 1947. The case revolved around Tola's sale of the rights of *Sorry, Wrong Number* to Hal Wallis Production for $100,000, after buying them from author Lucille Fletcher for $15,000. Tola reported the transaction as a capital gain item, but the tax collector contended it was subject to a considerably higher straight income tax rate. Judge Arnold Raum ruled that Tola had bought the story in connection with his business as a director and not primarily for resale. Therefore the sale was not Tola's normal line of business and could qualify as a capital gain.

Tola had spent almost a year in Paris preparing and producing his new film *The Deep Blue Sea,* based on a successful play by British playwright Terence Rattigan. Tola worked very closely with the author, who visited him in Paris. The film was going to be the first British production shot in CinemaScope, an unsuitable format for a claustrophobic drama played in a crummy apartment. Yet Tola's producing partners, Fox and London Films, owned by Alexander Korda, insisted in making the film in color using the new trendy CinemaScope format. *The Deep Blue Sea* told the story of Hester Collyer, middle-aged wife of a high court judge, who falls madly in love with a frivolous and unstable former R.A.F. pilot. For him, she loses her dignity and her financial stability. The picture was entirely shot in London, partially on location around the city and partially at Shepperton Studios. Korda wanted Marlene Dietrich to star; the names of Greta Garbo, Deborah Kerr and Olivia de Havilland were also mentioned. When Dietrich was unavailable, Vivien Leigh was cast. It proved to be a bad choice because of Leigh's stiff performance and her lack of chemistry with Kenneth More, who played her lover. More had performed that role in the original stage production opposite Peggy Ashcroft, Celia Johnson and Googie Withers and wanted Ashcroft to be the leading lady, but Korda dismissed that idea, convinced that a solid name like Vivien Leigh was necessary to create more interest in the film. More still thought that Leigh was miscast since she was supposed to be a plain woman but secretly high-sexed and she was too beautiful to be believable in such a role. After reading the final script, More was very disappointed since it was too unlike the play. At a pre-shooting conference with Tola, Korda and Vivien Leigh, More said bluntly, "Gentlemen, we can't start this film. The script is no good." Tola was speechless, but before anyone else could intervene, More explained, "Frankly the trouble with the script is that there is too much Litvak in it and not enough Rattigan.... I'd almost go so far to say that all Rattigan has come out and all Litvak has gone in." The playwright tried to calm everybody down, saying, "Oh, that's not true! Litvak and I spent months in Paris preparing this script. I was leaning over his shoulder the whole time."

The next morning Korda summoned More to his office, "You stupid young idiot," he began. "I've spent all this money on you, thousands and thousands of pounds, and months of time and effort to build you into an international star. And what do you do? You insult Litvak, who I consider one of the greatest living film directors. You read a script in an evening, and although you've never written a line in your life, you say it's rubbish. You upset the rest of the cast and the whole production team, and you know nothing, nothing, *nothing* at all about it."[20] More apologized and promised not to cross Tola again. "By the time we had finished I was very attached to him,"[21] More admitted in one of his autobiographies.

Principal photography started early in 1955 but the atmosphere on the set was often tense. Tola was rarely satisfied and frequently required up to twenty takes of every single shot before printing it. More recalled,

> Although he often had as many as five good ones in the can, he said, Just one more please. None of us laughed or spoke on Tola's set. He is too intense. The only time events moved outside his control was when we went to Klosters [Switzerland] for the winter sports scenes. He arranged a marvelously spectacular sequence of skiers sweeping down the mountainside towards the camera. We spent a full, exhausting day getting this right. "I am happy!" he said afterwards as we trudged back to our hotel. "Our best day's shooting so far." But the negative got ruined. The printing machine broke down while the film was still being processed in the laboratories. It was a terrible blow. The insurance company bore the cost of the loss, but of course couldn't replace the film. We had no chance of going back and shooting the sequence again because the snow was melting.[22]

Actress Moira Lister, who played a secondary role, remembered Litvak as "a horrifying director": "He had this theory that you have to destroy somebody first to get a good performance out of them and he used to—systematically—every day—destroy Vivien until he got her to cry, and he said 'Right. Now you're in a mood to do the scene. We'll do the scene.' He was really, really harsh with her."[23] On the other hand, when *Picturegoer* asked if she enjoyed making the film, Vivien replied, "Very much. Although I would have liked to have had more time.... I thought [the film] was very good, But I wasn't very happy about the flashbacks. I felt the picture should have retained the claustrophobic, intimate quality of the play." Commenting on working with Tola: "He's a fine director. Very understanding and very patient."[24] If Vivien hit it off with Emlyn Williams, with whom she enjoyed playing card games between sequences, she did not get along with More, with whom she had a lot of quarrels. "She wanted glamour and continuous praise for her physical beauty in a script which basically depended upon a woman who had unattractive and tiresome sides to her," More told one of Leigh's biographers. "I fought against this, to the point of quarrelling with Korda and the film's director Anatole Litvak. I lost the argument, and Vivien never forgave me for arguing in the first place.... While her beauty was beyond question, her acting talent was not!"[25] Years later, when asked to comment about the film and her co-star, Vivien responded, "Oh, Kenneth More, was he in that film?" *The Deep Blue Sea* was shown in competition at the Fifteenth Venice International Film Festival where More won the Coppa Volpi for Best Actor Award. The film was a commercial flop, receiving a tepid reception from critics and spectators.

Kenneth Moore and Vivien Leigh in *The Deep Blue Sea*.

In the spring of 1955, Tola returned briefly to the United States, then with indomitable strength flew back to Europe for a short holiday before sitting as a jury member at the Cannes Film Festival. He announced in the press his hope to interest Orson Welles and Alec Guinness in a film adaptation of an old German play he wanted to make in America after completing the supervision of the editing and dubbing of *The Deep Blue Sea*. His plans changed and when he returned to America at the end of the year, he surprised his friends announcing his imminent wedding only three days in advance! The announcement was made at a dinner party given by Charles Feldman at his house. Tola and thirty-two-year-old French model and fashion editor Simone "Sophie" Malgat Steur had been seen in each other's company for several years already and their upcoming marriage had been reported from time to time. A natural blonde, taller than Tola, with a slim figure; she modeled for the most prestigious fashion houses in Paris and New York. According to Peter Viertel, Malgat was "endowed with a good sense of humor, although often cuttingly sarcastic, she was flirtatious by nature, knowing that her hold on Tola was enhanced by her ability to make him jealous."[26] Michael Gross, author of the book *Model*, tells a funny anecdote about Litvak's bride when she worked in New York with Eileen Ford, owner of the famous model agency. "When Ford got Sophie a job modeling on a Seventh Avenue show, the designer called her screaming. 'She'd come to a fitting without underwear,' Ford remembers, 'and the designer was just about to die.'"[27]

Tola and Sophie tied the knot on December 2, 1955, at 9 p.m. at the Sands Hotel in Las Vegas. Jack Entratter, manager and impresario of the hotel, arranged a private ceremony in the bridal suite performed by Justice of the Peace John Mendoza, followed by a small reception. After a brief honeymoon, Tola returned to Hollywood for a meeting with Zanuck concerning his assignment to an upcoming international production. After two flops, Tola's reputation was fading and *Anastasia* came to his rescue.

9

Far from Hollywood

"Anatole Litvak was a tough taskmaster."
—Helen Hayes

In September 1953, Warner Bros. optioned the rights to the London stage production *Anastasia* as a vehicle for Jane Wyman; that picture was never made. In January 1956 it was announced that Darryl F. Zanuck was to produce *Anastasia* in Vienna, after his associate Buddy Adler had bought the rights to Marcelle Maurette's play for $400,000. The story was based on the life of a woman still living in Germany, who was persuaded to proclaim herself the youngest daughter of the last Tsar Nicholas II and claim the Romanov fortune deposited in the Bank of England. Tola, who had always expressed a deep interest in the Romanov culture, was excited that the film was to be produced entirely in Europe at a cost of $3,500,000—the most expensive motion picture ever made abroad by 20th Century–Fox.

Tola asked Arthur Laurents to write the script. He accepted on one condition: to tell the story like a fairy tale and not as a serious non-fictional event. Tola gave him carte blanche, and Laurents started to work on it immediately

Yul Brynner, the first to be cast, took on the role of General Bounine, a former White Russian army officer who tries to collect the fortune of the tsars by training an imposter to pose as Anastasia, daughter of the last tsar of Russia. Brynner was emerging as a new screen phenomenon and had just completed *The King and I* for which he would win an Oscar. The bald star was himself a Russian and hit off with Tola immediately; together they would discuss the script and their conversation would flow without interruption from Russian to French to English.

Both agreed that Ingrid Bergman was the perfect choice to play Anastasia. Buddy Adler, Zanuck and Spyros Skouras, president of 20th Century–Fox, backed by the sales department, opposed casting the Swedish actress. Bergman had been ostracized in the U.S. after having a child with Italian director Roberto Rossellini while still married to Peter Lindstrom. "Americans have

Akim Tamiroff, Yul Brynner and Ingrid Bergman in *Anastasia*.

never forgiven Miss Bergman and she will not be received at the box office," maintained Skouras.[1] Litvak threatened not to make the film, and without Fox's approval he and Ingrid met in the bar of the Plaza Athénée Hotel. As Bergman recalled in her autobiography, "Tola said; 'I just want to know if you will do it if I can make the other people agree.' The 'other people' in 20th Century–Fox thought I was box-office poison, anything they put me in would be destroyed. The picture was going to be made in England. Was I interested? Yes. I was interested. It was a marvelous part."[2] Only after exhausting meetings between Tola and the studio did Fox agree to cast her; *Anastasia* marked her return to the American screens after a seven-year-absence.

In the role of the Dowager Empress, Tola wanted the English actress Helen Hayes, who had played that role on stage, but through a series of misunderstandings he got the American actress Helen Haye, who reluctantly accepted (she was still mourning the death of her husband) after she realized that the producers wanted someone with a moral and upright reputation to co-star with Bergman, someone who could lead the way to public reacceptance of the Swedish actress.

To bring authenticity to the production, Litvak used as extras members of the large Russian exile community that resided in Paris and London, most of whom fled Russia during the Revolution and had been making a precarious living as taxi drivers, doormen, restaurateurs, jewelers, etc. Brynner pressed the producers to hire a family of gypsy musicians to perform a tzigan song with him in a scene in a nightclub modeled after one of the actual clubs where he had performed with them as a singer prior to his movie career.

Shooting began May 21, 1956, in Copenhagen where the palaces, squares and restaurants of the lovely city were used as natural locales and photographed by Jack Hildyard and his camera crew. Meanwhile Brynner and Bergman flew to London where costume fittings and rehearsals began. Laurents constantly modified the script according to Tola's wishes. Litvak's habit of correcting the dialogue, even though he spoke English with a French-Russian accent, often annoyed Laurents.

"We had battles," the screenwriter recalled. "Like: [Tola] would say, she can't say 'I don't.' She has to say 'I do not.' I'd say, No, she can't say 'I do not.' She has to say 'I don't.' I would say, 'Tola, you do not speak English, you don't understand about colloquial English....'"[3]

For more than a week the crew worked at night in a light rain filming on the banks of the Seine in Paris. Tola had insisted on inserting a Russian Easter scene because he loved that Russian tradition, and planned to film that sequence around St. Alexander's Cathedral, one of the three Greek Orthodox churches in Paris. At the last moment the ecclesiastical authorities wavered about granting the necessary permission, compelling the crew to move to Nice where there was a small Russian church. Tola was dissatisfied so he had no choice but to have a $56,000 replica built of the Parisian church on the Borehamwood Studios back lot outside London.

During the entire shooting, Bergman and Hayes had a Russian coach to help them speak with believable Russian accents. Brynner would use the excuse of helping Bergman with the language and be in her dressing room for hours. They began a secret romance that lasted during filming.

"Anatole and I got on very well," Bergman recalled. "Though he was a bit worried occasionally about my slowness in learning the dialogue. I remember him saying, 'Ingrid, you are marvelous in this picture, but think how much better you would be if only you knew your dialogue.' Then one day he passed me in my little trailer, and there I was reading the script. 'Great! You are actually studying the dialogue,' he said. I didn't have the heart to tell him I was studying *Tea and Sympathy* [Bergman's upcoming stage engagement] in French."[4] On June 11, shooting switched to London where the company completed the picture at the Borehamwood Studios. When the press asked the status of the production, Tola reported progress with "no more than the average number of headaches."[5] According to Helen Hayes, "It seemed to take forever to finish. The director Anatole Litvak was a tough taskmaster, though he did turn out good films."[6]

In early July, while the picture was still in production, Ed Sullivan, popular host of an American Sunday night television show, flew to London to film a brief interview with Bergman and some documentary footage of the production in progress to be used on his program. On his return he announced that he would show this film on a forthcoming Sunday night, and at the same time Bergman would make a "live" appearance. He also asked if his viewers approved or disapproved of the Swedish actress visiting the United States after seven years' "repentance." A total of 5,826 letter-writers were in favor of her appearance on the show, but 6,433 were not. Shocked by the response of his audience, Sullivan had to keep his word and canceled her appearance.

Anastasia wrapped by the end of August 1956, and was quickly edited and scored for a Christmas release. In early December Fox held a press and industry preview in the Beverly Hills Theater of the Academy of Motion Picture Arts and Sciences. When Bergman's name appeared on the screen, the audience burst into applause. The press was impressed and the reviews were unanimously positive. *Variety* praised the picture "under the sensitive and imaginative direction of Anatole Litvak here also doing his best work in years."

The film premiered at Radio City Music Hall in New York. Brynner and Bergman, tied up by previous work engagements, were unable to attend. Tola begged Hayes to escort him to the opening. Hayes, who on that same day was celebrating her son's birthday in a club, declined the invitation. Tola urged her to leave the party for a while and then return to the club after the premiere, but Hayes refused firmly, leaving him with no choice but to show up alone at the event. A few days later, the New York critics voted Ingrid Bergman "best actress of the year" making her comeback a triumph. *Anastasia* received international acclaim; however, all the industry awards snubbed Tola. Composer Alfred Newman received an Academy Award nomination for Best Music Score, while Bergman won a Golden Globe and the Oscar as Best Actress.

In November 1956, while the editing and the dubbing of *Anastasia* were still in progress, Tola arrived in New York to start working on a new, ambitious project: a live telecast of *Mayerling* for NBC-TV. Although the date of the broadcast was five months away, Tola devoted all his time to the perfection of his television debut. He started to polish the script, adapted by Michael Dyne, and supervised all the sets, designs, costumes, etc., scheduled to be finalized before stars Audrey Hepburn and Mel Ferrer started rehearsing at the end of December.

Henry and Saul Jaffe were the producers of *Producers' Showcase,* an anthology series of plays and musicals that aired once a month on NBC. The Jaffes decided to hire Tola after he had offered to produce a TV remake of *Mayerling*. The producers liked the idea hoping that Litvak could convince Hepburn, at the time one of the hottest actresses in Hollywood, to star. Hepburn and her husband Ferrer were Tola's old friends. Two years earlier the couple had traded their Swiss chalet for Tola's oceanside house in Malibu through their common agent Kurt Frings, who later negotiated their fees to appear in the TV production.

According to NBC's production manager Alvin Cooperman,

> Litvak insisted in his contract that he direct it. This was a live show where he would actually sit behind the director, who was going to be, in his mind, a technical person, and he would tell him, camera one, camera four. And Saul Jaffe came to me and said, "It's the only way he'll do the show," and I said, "Well, you can't do the show that way because he doesn't understand, it's not going to work." "Well, he is not going to do the show." So I said, "Well, why don't you let him sign the contract that way, and when he gets in the control room—he's not an idiot—he will see he can't do it." So we did that: We in fact did a contract with Litvak that would actually have hands-on in the control room.[7]

Hepburn loved the script as well the opportunity to earn $150,000 for only three weeks' work. But she insisted that NBC cast Ferrer in the male lead. The Jaffe brothers did not think it was such a bad idea having husband and wife playing the role of the doomed lovers and hired Audrey's husband for $25,000.

Mayerling was budgeted at $620,000 with a cast of 107 performers, 317 stagehands, costumers, musicians and cameramen, 30 lavish indoor sets, expensive costumes copied from nineteenth-century originals, and two rehearsal locations—one at the St. Nicholas Arena on West Sixty-sixth Street and another in a former department store on Sixth Avenue. The ninety-minute program was shot and broadcast in color, as most of NBC's special were, to create a buzz about color television sets, which had just came out on the American market.

Rehearsals began on New Year's Day 1957. The Ferrers punctually arrived on the set and were welcomed by an eager Tola, ready to begin. The large cast included notables Raymond Massey, Judith Evelyn, Diana Wynyard, Lorne Greene and Basil Sydney. The presence of the husband-and-wife acting team put Tola in a delicate situation, as he revealed three weeks later to *Life* magazine: "When Audrey plays Marie, speaking to the prince, she is also Audrey speaking to her husband.... It is very difficult to get Mel to treat her roughly. I had to work with him to get him to do it."[8] Tola was also photographed embracing Hepburn while Ferrer looked at them. The caption read, "Litvak as lover shows Ferrer how he should hold his wife, Audrey, to get the best effect at romantic moments." The director later explained, "I had a lot of trouble getting them to turn on the heat. Audrey seemed to have a better rapport with that Yorkshire terrier of hers."[9]

Tola had insisted on all the costumes and furniture to be there for rehearsals, something unheard of in the TV industry where everything was done with only the most essential props until the real broadcast. The huge space of the St. Nicholas Arena had to be rented to allow the cast to rehearse it like a film.

On January 15, a press conference was attended by the director and the two stars. Tola said that because of "the spontaneity of a performance running from beginning to end," TV had more "sparkle" to it than film. He thought that the live broadcast was going to be "very tough, very exciting," but he added later that he didn't think it was going to be as difficult adjusting to a different medium as some people would have him believe.[10]

After special material that Tola had shot in Vienna was chosen for inclusion in the episode, the production moved into the broadcast studio for the final five days of rehearsals on camera. On February 4, as Alvin Cooperman remembered,

> *Producers' Showcase* goes on the air at eight o'clock and Litvak is sitting in front of me, behind Kirk Browning and the technical director and the assistant director and all the audio people, and we go on the air. And Anatole Litvak sat silently for ninety minutes, never said a word, and when it was finished he tapped Kirk Browning on the back and said, "Congratulations." He didn't understand, because once he got in the control room... What you have in the control room is, you have your five monitors showing all five cameras. Then you have your one monitor which is your on-air camera, and what Kirk Browning is doing is selecting.... That goes right into the air.... [Litvak] thought he could make changes.[11]

Mayerling had better ratings than any *Producers' Showcase* program since Mary Martin's acclaimed *Peter Pan* in March 1955. Critics praised the lavish production in general along with Hepburn's performance but Ferrer was considered miscast because of his stiff acting. To cover some of the high expenses, NBC made a deal with Paramount to release the program as a theatrical movie in Europe, where it performed disappointingly at the box office.

While Tola was making *Anastasia* in London, the Hungarian revolution dominated the news. British producer Anthony Havelock-Allan recognized the world drama as one of the most absorbing events of history and started to look for a screenwriter capable of writing a story based on the current crisis. The producer had in mind for the leading roles Italian actress Anna Magnani and Yul Brynner. Brynner immediately liked the idea and wanted Tola as director. But Havelock-Allan was not convinced that Litvak was the right choice and backed off; the project fell into the hands of Brynner and Tola. They were the perfect team to make the uprising of Hungary's patriots into a film and combined forces and fortunes to make it independently. They formed a company called Alby. Tola contacted his old friend Joseph Kessel, asking him to write a script based on one of his stories mixed with the current events, but the French writer had no interest in the idea. Tola assigned the task to screenwriter George Tabori, a Hungarian immigrant in Hollywood, who wrote a first draft set in China. Tola and Brynner asked him to change it and get an inspiration by the real political events generating local resistance after the Red Army invaded Hungary. Tabori's final script (loosely based on Guy de Maupassant's short story "Boule de Suif," which had also inspired John Ford's *Stagecoach* [1939]) contained exactly what the director was looking for. After Anna Magnani turned down the chance to star opposite Brynner, the actor suggested his old friend and *King and I* co-star Deborah Kerr. The Scottish actress liked the idea of working again with Brynner under the direction of a respected filmmaker like Tola and accepted the part.

The Journey tells the story of sixteen international travelers stranded in Hungary after the sudden political changes. The Russian militia led by Major Surov (Brynner) interrupts their evacuation. Kerr was Lady Diana Ashmore, an elegant British aristocrat who tries to help her Hungarian lover (Jason Robards Jr.) flee the country. Tola devoted almost a year to the selection of a truly international cast. Among the artists who made significant contributions were the French Anouk Aimée, as one of the leaders of the Hungarian resistance, British character actor Robert Morley, American Anne Jackson and Asian-American Jerry Fujikawa, who Tola had seen in the play *The Teahouse of the August Moon*.

Almost a year before principal photography began, Tola flew to New York to try to arrange for filming exterior scenes in Hungary, yet he was unable to obtain permission. He opted instead for a location in the hills outside Vienna and at the Rosenhügel studios. There was a great amount of interest in *The Journey* because it was reuniting Kerr and Brynner after the international success of *The King and I*. There was unfounded speculation about a romance; the truth would be known several weeks later.

Just a few days before Tola began shooting, he decided to call his old friend Peter Viertel to ask if he would consider joining him to do some work on the script. Viertel was not particularly eager to do it but agreed to help him fix a few scenes. Viertel was then introduced to the cast. "Deborah, with her beauty, her simple and direct manner, stood out above all the others," he wrote in his 1992 memoir *Dangerous Friends*. "Tola had told me that she was an exceptional woman, and I soon realized that his glowing description had not been an exaggeration."[12] After a press conference, Litvak hosted a dinner for the crew and actors. Viertel was seated on Deborah's left. "We talked with complete disregard for any of the other people present," recalled the writer. "And before the evening had ended I had fallen in love with her."[13] From that day on, the two embarked on a romantic affair that led Kerr to leave her husband Tony Bartley after 12 years of marriage. As soon as the news of Kerr's imminent divorce reached the press, Tola had to ban all visitors from the set to avoid the paparazzi photographing the couple. Tola went around trying to re-establish good will, and had just about calmed the media when another explosion shattered the frail peace on the set

Several newspapers accused the film of doing anti–Soviet propaganda in neutral Austria, while others maintained that it was against the Hungarian resistance. All accusations were pure speculation. Nevertheless, the quarrels kept inflaming the pages of the eleven Viennese daily papers, forcing Tola to release a statement in which he declared his firm intention to continue his work in peace, condemning those who criticized the film without even knowing what it was about.[14] Many of the extras playing Russian military men were former soldiers, appearing before the cameras in their own uniforms and medals. They signed for the picture under false names, being all refugees or defectors from the Red Army during World War II, finding sanctuary in Austria. Most of them had been found by Tola in Munich, where about one thousand Russians had resettled. Uneasy about travelling to Vienna for

Yul Brynner and Deborah Kerr embrace in *The Journey* (1959).

their roles, the ex–Soviets were sick with fear when the set moved to the Austrian border. But shooting there went smoothly.

While the professional relationship between Kerr and Tola was idyllic, Brynner and the director were not so amicable. Especially when the bald actor wanted to enter his Mercedes Benz 300 in a sports car race in Vienna, and Tola refused to allow him to risk his neck *and* the film. The argument was so heated that at one point some bystanders were afraid it could turn physically violent. Brynner stormed off and refused to work the rest of the day, returning the following morning after he cooled down.

The making of *The Journey* dragged out for several extra weeks. Anne Jackson, who was pregnant, used to joke that she would have to give birth to the child on the location bus. In the film, one of the two kids playing the children of Jackson was four-year-old Ron Howard, who later became the acclaimed director of *The Da Vinci Code* (2006), and *Rush* (2013), et al. *The Journey* was his screen debut.

The picture premiered at New York's Radio City Music Hall on February 18, 1959. Tola could not participate at the event since he was stuck in his London hotel bed with shingles. A few days before the premiere, he told the press that the Soviets had attempted, unofficially, to pressure the Austrian government to halt the production of the film. In addition he revealed that *The Journey* had been subjected to violent criticism in the Communist press while it had received the wholehearted endorsement of Radio Liberation and the Voice of America. He explained that his approach to the film resulted in acclaim from the people in Europe. His objective was to let both sides speak. There was amazement that an American film company had the courage to indulge in "fair play" in dealing with a subject of that kind. "They consider it a tribute to the American motion picture industry," he added, "and to the people of the United States."[15]

In spite of all the press coverage received during production, the picture did very poorly at the box office. Reviews were generally good but not enough to generate much public interest.

After the completion of *The Journey,* Tola planned to take eight months off to develop two or three properties so he could maintain continuity through his own independent operation. He planned to partner again with Yul Brynner in two films, *Two Different Worlds* and *The Mad King*. The first was scheduled to be made between Istanbul and Paris, some time during 1958, as soon as Brynner was free of his previous commitments. *The Mad King* was announced in the press in early November 1959. The script was to be based on the life of Paul of Russia, son of Catherine the Great. Tola intended to write, produce and direct with Brynner as co-producer and star. Both films were supposed to be financed and released by United Artists, but they were never made. Instead, Tola produced *Mission to No-Man's Land*, a 30-minute documentary reporting on the conditions of refugee children in Eastern European camps. The film, narrated by Brynner, was made in collaboration with the BBC for the United Nations High Commissioner for Refugees and aired on American television in January 1960.

In February 1960, Tola flew to California to attend the ceremony as he got a star on the Hollywood Walk of Fame. It is located at 6635 Hollywood Boulevard. It was a proud event for him as a filmmaker. It was a short trip that brought back a lot of memories from his past in Hollywood; however he did not have any regrets about living and working in Europe. "Slowly, slowly the American film industry is losing ground abroad ... losing prestige ... losing audiences too," he said in an interview.[16] He also remarked that the Italians and the French were the ones challenging world interest with films that were daring in theme, often made without stars, and were proving both artistic and financial successes.

That year Tola read *Aimez-vous Brahms?*, a novel by best-selling French author Françoise Sagan (whose books *Bounjour Tristesse* and *That Certain Smile* had been already adapted into films by Otto Preminger and Jean Negulesco). Litvak liked the romantic story of Paula, a middle-aged woman neglected by her lover, who finds temporary happiness with a man half her age. He optioned the film rights, thinking that it was a perfect vehicle for Ingrid Bergman. Yet the Swedish actress was very hesitant to accept that role, as she told a close friend in a letter dated August 16, 1960: "At last I have a script. It is not as good as I hoped. I wrote three pages typewritten to Tola Litvak with complaints. Sagan after all is an artist. Of course not much happens in the book, and it's hard therefore to get any action in the picture. But I hope that Tola himself and his cast will put back the atmosphere that I feel is lost."[17] Eventually Bergman signed the contract and joined the cast that included Anthony Perkins and French singer-actor Yves Montand. Perkins, one of the hottest young stars in Hollywood, had just finished Alfred Hitchcock's *Psycho* (1960) but it had not yet been released. Perkins said in an interview:

> Anatole Litvak, the producer-director, had seen me in *Look Homeward Angel* [on Broadway], and he wired me about the role. I was on stage in *Greenwillow* at the time and could not get away. I said to myself, "too bad, this is a real nice part," but I told Litvak I was unavailable and he offered it to Laurence Harvey. Well, it seems they negotiated but couldn't get together. My show closed, I wired fast that I *was* available. Twenty-four hours later I was in Paris. Right away I was introduced to Ingrid, and we went to work with my head on her shoulder! I found Ingrid marvelous to work with, in top form with great stability, and I liked the picture much better than any other they're done from Françoise Sagan's novels."[18]

The third co-star Yves Montand had just returned from making two films in America. Tola cast him as Bergman's womanizing other lover, because he thought having the popular French performer in the film would appeal to European audiences. To get the three leading stars better acquainted, Tola organized a dinner at his house but Bergman canceled at the last moment due to some personal emergency.

Sagan, who had been dissatisfied with the two screen versions of her novels, seemed very confident in Tola's ability as filmmaker. She expressed her approval first in a letter sent to him just before the beginning of the shooting and later accepting his offer to work as an extra in a scene. "I think the movie Litvak is making of my book will be—for the first time—a good movie," she remarked in an interview for a French newspaper.

Principal photography began on September 19, after a couple weeks of rehearsals. The evening before the first day of the shooting, Tola threw a cocktail party at which Brahms' First Symphony was played incessantly. After the movie "wrapped," there was a farewell production party at the Salle Pleyel, part of which had been reproduced on the sound stage. There, Brahms' *Third* Symphony played continuously. Both symphonies played a major part in the film soundtrack.

To heighten the story's dramatic mood, Tola decided to film in black and white, keeping the novel's original locations. The crew flew to London just for a single sequence (Perkins rushing out of the Admiralty Court). Other sites used, besides Paris, were Deauville and the picturesque village of Montfort-L'Amaury. In Deauville, the script called for a dark and overcast sky but when the production arrived, they found Indian summer—not a cloud in the sky. While the camera crew fussed around with scaffolding to blot out the light, Tola and Montand sunbathed on the beach. The majority of the film was staged at the Studio de Boulogne. There, forty-one sets were designed and built by the art directors. A Polynesian nightclub called the Ivory Club, the famous restaurant Chez Maxim's, and the Epic, another popular Left Bank nightclub, were duplicated on the sound stage. The scene shot at the Epic included a lot of famous people as extras: Tola, playwright Marcel Achard, singer Sacha Distel, novelist Maurice Druon, Françoise Sagan and Yul Brynner. The latter also worked for two weeks as the official still photographer. Brynner, a skilled photographer, enjoyed taking the photographs, most of them candids of the cast and crewmembers.

Bergman got along magnificently with Perkins and Montand. "These two actors are wonderful for their parts," the actress told a friend. "It's a long time since I worked with two actors I enjoyed so much. They are both charming, both great personalities and very different, and you understand why I—

in my part as Paula—love them both."[19] On the set, the only moment of tension was when Tola had to shoot the love scenes between Ingrid and Tony. Wishing to practice privately, she took her co-star in her dressing room and said, "For heaven sake kiss me!" He did a double-take, then laughed and asked, "Why? What for?"

> I said, "Because we've got to do it later in the film, and I don't know you. I'm hardly acquainted with you, and I'm shy and I blush. Much better we do our first rehearsal in my dressing room, so I shan't start dreading the moment when we have to do it in front of a hundred technicians." He grinned and understood, and said "Okay," then he kissed me "That hurt? No? Good." He was very sweet, and it was easier for me after that, I knew him. We were friends.[20]

In an interview in the '80s, Perkins claimed that Bergman had tried to seduce him; later he denied he'd said that.[21] Commenting on his role in an on-set interview, Perkins said, "For me Philip is a real change of pace. I've played a disturbed ballplayer [*Fear Strikes Out*, 1957], a young deputy sheriff [*The Tin Star*, 1957] and, most recently, a homicidal maniac in *Psycho*. Of course one of the dangers of the love story is that it can get too mushy. But Mr. Litvak has promised not to have those one hundred violins sawing away the sound track, and he's using some wonderful Paris backgrounds that will make the

Anthony Perkins and Ingrid Bergman in *Goodbye Again* (1961).

9. Far from Hollywood

atmosphere convincing."[22] Perhaps the most uncomfortable person on the set was Yves Montand. He told Bergman that he preferred to be a singer, not an actor, since as a singer he could "hear his performance," but as an actor, he couldn't judge his own work.[23]

Off the set Tola enjoyed inviting his stars over for dinner or to go out with them. One night with his wife Sophie and Françoise Sagan, he took Perkins to a Judy Garland concert and later they all went backstage to visit the singer.

During the making of the film, Tola worried about the French title *Aimez-vous Brahms?*, which he thought would be incomprehensible to American audiences. So he asked around for suggestions. *Variation on a Theme, The Way We Are, Time on Our Hands* and *Paula* were all options. Perkins proposed *Goodbye Again,* because it had been the title of one of his actor-father Osgood Perkins, Broadway successes. Tola liked it and the film was released in North America as *Goodbye Again.*

The shooting was completed on December 13, 1960, and the picture was screened at the 14th Cannes Film Festival the following May. *Aimez-vous Brahms?* was highly praised in Europe and Perkins received several prestigious European awards including the Palme d'Or in Cannes. Nonetheless *Goodbye Again* met with no success whatsoever in the United States where many reviewers panned it, reflecting the American opinion that the story of an unmarried couple living together, and the woman who later takes a lover young enough to be her son, was shameful and far "too French."

10

Fading Away

> "Litvak understands an actor's problems and he'll do all he can to get the best out of performance.... What more can an actor ask for?"
> —Anthony Perkins

It took exactly a year for Tola to get back behind the camera. His next project had a lot in common with *Goodbye Again*, and proved to be one of the biggest flops in his carrier. Inspired by the success of Alfred Hitchcock's films, he decided to enter the suspense thriller genre. The plot came from an idea of actor-screenwriter André-Michel Versini, which Tola asked Peter Viertel and Hugh Wheeler to adapt into a full script. The original title was *All the Gold in the World* and Tola insisted that Tony Perkins take the lead. The actor, who was at the peak of his popularity after *Psycho*'s extraordinary success, was happy to work with him again, especially when he heard that his co-star would be Sophia Loren, who had replaced the previously announced Jeanne Moreau. "I felt very stimulated working with Litvak the first time," said Perkins. "And he's a man to whom—if he calls up and says, 'Will you do a picture with me?'—I'll say yes. There are not many going like that. He's a rare worker in that he is a flexible pro.... Litvak knows, he understands an actor's problems and he'll do all he can to get the best out of performance. That's why I trust him. He's the guy that holds a picture together. And I respect his knowledge and his instincts. What more can an actor ask for?"[1]

Loren and Perkins had previously worked together in *Desire Under the Elms* (1957). Tola was very excited to re-team the couple on the screen. This was big news in France since they had both won the Palme d'Or as best actors that previous spring (Loren with De Sica's 1960 film *Two Women* and Perkins with *Goodbye Again*). Tola told the *New York Times,*

> In casting Sophia and Tony in this film, I was interested in the contrasting personalities of the two. Sophia is outgoing, serene, and cheerful. She has to play the role of a girl from a humble home in Naples who is making good in the sophisticated world of the Paris fashion houses. Well, Sophia knew poverty as a child in Naples

and she is certainly a success in the sophisticated world of international picture-making. Tony has a gentle boyish quality, which also contains the seeds of violence. I am trying to blend the gentle young boy I directed with Ingrid Bergman in *Goodbye Again* with the dangerous quality he revealed in *Psycho*.[2]

Loren was offered $300,000 to play Lisa, an Italian girl working as a part-time model. The actress flew to Paris in the fall of 1961 for the fitting of her gowns at the house of fashion of couturier Guy Laroche, who exclusively designed her wardrobe for the scenes taking place in his atelier. Tola used his model–fashion designer wife as costume supervisor. It was the first time that Sophie Litvak worked on one of her husband's films.

Interviewed on the set, Loren commented about her ongoing work experience with Tola:

> I must ... rely more than ever upon the director. He must be there to help me find the right emotional charges, the right tensions. Litvak discusses the action with me, scene by scene. He illuminates the silences. In a suspense picture the silences are important. It can be very difficult to go through a scene without lines to say. One has to avoid the danger of becoming monotonous, or too relaxed. Litvak understands this and works with me. He has deep insights into human psychology. I feel this all the time with him, and it gives me strength. I know that I can trust him. He has the right vision.

The only complaint Tola had regarding the Italian star was her social life off the set:

> In all the weeks in Paris, she only went out twice. One can't even get her to a nightclub unless she convinces herself it's a question of public attention. Actually, once she's there she has a great time, but she'll never let herself have fun for fun's sake. A good actress needs human experience of all kinds and must live broadly in order to feel. I kept telling her, "Sophia, go out and live a little," but there's nothing doing. Even her rare vacations are a big bore, concentrated on physical recuperation, which is also part of the plan."[3]

In spite of his disapproval of her quiet social life, Tola had wonderful words for Sophia when NBC decided to run a one-hour special called *The World of Sophia Loren*. The American network followed the actress on the set, filming her having fun between takes, interviewing Tola, Perkins, columnist Art Buchwald and other crew members.

During the entire shoot, Tola was a perfectionist, covering each scene to the minutest detail. The picture was shot in black and white and in both English and French versions at the St. Meurice Studios outside Paris. The production proceeded smoothly, except when on March 10, 1962, Tola was taken unconscious to the American Hospital in Neully after a fall. He was on top of a platform when he suddenly made a false step. He plunged down ten feet.

Loren and Perkins rushed to help him along with others who were on hand. At the hospital the doctors determined that he had suffered a concussion and a few cracked ribs. Luckily he was able to recover in a few days and complete the film.

All the Gold in the World went through an endless series of title changes before its release. First it was renamed *The Third Dimension,* but Tola was concerned that it might be mistaken for a 3-D movie. United Artists then proposed *The Fourth Dimension,* then *Deadlock* or *L'Impasse,* before finally settling for the cryptic *Five Miles to Midnight* for the English version and *Le couteau dans la plaie* for the French market. In France the film was fairly received by the public during the Christmas holiday of 1962. Two months later, the American press roasted it. Reviewers called the script "idiotic" and the film was a box office disaster. Tola, who had invested a hefty sum in it, was so disappointed that he directed no more films for almost four years.

During this long break from being on a set, Tola looked carefully for the perfect script to produce and direct. He spent his free time between his duplex in Paris and a house in St. Tropez, on the French Riviera. The Parisian apartment was renowned for Tola's amazing art collection. He had always been a collector of modern paintings and the walls of his duplex reflected the sureness of his instinct as a discriminating buyer. A few years before, there was a bidding war between Tola and concert pianist Arthur Rubinstein at a famous Paris auction house for an oil sketch by Delacroix entitled *Asiatic Studies.* Sophie's only real collection was in her large dressing room: many years of shoes in a floor-to-ceiling open cupboard, all arranged methodically. Her amazing taste was reflected most in the St. Tropez house, for which she had been both the architect and the decorator. The job took her three years to complete. The elegant Litvaks' summer residence was photographed for a popular French magazine.

In the early 1960s, Tola's name was attached to a couple of major projects, neither of which materialized. For months Walter, Harold and Marvin Mirisch of United Artists had been talking with him about his doing a film. In November 1963, Tola proposed that the producers acquire the rights to a new, highly successful Broadway play, *A Shot in the Dark,* which was based on the French play *L'idiote* by Marcel Archard. It had been adapted for the American stage by Harry Kurnitz and starred Walter Matthau. The three brothers saw the play and agreed to acquire it. Tola suggested that Alec Coppel write the screenplay. As the project developed, Tola wanted Sophia Loren to play the lead, but her husband, producer Carlo Ponti, disliked the script and advised her not to accept it unless it was re-written. The Mirisch brothers asked screenwriter Norman Krasna to intervene. Tola decided to drop out of the project, claiming "illness." The producers were very upset because they had invested a lot of

10. *Fading Away*

Sophia Loren, Anatole Litvak, center, and Anthony Perkins on the Parisian set of *Five Miles to Midnight* **(1962).**

money in the film which was Litvak's idea. They asked director Blake Edwards to replace Tola. The director accepted, hired writer William Peter Blatty (who later become an acclaimed filmmaker), and involved Peter Sellers and his successful Inspector Clouseau character from *The Pink Panther* (1963) in the

Sophia Loren, and Anthony Perkins in *Five Miles to Midnight* (1962).

story. *A Shot in the Dark* turned out to be a much finer and more successful film than the original *Pink Panther*.

In March 1964 Tola formed the production company Jorilie with filmmaker Jules Dassin, known for his film noirs *Brute Force* (1947), *The Naked City* (1948) and the acclaimed *Rififi* (1955). Together they announced the making of *10:30 p.m. Summer* starring an international group of artists including Greek actress (and Dassin's wife) Melina Mercouri, Austrian star Romy Schneider and British actor Peter Finch. Originally Dassin and Tola asked Joseph Losey to direct the picture. As early as 1961, Losey had been interested in the novel by Marguerite Duras (author of *Hiroshima Mon Amour* [1959]). At the time Simone Signoret held an option on the screen rights, which she then passed to Tola, who had been one of Losey's colleagues during service with the Army film unit in 1944. The British director was eager to direct the film and agreed to accompany Dassin to scout Spanish locations in November 1964. It was one unhappy trip with Losey and Dassin arguing constantly. Four weeks later, after a meeting that included Tola, Dassin explosively told Losey: "Let's forget it—drop it—it has become a nightmare to me. I cannot support your

10. Fading Away

condescending attitude, you *tolerating* me, your insults. I told you some months ago that I did not believe we could collaborate.... In Spain you offended me time and again.'[4] Apparently the two directors had a history of spats and rows but this time Losey had crossed the line and he was taken off the project. Dassin took charge of the direction. *10:30 p.m. Summer* was a complete flop as Mercouri stated in her autobiography: "Everybody called it a disaster." Peter Finch described it as "murky and confused." The name Anatole Litvak did not appear in the credits, therefore only a few knew of his involvement in this film that many reviewers called "dreadful," "pretentious" and "boring."

Later that year Tola was interested in making a picture of Rolf Hochhuth's controversial play *The Deputy*. The story was an indictment of the alleged silence of Pope Pius XII (God's "Deputy" on Earth) regarding the Nazi persecution of the Jews during World War II. Marlon Brando was very eager to star in it, as he stated in an interview: "I don't care if *The Deputy* doesn't make a penny. I'd do it for nothing.... But I hope Mr. Litvak doesn't read the *New York Times*."[5] The film was never made.

Finally the right opportunity came from Tola's old friend and gin rummy companion: Producer Sam Spiegel optioned the rights for a screen version of *The Night of the Generals*, a highly praised novel by German author Hans Hellmuth, published in the United States in February 1964.

In an interview, Litvak said that he hadn't made a picture in two years because "I was looking for a subject that somehow would attract me more than some of the pictures I've done lately." He continued:

The subject matter becomes more and more important to me. We used to do, a long time ago, pictures mainly because we could get a star or a couple of stars—a woman and a man—that would attract commercially the public to see the picture—and somehow after my two last pictures I decided I would like to wait and see if I can get a subject that will be the star of my project instead of the stars themselves. I think the subject is more and more growing to be the most important thing in movie-making....

Omar Sharif in *The Night of the Generals* (1967).

The script is written by Robert Anderson. For the first time in a long time I'm really acting mostly as a director but I'm delighted to do so because it gives me more time to think about how to get the picture creatively instead of thinking about how to get the money, how to get the actors.[6]

The Night of the Generals was a big-budget film like Spiegel's previous productions *The Bridge on the River Kwai* (1957) and *Lawrence of Arabia* (1962). Peter O' Toole was signed to play the principal role of General Tanz, a psychotic Nazi commander, worshipped by his soldiers, who goes through the war a great hero, but gets away with some horrible murders. Spiegel and O'Toole were joining forces again after the Irish actor had successfully starred in *Lawrence of Arabia*, financed by the independent producer.

Despite their long-standing friendship, Spiegel and Tola argued frequently during the making of the film. The producer would often disappear from the set with his mistress, making Tola furious. He told everyone that Spiegel was more taken with his new girlfriend than the business side of the production. Instead of making up with Tola, Spiegel's attitude toward him became worse and worse. Author Gore Vidal was called in to re-write a few scenes; he recalled: "Sam was constantly insulting Tola, he said, 'If you can't direct, you should quit, you know.' He would say stuff like that in front of the crew. It was unforgivable. And the way Tola would take it: He had a spray for his asthma and he would spray into his mouth."[7] Tola in fact had developed a serious bronchial ailment as well as being plagued with diseases of the respiratory tract and sinuses. As a result of his illnesses, another $50,000 had been attached to the picture's medical insurance.

The only time Tola and Spiegel both agreed was when Vidal suggested Dirk Bogarde for the role of Major Grau, but Spiegel dismissed the idea with a homophobic comment and Tola confirmed it, casting in his place Omar Sharif. The Egyptian actor had accepted the role of a Nazi just to work once again with his friend O'Toole. "Being with Peter again delighted me," Sharif said in his autobiography, "but wearing a German uniform struck me as incompatible with my physique and character. 'It's grotesque,' was my first reaction. The director, Anatole Litvak, insisted: 'Let's do a little test.' And the test proved fairly convincing. My moustache reshaped, the uniform made me into a different man."[8]

There was an international crew of French, English, and Americans along with Polish technicians temporarily hired during the shooting on location. The cast also included Christopher Plummer, Donald Pleasence and French actor Philippe Noiret. Plummer, who was cast as Field Marshal Erwin Rommel, recalled vividly his first meeting with Tola in the small French village of LaRoche-Guyon:

10. Fading Away

He was impeccably mannered, smooth and civilized and it was a privilege to work with him, if ever so briefly. Together we lunched at this delightful pension. Two of the waiters were very old and had been kept on by Rommel and both related in reverent tones that even though he was the enemy he had treated the whole French staff with great respect ... the only good German in the military, they told us, and he was killed so soon after he left us. *Comme c'était triste—un homme tres gentil comme ça.* Mr. Litvak turned to me, "You see? He was a most remarkable man." I suddenly wished that my role was a much larger one.⁹

Once Philippe Noiret signed on to play Inspector Morand, Tola assigned him an English coach and made him go through numerous rehearsals to have him deliver his lines in perfect English. In spite of the hard work, Noiret enjoyed working with Tola: "Litvak was a charming, nice man, who I loved to hear speaking. We should not forget that he had begun in Russia as a film editor! Those are the people who have a lot to tell."¹⁰

O'Toole thought *Night of the Generals* had a good screenplay but he disagreed with many changes made by Tola and Spiegel while the film was going on. "*The Night of the Generals* could have been a smashing movie," he reportedly said, "but once again, I adhered faithfully to what had been the original material and everybody else was in a different movie. Unless you have conviction in your material, how do you start?"¹¹ O'Toole's relationship with Tola was of great mutual respect and when the Irish actor wanted to travel to England for a celebration of the Bristol Old Vic Theatre, Tola agreed to rearrange the schedule so he could attend the event.

In February 1966, the company travelled to Warsaw for the first month of filming. It was the first western film made in Warsaw since the end of the war. In order to obtain the permission of the Polish Minister of Cultural Affairs, a script had to be submitted. The producers found it necessary to make several changes from the original novel in order not to upset the local authorities.

Dialogue coach Frawley Becker described the first day of filming in his memoirs:

[It] was a night scene with Gordon Jackson and Omar [Sharif] in front of Lazienki Palace, an eighteenth-century marvel most of which had miraculously remained intact through World War II.... The night was limpid, the snow crisp, and the palace, bathed by powerful brut arc lamps, shimmered. Dolly track, one of Litvak's constant instruments, was laid down easily on the packed snow. It all went without a hitch, and joyously, at 2 a.m. we went back to the hotel to go to bed. And while we slept, a searing sun came out. By early afternoon all the snow had melted. At four o'clock, Litvak announced he would not shoot because Warsaw's streets had been completely stripped. He spoke to Spiegel in London, who agreed to wait a day or two. Surely, it would not take more than that for the snow to return. Three days later, I was with the despondent director in his suite in the Hotel Europejski as he eyed the clean spring-like street below his window. Suddenly, Peter O'Toole burst into the room.

"Tola, let's shoot it!"

"We can't. There is no snow."

"The script says February in Warsaw. Well, it's February and we're in Warsaw, so let's shoot it!"

"If there's no snow, it'll just look like we shot it on the back lot somewhere." And his face turned into a mask of Slavic suffering. It seemed incredible that the famous Warsaw winter was not there for us. Then Litvak headed for the phone and another call to Spiegel while Peter and I looked down on the sunlit street below. The next day, the snow still didn't arrive. What did arrive were the snow-making machines that Spiegel had had flown in. For the next three weeks, the streets of Warsaw were winterized into whiteness with Styrofoam. The air was cold and clear, but not a flurry of real snow fell in Warsaw in February 1966."[12]

Tola explained that even though the film had been shot in color, he and cameraman Henri Decae tried to stay away from color as much as they could: "Color can be bad, particularly with the war; it takes away from reality in the most horrible way."[13]

"It seems to me that we accomplished some East-West accord with our trip to Warsaw—at least cinematically," Tola said to *The New York Times.*

> It was a pioneering venture and we found an eagerness to cooperate on all levels and a great curiosity about our methods.... The Polish Army supplied us with 200 soldiers to act as Nazi troops and the Polski film organization provided civilian extras. We were given German tanks, army Jeeps and weapons, and the walls of the street in which we were to work were plastered with German posters from 1942. The Vajda Studios offered stage space for a few interior scenes and the Lazienkowski Palace, once the residence of Polish monarchs, then the German generals' headquarters during the Occupation and now a history museum, was decked out with swastika flags, as one of the major sequences takes place before it. The only opposition we encountered came when we were at work on a night scene in central Warsaw. We had asked the tenants of the buildings on which our cameras were focused to take down their televisions antennas and to keep the lights out in the first apartments. A professor refused to do either—in protest, he said, against the Vietnam war. We didn't argue, but simply shifted the camera angle.[14]

After shooting in bitter cold Warsaw, the crew moved to Paris. With the help of Alexander Trauner, the set designer, who had studied every detail of the interior of the Lazienki Palace, Tola was able to build replicas of some of the rooms at the Studios de Boulogne Billancourt. Later some cast members, including O'Toole, had to fly to London where some dialogue, shot with outdoor sounds interfering, had to be dubbed. *The Night of the Generals* took two and a half years of Tola's life. It premiered in London on January 29, 1967, and a month later in New York. Mixed reviews and a poor box-office performance (only $2.4 million) sunk the film that by 1972 would lose more than $3 million

On the occasion of the American release of *The Night of the Generals,* a journalist asked Tola about his professional future. "Nothing definite till I find something I like," was his reply. "There aren't that many good stories around"[15] In fact three months later producer Joseph E. Levine, founder of Embassy Pictures, announced that Tola would direct *The Ski Bum* with O'Toole, Arthur Kennedy and Katharine Ross. The picture, based on a story by Romain Gary adapted by Sidney Carroll, was going to be shot in Switzerland, with interiors at the Ardmore Studios in Ireland. However due to script difficulties, O'Toole and some crew members connected with the project were reassigned to a different production. With O'Toole's gone, Tola decided to withdraw his participation. In February 1968, Embassy Pictures filed a suit against him in New York Supreme Court for a breach of contract for alleged failure of performance in his obligations as director. Apparently the case was settled outside of court.

Samantha Eggar and John McEnery in a scene from *The Lady in the Car with Glasses and a Gun* (1970).

At sixty-six years old, Tola demonstrated no signs of wanting to retire. He was still very active and eager to go back to work, despite the disappointment of his last films. After purchasing the rights to the thriller novel *The Lady in the Car with Glasses and a Gun*, written by French author Sebastien Japrisot, he planned to start shooting in France in the summer of 1968. But the difficult political climate created by the French student movement forced him to postpone the filming. Because the story was set in the summer, Tola had to delay the production for one year. The thriller followed the journey by car of an English secretary, from Paris to the South of France during a long, summer holiday weekend. The woman arrives at her destination after a series of scary and strange adventures, convinced she is either crazy or an amnesiac.

Casting choices were announced in the press in the spring of 1969. Tola teamed British actors Samantha Eggar and Oliver Reed in the leading roles. The picture was shot on location in the South of France with interiors at Pinewood Studios in England in July 1969. The two stars got along very well. They were in fact old friends and playmates from childhood who grew up together in the same village in rural England. Tola's enthusiasm to be back at work was described by set photographer Bob Willoughby as "contagious ... he was so filled with energy that after shooting all day he would make special things in the hotel kitchen for the cast."[16] A skilled cook, Tola often cooked for friends and family. His favorite dish to prepare was a special salad based on an old Russian family recipe. One evening the catering people had their television on, and *Anastasia* happened to be playing. All members of the crew took their plates of food and stood around watching it. It was a very moving moment for Tola and the young French and British crew members could see just what he was about. The only moment of tension seemed to be when Yul Brynner, on the set at Tola's invitation, tried to take some pictures of Eggar in the nude. The actress kept throwing him out of the dressing room and he complained to Columbia Pictures that she was acting unprofessionally.

The Lady in the Car with Glasses and a Gun opened in France in the fall of 1970 and on Christmas Day in the States. The critics accused Litvak of making a thriller with an implausible plot, little tension and a rushed ending. Oliver Reed in his autobiography called it "a terrible movie." The picture had a limited release and disappeared quickly from the theaters. It was Litvak's last film.

Tola spent his last four years mostly between his two houses in Paris and St. Tropez. Jean Witta remembered bumping into him at the bar of a studio in 1973, twenty years after her last meeting on the set of *Act of Love*: "Because of his warm and happy welcome, I experienced once again the affection that had bound us thanks to common efforts."¹⁷ Jean Negulesco had lost with Tola, then saw him in Paris during a business trip. He found him lacking his usual

> Russian sparkle and his asthma was bothering him seriously. We talked the whole afternoon—reminiscences of old times, of fun, work and future plans.... When we left, Tola asked me a strange favor. "Johnny, could I come and spend some time in your flat in London? I may find some of my sanity." I called his Paris apartment from London two weeks later. His faithful secretary Anne Sallepenko [sic] told me that he had gone to Vienna for a possible deal. He never made it. The deal or London.¹⁸

In the fall of 1974, Tola was diagnosed with stomach cancer. After consulting with several specialists, he decided to be hospitalized in a private clinic in the affluent Paris suburb of Neuilly-sur-Seine. On December 15, 1975, after several weeks in the hospital, Anatole Litvak died at age 72. His beloved and caring wife Sophie was with him at the end. A funeral service was held at the crematorium of Père-Lachaise cemetery in Paris. Tola's closest friends, technicians, writers, actors and producers showed up to pay tribute of their friendship. The service was heightened by mournful Russian music Sophie had chosen. The moving and intense ceremony involved the sliding of the coffin into an open crematorium seen by the congregants, who heard the flames crackling and later saw a box of ashes emerging from the other side. Irwin Shaw and his wife Bodie, together with Peter Viertel and Deborah Kerr, were so shaken by that sad event they adjourned to the Ritz Hotel bar to drink to Tola's memory. According to Tola's wishes, after a brief period at Père-Lachaise cemetery his ashes were removed by Sophie and scattered in an unknown location.

In a will written five years before his death, Tola left Sophie his entire estate estimated at $750,000, including the apartment in Paris, the villa in St. Tropez and other assets in California exceeding $50,000. In September 1975, a petition for probate of the will was filed in Los Angeles Superior Court to allow the distribution of Tola's American properties to his widow.

Sadly, Anatole Litvak's legacy was quickly forgotten after his death. Many film historians and movie critics have unfairly overlooked his name and filmography. His unjust exclusion from the list of directors who made history during Hollywood's golden age made him a forgotten filmmaker.

Filmography

As Director

Tatiana
B&W; short silent film; Released in 1923
CREDITS: *Director*: Anatole Litvak; *Producer*: Nordkino Studios
CAST: Nikolai Petrov.
NOTES: No further information is available about *Tatiana*. In an interview, Litvak called it "a film for kids."

Serdtsa i Dollary
(*Hearts and Dollars*)
Kino-Sever; B&W; 87 minutes; silent film; Released in 1924
CREDITS: *Director*: Anatole Litvak; *Screenplay*: Dukh-Banko (Glikman), Vladimir Korolevich; *Photography:* Nikolai Kozlovsky, Evgeny Mikhailov; *Production Designer*: Vladimir Yegorov
CAST: D. Cherkasov, Sergei Shishko, Ivan Lersky, Nikolai Petrov, Maria Babanova, Sofya Magarill
PLOT: In the years of NEP (New Economic Policy), two men with the same last name live in Leningrad: Ivanov, a draftsman, and Ivanov, a "Nepman" (a nouveau riche). Jane, an American relative of the draftsman, comes to Leningrad on a visit at the same time as Harry, an American relative of the Nepman. A comedy of errors begins and chaos ensues.
NOTES: Released in France in 1925 as *Le Coeur*.

Dolly Macht Karriere
(*Dolly Gets Ahead* aka *Dolly's Way to Stardom*)
Universum Film A.G. (UFA); B&W; 87 minutes; Released in Berlin on October 24, 1930
CREDITS: *Producers:* Noé Bloch, Gregor Rabinovitch, Arnold Pressburger; *Director:* Anatole Litvak; *Screenplay:* Irma von Cube, Peter Heimann, *Idea*: Alfred Halm; *Photography*: Fritz Arno Wagner, Robert Baberske; *Production Designers*: Heinz Fenchel, Jacek Rotmil; *Music:* Rudolf Nelson, Willy Schmidt-Gentner, Alfred Strasser; *Costumes*: Ernst Stern

CAST: Dolly Haas (Dolly Klaren), Oskar Karlweis (Fred Halton), Grete Natzler (Mariette), Vicky Werckmeister (Orelly), Alfred Abel (Count Eberhad von Schwarzenburg), Herman Blaß (O.W. Pietsch), Kurt Gerron (Silbermann), Paul Kemp (Jack), Theo Lingen (Conny Coon), Gustl Stark-Gstettenbauer (Boy), Hansi Arnstaedt, Lucie Euler, Trude Lehmann, Valeska Stock, Ellen Plessow, Paul Henckels, Erich Kestin, Géza L. Weiß, Manfred Voß, Bernhard Veidt, Charlie Dodo, Georg Schmieter, Kurt Lilien, Julius E. Herrmann, Hans Zesch-Ballot

PLOT: When young Dolly Klaren loses her job, she returns home to a big Berlin tenement where her boyfriend, composer Fred Halton, and his buddy, clarinet player Jack, also live. The two young men are determined to help Dolly realize her dream of going on stage. She tricks cabaret owner and theater director Silbermann into giving her a chance to appear in place of a missing leading lady in a new revue. Dolly gets stage fright and almost makes a failure of Silbermann's much-advertised premiere. But a kind elderly man in the audience cheers her on and she finally recovers her self-control, making the show into a success. The elderly man turns out to be Count Eberhad von Schwarzenburg, whose name has been linked with Dolly's by Silbermann for publicity purposes (Silbermann was under the impression that the count was hunting big game in Africa). The count is entertained by Dolly at the supper after the show, but his rather half-hearted advances are easily foiled by the clever Berlin girl. At the end the old man plays a leading part in effecting the inevitable reconciliation between Fred and Dolly.

REVIEWS:
"The acting and photography are excellent."—*New York Times,* July 18, 1931
"This is the best picture Ufa has yet shown at its New York Cosmopolitan."—*Variety* July 31, 1931

REWIEWS FOR ANATOLE LITVAK:
"Litvak, once an assistant, has got ahead, managing with ease the sound and the performances of the leading lady."—*La Cinématographie française,* June 27, 1932

ADDITIONAL REVIEWS AND ARTICLES:
New York Times November 23, 1930; *Cinémonde* May 14, 1931; *Pour Vous* November 20, 1931

NOTES: *Dolly Macht Karriere* opened in New York at the Cosmopolitan Theatre on July 17, 1931.

Nie wieder Liebe!

Universum Film A.G. (UFA); B&W; 82 minutes; Released in Berlin on July 27, 1931

CREDITS: *Producers:* Noé Bloch, Gregor Rabinovitch; *Director:* Anatole Litvak; *Production Manager*: Noé Bloch; *Assistant Director*: Max Ophüls; *Screenplay:* Irma von Cube, Anatole Litvak; *Based on the play* Dover-Calais *by* Julius Berstl; *Photography:* Franz Planer, Robert Baberske; *Production Designers:* Robert Herlth, Walter Röhrig; *Art Director*: Werner Schlichting; *Editor:* Alexander Uralsky; *Music:* Mischa Spoliansky; *Music Director*: Hans-Otto Borgmann; *Lyrics:* Robert Gilbert; *Sound:* Erich Leistner; *Makeup:* Ernst Schulke

CAST: Lilian Harvey (Gladys O'Halloran), Harry Liedtke (Sandercroft), Felix Bressart (Jean), Margo Lion (Eine Stimmungssängerin), Oscar Marion (Jack), Julius Falkenstein (Dr. Baskett), Hermann Speelmans (Tom), Theo Lingen (Rhinelander), Raoul Lange (der Spanier), Lovis Brody (Der Koch), Constantin Kaiser (Schiffsjunge), Rina Marsa (Claire), Hans Behal (Charlie), Mischa Spoliansky (Klavierspieler).

PLOT: After nearly being bankrupted by a series of a disastrous love affairs, Mr. Sandercroft, a rich young American, promises that he will not go anywhere near a woman for five years. To strengthen his resolution, he backs up his promise with a $500,000 bet with his friend Jack. He hires a yacht, swears his crew to female abstinence and off they sail. With the help of Jean, his faithful butler, Sandercroft successfully eludes women. But just before the five-year time limit is up, he is obliged to rescue from the ocean Gladys O'Halloran, a beautiful girl who claims to be a Channel swimmer. In order to get rid of the woman, the butler breaks into his master's desk and arranges evidence so that it will look as if the girl were the thief. It turns out that Gladys had been hired by Jack to make certain that Sandercroft would lose his bet, but just before she kisses him as planned, she realizes that she's fallen in love with him. Eventually Gladys dedicates herself to making sure that Sandercroft will keep his promise but allowing him to marry her after the five-year period.

REVIEWS:

"An amusing idea back of this latest German musical.... For non–Germans it's liable to prove a bit too slow.... With 20 minutes cut out and the action speeded that much it would prove a first rate musical comedy fancy."—*Variety,* January 19, 1932

"A merry German version of the old story of the Don Juan who 'swears off' from all the women for a terms of years."—*New York Times,* January 16, 1932

REVIEWS FOR ANATOLE LITVAK:

"[Litvak] has caught many moments where melody and action could be combined to the rhythms of Mischa Spoliansky's skillful music."—*New York Times,* October 4, 1931

ADDITIONAL REVIEWS AND ARTICLES:

Lichtbild-Bühne July 28, 1931; *Kinematograph* July 28, 1931; *Film-Kurier* July 28, 1931; *Der Film* August 1, 1931; *Frankfurter Zeitug* August 3, 1931; *La Revue du Cinéma* October 1, 1931; *New York Times* October 4, 1931

Calais-Douvres

Universum Film A.G. (UFA), L' Alliance Cinématographique Européenne, B&W, 87 minutes, Released in Paris on September 18, 1931

CREDITS: *Producers:* Noé Bloch, Gregor Rabinovitch; *Directors:* Anatole Litvak, Jean Boyer; *Screenplay*: Irma von Cube, Anatole Litvak; *Based on the play* Dover-Calais *by* Julius Bernstl; *Dialogue*: Jean Boyer; *Photography:* Franz Planer, Robert Baberske; *Production Designers:* Robert Herlth, Walter Röhring; *Set Decorator*: Werner Schlichting; *Editor:* Alexander Uralsky; *Music*: Mischa Spoliansky; *Music Director*: Hans-Otto Borgmann; *Sound:* Erich Leistner

CAST: Lilian Harvey (Gladys O'Halloran), André Roanne (MacFerson), Armand Bernard (Jean), Margo Lion (Eine Stimmungssängerin), Robert Darthez (Jack), Sinoël (Dr. Baskett), Andrè Gabriello (Tom), Guy Sloux (Rhinelaender le chef d'equipage), Frédéric Mariotti (un marin espagnol), Louis Brody (Der Koch), Rina Marsa (Claire), Margo Lion (La diseause de Zanzibar), Willy Rozier, Fred Casamini, Yvette Darnys

PLOT: *Calais-Douvres* has the same plot as *Nie wieder Liebe!,* which is synopsized above, but with different character names.

REVIEWS:

"*Calais-Douvres* is a film with no importance, but charming and lively."
—*La Cinématographie française,* September 26, 1931

REVIEW FOR ANATOLE LITVAK:
"Excellent script."—*La Cinématographie française* September 26, 1931
ADDITIONAL REVIEWS AND ARTICLES:
Pour Vous September 24, 1931; *Cinémonde* September 24, 1931; *Pour Vous* October 15, 1931; *Cinémonde* November 19, 1931
NOTES: This French version of *Nie wieder Liebe!* was shot in Berlin simultaneously, sharing half of the cast. André Roanne substituted for Harry Liedtke. The film was briefly released in New York as *Never Love Again*.

Coeur de Lilas

(Released in the U.S. as *Lilac*), Fifra, Les Artiste Associés, S.A., United Artists, B&W, 90 minutes, Released in Paris on February 13, 1932

CREDITS: *Producers:* Jean Hulswit, Dorothy Farnum, Maurice Barber; *Director*: Anatole Litvak; *Screenplay*: Dorothy Farnum, Anatole Litvak, Serge Veber; *Based on a play by* Tristan Bernard and Charles Henry Hirsch; *Cinematography*: Curt Courant; *Music*: Maurice Yvan; *Lyrics*: Serge Veber; *Music Conductor*: Pierre Chagnon; *Set Decorator*: Serge Pimenoff; *Camera Assistant*: Louis Née; *Assistant Directors*: Dimitri Dragomir, H. Blanchon; *Sound*: Roger Loisel; *Sound Editor*: Victor Fastowich; *Production Manager*: Grégoire Metchikian

CAST: Marcelle Romée (Lilas Couchoux), André Luguet (André Lucot), Madeleine Guitty (Mme. Charigoul), Carlotta Conti (Mme. Novion), Lydie Villans (La Crevette), Fordice (Mme. Darny), Fréhel (La Douleur), Marcel Delaître (Darny), Paul Amiot (Merlu), Georges Paulais (The judge), Pierre Labry (Charigoul), Fernandel (Boy of honor), Jean Gabin (Martousse), Jean Max, Georges Pally, Edouard Rousseau, René Maupré

PLOT: A group of children accidentally discovers the body of Novion, an old businessman who's apparently has committed suicide by throwing himself into the Seine. After examining the body, Inspector André Lucot does not share the opinion of the examining judge who calls it a suicide. A glove belonging to well-known prostitute Lilas Couchoux was found next to the corpse, and Lucot decides to investigate on his own. He assumes the identity of an unemployed mechanic and rents a room on the bank of the Marne in order to meet the woman. In a bar where Lilas hangs out, the inspector meets Martousse, bouncer of the dive and Lilas' former lover. The two men violently quarrel and Martousse is arrested in the course of a police raid. Lucot, who is falling in love with Lilas, takes her back to his hotel room. Martusse, escaped from prison, finds the couple and reveals to Lilas that her new lover is a police officer. Upset by the revelation, she tries to flee but she is quickly found by a policeman. Finally she confesses her crime.

REVIEWS:
"[*Coeur de Lilas*] is obviously a special film.... It's a very human piece of work."—*La Cinématographie française,* February 20, 1932
"The director works with such a virtuosity, with such a firm hand, that we can follow his gestures with increasing interest...."—*Le Journal,* February 20, 1932
"So far the best picture of the French underworld."—*Variety,* March 1, 1932
REVIEWS FOR ANATOLE LITVAK:
"Direction is very good and cleverly skips unsafe bits, such as the battle in the dive...."—*Variety,* March 1, 1932

"There is a wealth of just and piquant images integrated with fertile invention and precise sense of cinema by the director Anatole Litvak."—*L'Intransigeant,* February 20, 1932

ADDITIONAL REVIEWS AND ARTICLES:
Pour Vous February 18, 1932; *Cinémonde* February 18, 1932; *L'Echo de Paris* February 20, 1932; *La Liberté* February 20, 1932; *Cinémonde* March 3, 1932; *Jeune Cinéma* January 1989

Das Lied einer Nacht

(*The Song of the Night*)
Cine-Allianz-TonFilm (GmbH), Universum Film A.G. (UFA), B&W, 85 minutes, Released in Berlin on May 27, 1932
CREDITS: *Producers:* Hermann Feliner, Arnold Pressburger, Gregor Rabinovitch; *Director*: Anatole Litvak; *Screenplay*: Albrecht Joseph, Irma von Cube; *Dialogue*: John Orton; *Photography*, Fritz Arno Wagner, Robert Baberske; *Assistant Director*: Victor von Struve; *Camera Assistant:* Igor Obeberg, Ekkehard Kyrath; *Music*: Mischa Spoliansky, Willy Schmidt-Gentner; *Lyrics*: Marcellus Schiffer; *Sound*: Hermann Fritzsching, Walter Rühland; *Art Director*: Werner Schlichting; *Editor*: Henri Rust; *Production Manager*: Fritz Klotzsch; *Costumes:* Walter Leder, Otto Suckrow, Gertrud Wendt

CAST: Jan Kiepura (Enrico Ferraro), Fritz Schulz (Alexander Koretsky), Magda Schneider (Mathilde Pategg), Otto Wallburg (Mayor Pategg), Ida Wüst (Mrs. Pategg), Margo Lion (Manager of Ferraro-Dragon Lady), Julius Falkestein (Balthasar)

PLOT: Enrico Ferraro, an attractive young tenor, is being bossed around by his domineering female manager. Driven to desperation, the singer makes a bolt for it and eludes his companion while en route to Bucharest. Falling in with Koretsky, a suave confidence man, whose carefree sense of humor appeals to the tenor, he makes for Zern, a pretty Swiss village. There, by a series of coincidences, Koretsky is mistaken for Ferraro. Ferraro allows the confusion of identities to continue because it will give him some freedom from his adoring fans. The crook even passes off the singer as his secretary. On a car trip, Ferraro is served at a gas station by the beautiful Mathilde, the adopted daughter of the local mayor; she pretends to be a mechanic just for fun. Promising he will sing to Mathilde, Koretsky mouths the words as Ferraro, hidden by shrubbery, sings the ballad. Suspecting that all is not as it should be, the girl discovers the trick and gives the confidence man a hearty slap in the face. Ferraro, who has taken Koretsky's name, is arrested by the police, who have looked up the crook's record. In order to prove his identity, he performs arias from famous operas for the local gendarmerie and is eventually prevailed upon to fulfill a promise given by Koretsky to play the lead in an amateur performance of *La Boheme*. Mathilde, still angry about being deceived, plans to spoil Ferraro's performance with the help of some girlfriends. But when Koretsky tells her that the tenor really loves her, she abandons her scheme. At the end of the show, Korentsky is caught and Mathilde goes off with Ferraro, who has locked in his dressing room his bossy manager, who has tracked him down and is already planning dozens of bookings for him

REVIEW:
"[The film is] altogether cheerful and sentimental...."—La *Gazzetta di Venezia,* August 13, 1932

REVIEWS FOR ANATOLE LITVAK:
"Graceful, directed with musical sense by the filmmaker Anatol Litwak."—*Film Kurier,* May 28, 1932
"As a director Anatol Litwak makes quite an outstanding job."—*Lichtbild Bühne,* May 28, 1931
ADDITIONAL REVIEWS AND ARTICLES:
La Gazzetta di Venezia August 14, 1932
NOTES: *Das Lied einer Nacht* was shown at the first Venice Film Festival on August 13, 1932.

La Chanson d'une nuit

Cine-Allianz-TonFilm (GmbH), L'Alliance Cinématographique Européenne (ACE), Films Osso, B&W, 85 minutes, Released in Paris on February 3, 1932
CREDITS: *Producers*: Arnold Pressburger, Gregor Rabinovitch, William A. Szekeley; *Directors*: Anatole Litvak; *Director of Additional Scenes:* Pierre Colombier; *Screenplay*: Albrecht Joseph, Irma von Cube; *Dialogue*: Henri-Georges Clouzot; *Photography*, Fritz Arno Wagner, Robert Baberske; *Assistant Director*: Henri-Georges Clouzot; *Camera Assistant:* Igor Oberberg; *Music*: Mischa Spoliansky, Willy Schmidt-Gentner; *Lyrics*: Serge Veber, *Art Director*: Werner Schlichting; *Editor*: Salabert
CAST: Jan Kiepura (Enrico Ferraro), Pierre Brasseur (Alexander Koretsky), Magda Schneider (Mathilde Pategg), Lucien Baroux (Pategg), Charlotte Lysès (Mme. Pategg), Clara Tambour (Le manager de Ferraro-la reine mère), Charles Lamy (Balthasar), Pierre Labry (L'inspecteur), René Bergeron (L'employé des contribution), Sinoël
PLOT: *La Chanson d'une nuit* has the same plot as *Das Lied einer Nacht,* which is synopsized above.
REVIEWS:
"Tasteful cinema, light-heartedness and good humor without any vulgarity."—*Pour Vous,* February 9, 1933
"If you ask a film to charm you, to be likable, to be interesting, to give you that impression that will make you say: 'what a lovely evening I spent' then you'd be satisfied."—*L'Ami du Film*, February 1933
REVIEWS FOR ANATOLE LITVAK:
"This film is among the best made by Anatole Litvak."—*Bordeaux Ciné,* February 17, 1933
"Litwak's adaptation is skilled with great artistic qualities."—*Semaine Cinématographique,* February 1933
ADDITIONAL REVIEWS AND ARTICLES:
L'Intransigeant February 1933; *Semaine Cinématographique* February 1933; *La Cinématographie française* February 1933; *Cinémonde* February 9, 1933; *Pour Vous* March 9, 1933; *Cinémonde* May 3, 1934; *Télérama* February 4, 1998

Tell Me Tonight

(Released in the U.K. as *Be Mine Tonight*)
Gaumont-British Universum Film A.G. (UFA); B&W; 81 minutes; Released in London on October 30, 1932

CREDITS: *Producers:* Hermann Feliner, Arnold Pressburger, Gregor Rabinovitch, Josef Somio; *Director*: Anatole Litvak; *Screenplay*: Albrecht Joseph, Irma von Cube; *Dialogue*: John Orton; *Photography:* Willy Goldberger, Fritz Arno Wagner; *Camera Assistant:* Igor Obeberg; *Music*: Mischa Spoliansky; *Lyrics*: Frank Eyton

CAST: Jan Kiepura (Enrico Ferraro), Sonnie Hale (Alexander Koretsky), Magda Schneider (Mathilde Pategg), Edmund Gwenn (Mayor Pategg), Athene Seyler (Mrs. Pategg), Betty Chester (Miss. Barker), Aubrey Mather (Balthasar)

PLOT: *Tell Me Tonight* has the same plot as *Das Lied einer Nacht,* which is synopsized above.

REVIEWS:

"One of the most perfect blendings of romance, music, song and comedy we have yet had on the screen."—*Picturegoer,* January 7, 1933

"Never heavy or cumbersome in plot, yet always providing enough story, the picture acquires a certain charm that's among its important assets."—*Variety,* April 18, 1933

"A romantic musical of much charm, cleverly mixed with a story of a transfer of identities...."—*Kinematograph Weekly*, May 18, 1944

REVIEWS FOR ANATOLE LITVAK:

"Anatol Litwak's direction is full of point and humour"—*Daily Express,* October 30, 1932

"Director Anatol Litwak has devised business for supplementary characters or directed attention to the beauty of natural scenic backgrounds. The result is a neat blending of entertainment for eye and ear."—*Hollywood Reporter* February 4, 1933

ADDITIONAL REVIEWS AND ARTICLES:

Cinema Quarterly Winter 1932; *The Cinema Booking Guide Supplement* January 1933; *Motion Picture Herald* February 18, 1933; *Harrison's Reports* March 25, 1933; *New York Times* April 14, 1933; *The Cinema News* May 17, 1944

Sleeping Car

(aka *Love and Let Love*)

Gaumont-British; B&W; 82 minutes; Released in London on June 13, 1933

CREDITS: *Producer:* Michael Balcon; *Director:* Anatole Litvak; *Screenplay*: Michael Gordon; *Story:* Anatole Litvak, Franz Schulz; *Dialogue:* Roland Pertwee; *Photography:* Günther Krampf, Glen MacWilliams; *Music*: Louis Levy, Noel Gay; *Lyrics*: Clifford Grey; *Editor:* Henri Rust; *Sound:* A. C. O'Donughe; *Production Manager:* Geoffrey Boothby; *Art Director*: Alfred Junge, *Jewellery*: Lacloche Frères.

CAST: Madeleine Carroll (Anne Howard), Ivor Novello (Gaston Bray), Laddie Cliff (Pierre Concombe), Kay Hammond (Simone), Claude Allister (Baron Delande), Stanley Holloway (Francois Dubois), Vera Bryer (Jenny—Anne's Maid), Ivor Barnard (Durande), John Singer (Page Boy), Bobbie Comber, Pat Fitzpatrick, Sam Keen, Richard Littledale, Yvonne Dulac

PLOT: Gaston Bray is a handsome sleeping car attendant having numerous love affairs in different cities at which the Trans-Continental train stops. He really falls in love with wealthy English girl Anne Howard who, having refused to answer a summons for driving recklessly, is due to be expelled from France. It is explained to her that if she marries a Frenchman she will be allowed to remain in France and so she advertises for a husband. Many applicants arrive, amongst them Gaston, who gets the post. When a former sweet-

heart enters upon the scene, many complication ensue before matters are finally straightened out.
REVIEWS:
"The film has comedy, if not wit and piquant characters, if not real people. Pictorially, it is lavish and ingenious...."—*Film Weekly,* June 16, 1933
"*Sleeping Car* is a gay comedy, with a wealth of laughter arising from its many original and piquant situations."—*Sunday Pictorial,* June 18, 1933
"[T]he evident competence of the film deserves to be praised...."—*The Times,* June 19, 1933
REVIEWS FOR ANATOLE LITVAK:
"...first rate photography and direction."—*Variety,* June 27, 1933
"[S]tory writer [Franz Schulz] has left his director, Herr Anatol Litvak, badly in the lurch."—*The Illustrated London News,* July 1, 1933
ADDITIONAL REVIEWS AND ARTICLES:
Kine Weekly June 22, 1933; *The Cinema Booking Guide Supplement* July 1933
NOTES: The picture was entirely shot at Shepherd's Bush Studios in London. British actor Sonnie Hale, who had starred in *Tell Me Tonight,* was Litvak's uncredited assistant.

Cette Vielle Canaille

(Released in the U.S. as *That Old Bum* aka *That Old Rogue* aka *The Old Devil*)
Cipar Films; B&W; 95 minutes; Released in Paris on November 3, 1933
CREDITS: *Producer:* Simon Schiffrin; *Director*: Anatole Litvak; *Assistant Directors*: Claude Heymann, Georges Friedland; *Screenplay*: Anatole Litvak, Serge Veber; *Based on a play by* Fernand Nozièr; *Dialogue*: Serge Veber; *Photography*: Curt Courant; *Camera Assistant*: Bauer; *Music*: Georges Van Parys; *Lyrics*: Serge Veber; *Art Director*: Andrej Andrejew; *Sound*: William Robert Sivel, *Editor*: Henri Rust
CAST: Harry Baur (Prof. Guillaume Vautier), Alice Field (Hélène), Pierre Blanchar (Jean Trapeau), Christiane Dor (Suzanne), Paul Azaïs (Jacques), Madeleine Geoffroy (Germaine), Madeleine Guitty (la mère d'Hélène), Pierre Stephen (le professeur d'histoire), Saint-Allier, Andrée Doria, Kiki of Montparnasse, Ginette Leclerc, Josèphe Evelys
PLOT: At a funfair in Neully, Hélène, the pretty daughter of a stall holder, quarrels with a rival over Jean, a young acrobat. Prof. Vautier, a middle-aged Parisian surgeon, intervenes and tends her injuries. Hélène is arrested and ends up in jail. That same night, she is mysteriously released and taken to a luxurious private residence. There she again meets Vautier, who had bailed her out. The retired surgeon makes no attempt to restrain Hélène, but he offers her the house as her own home. Hélène accepts Vautier's kind offer and quickly she forgets her former life and her lover Jean. Although Vautier apparently has no amorous designs of his own, he manages to impede every attempt Hélène makes to find another man. One day Hélène encounters Jean and suddenly realizes that she still in love with him, leaving Vautier for the acrobat. When Jean is injured by a fall from the trapeze, the surgeon puts aside his pride and performs a delicate operation, saving the acrobat's life.
REVIEWS:
"Better than most French pictures."—*Variety,* December 12, 1933

"[T]he high-class photography and the quality of the performance go far toward overcoming the banality of the story."—*New York Times,* January 14, 1935
REVIEW FOR ANATOLE LITVAK:
"[*Cette Vielle Canaille*] is human, tough and cruel. Its set up made by Litvak is of incomparable integrity and richness."—*La Cinématographie française,* November 11, 1933
ADDITIONAL REVIEWS AND ARTICLES:
Pour Vous June 22, 1933; *Cinémonde* July 13, 1933; *Pour Vous* August 10, 1933; *Cinémonde* November 2, 1933; *Pour Vous* November 9, 1933; *Cinémonde* November 16, 1933; *Pour Vous* January 25, 1934; *Film Kritik* February 1960; *Cinématographe* June 1983; *Jeune Cinéma* February 1989; *Télérama* December 31, 1997
NOTES: Charles Boyer was Litvak's first choice for the role of Jean Trapeau. Paul Azaïs sings "Ah, c' qu'on est bête quand on est amoureux!" written by Serge Veber.

L'Équipage

(Released in the U.S. as *Flight into Darkness*)
Pathé Consortium Cinéma-Pathé Nathan France; B&W; 100 minutes; Released in Paris on October 22, 1935
CREDITS: *Producers:* Noé Bloch, Grégoire Metchikian; *Director*: Anatole Litvak; *Screenplay*: Joseph Kessel, Anatole Litvak; *Based on a novel by* Joseph Kessel; *Dialogue*: Joseph Kessel; *Story Editor*: J. Cubé; *Assistant Directors*: André Cerf, André Lang, Jean-Paul Dreyfus; *Photography*: Armand Thirard; *Camera Assistant*: Luis Née; *Music*: Arthur Honegger, Jean Wiener; *Music Conductor*: Maurice Jaubert; *Lyrics*: Louis Poterat; *Editor*: Henri Rust, Jean-Paul Le Chanois; *Production Designers*: Lucien Aguettand, Lucien Carré; *Costumes*: Boris Bilinsky; *Sound*: William Robert Sivel; *Technical Advisors*: P. Carretier, R. Phelizon
CAST: Annabella (Hélène/Denise), Charles Vanel (Le lieutenant Maury), Jean Murat (Le capitaine Thélis), Jean-Pierre Aumont (Jean Herbillon), Daniel Mendaille (Deschamps), Raymond Cordy (Mathieu), Suzanne Desprès (Madame Herbillon), Alexandre Rignault (L'amant de la patronne), Pierre Labry (Marbot), Geo Laby (Mézières), Bergeron (Fortin), Jean Heuze (Berthier), Roland Toutain (Narbonne), Yves Forget, André Lannes (Officiers), Serge Grave (Georges Herbillon), Guy Sloux (Michel), Davy (Brulard), Claire Franconnay (La patronne du beuglant), Raymond Aimos (Le crieur de journaux), Paul Amiot (Le soldat du 54e), Vera Baranovskaya (La veuve), Paulette Élambert (La petite fille), Marcel Melrac (Le planton), Viviane Romance (Une girl), Eugène Stuber (L'ordonnance de Maury Léon), Arvel, Jeanne Byrel, Charles Camus, Enrique Gómez
PLOT: During World War I, Jean Herbillon, a young lieutenant, makes the acquaintance of a beautiful woman. Despite the fact that he only knows her as Denise and doesn't even know her last name, the two are madly in love. Back at the front, Jean forms an "Equipage" with Lieutenant Maury and they become great friends. Jean and Maury enjoy many victorious flights together until Jean is given a fortnight's leave. Maury asks Jean to take a letter to his wife Helene, whom he loves dearly. Back in Paris, Jean and Denise are deliriously happy. Just as he is due back, he remembers his friend's letter. He calls on Maury's wife and discovers she is Denise. Jean is heartbroken at this discovery and dreads the thought of facing Maury, his best friend. He tries to forget Denise, but

every time he sees Maury the old wound opens. Maury cannot understand Jean's changed attitude. Denise, longing to see Jean again, decides to visit her husband. Jean does everything possible to avoid being left alone with her, but she manages to slip into his quarters. Denise tells Jean that life means nothing to her without him. Jean tries to make her understand about the friendship that exists between him and Maury and also the meaning of an "equipage," but Denise is deaf to everything but her great need of Jean. The war is nearing its end and a final attack is planned. Jean's squadron has received final orders. After a last meeting with Denise, Jean and Maury depart in their plane. Maury has guessed everything and the two friends now are bitter enemies. High in the skies the two men put aside all their personal feelings, showing great courage in their last mission. Once they get back to headquarters Maury discovers Jean dead and in his hand a photograph of his wife.

REVIEWS:

"It is, indeed, in the details and incidental action—life in the French escadrille, the grim reflections of war and the battle scenes in the air-that the picture is most impressive."—*New York Times,* October 17, 1938

"*The Flight into Darkness* is a dramatic picture, though too slow to be tensely dramatic."—*Daily News,* October 17, 1938

"There are a good many air raid shots—well photographed, too. But we're used to them. They hardly compensate for the mediocrity of the script."—*New York Post,* October 19, 1938

REVIEWS FOR ANATOLE LITVAK:

"Anatol Litvak is definitely one of the few foreign filmmakers in France, who belongs to us: because he respects our writers, because he made his own our way of understanding and feeling, and he has taste for quality."—*Pour Vous,* October 24, 1935

"[Litvak's] work as director tends to the humdrum, and here he only rises above the usual clichés when simple emotions coincide with real acting ability on the part of his cast."—*The Spectator,* May 13, 1938

"It is not hard to understand why Litvak's ability was spotted in this feature because the story construction, peculiar twists and original directional touches are much in evidence."—*Variety,* October 26, 1938

ADDITIONAL REVIEWS AND ARTICLES:

Pour Vous November 8, 1934; *Cinémonde* December 20, 1934; *La Cinématographie française* October 26, 1935; *Cinémonde* October 31, 1935; *Monthly Film Bulletin* May 1938; *Kinematograph Weekly* May 5, 1938; *World Film of News* July 1938; *New York World-Telegram* October 17, 1938; *New York Journal-American,* October 18, 1938; *New York Sun* October 18, 1938; *Brooklyn Daily Eagle* October 18, 1938; *The Daily Worker* October 19, 1938; *Télérama* August 17, 1983; *Ciné-Revue* August 18, 1983; *Télérama* May 7, 1994

NOTES: *L'Équipage* was shot at an airfield in Mourmelon-le-Petit and at Pathé Studios in Joinville, outside Paris. The novel upon which it was based was filmed as a silent in France in 1928 by Maurice Tourneur and released in the U.S. as *The Crew* in 1929.

Mayerling

Nero Films; B&W; 96 minutes; Released in Paris on September 13, 1936

CREDITS: *Producer*: Seymour Nebenzal; *Director*: Anatole Litvak; *Screenplay*: Marcel Achard, Joseph Kessel, Irma von Cube; *Based on the novel* La Fin d'une Idylle *by* Claude

Anet; *Dialogue*: Joseph Kessel; *Photography:* Armand Thirard, Jean Isnard; *Editor*: Henri Rust; *Music*: Arthur Honegger, Hans May; *Music Conductor*: Maurice Jaubert; *Costumes*: Georges Annenkov; *Production Designer*: Serge Piménoff; *Art Directors*: Andrej Andrejew, Robert Hubert; *Assistant Director*: René Montis; *Sound*: William Robert Sivel, *Production Managers*: Ralph Baum, Wilhem Löwenberg, Grégoire Metchikian

CAST: Danielle Darrieux (Marie Vetsera), Charles Boyer (Archduke Rudolph), Gabrielle Dorziat (Empress Elizabeth), Jean Debucourt (Debucourt Count Taafe), Jean Dax (Emperor Franz-Joseph), Marthe Régnier (Baronesse Vetsera), Suzy Prim (Countesse Marie Larisch), Yolande Laffon (Stéphanie), Gina Manès (Marinka), Jean-Louis Barrault, Gilbert Gil (Students), Raymond Aimos, André Siméon (Policemen), Nine Assia (Marie's Cousin), Junie Astor (la demi-mondaine), René Bergeron (Szeps), Jacques Berlioz (Helper in the camp), Henri Bosc (Schomberg), Jeanne Brindeau, Valentine Camax, Marguerite de Morlaye (Ladies-in-Waiting), Jean Davy (Count Hoyos), Lucette Desmoulins, Christiane Ribes (Girls), André Dubosc (Loschek), André Fouché (Georges Vetsera), Nane Germon (Anna Vetsera), Vladimir Sokoloff (chief of police), Odette Talazac (The Nanny), Henri Vilbert (Bystander), Fernand Ledoux (Philippe de Cobourg), Marian Michaud, Léon Arvel, Alla Donell, Henri Fabert, Philippe Hersent, Bernard Lancret, André Lannes, Louis Scott

PLOT: Vienna, 1888. The Archduke Rudolph, disgusted with the conservative policies of his father the aged Emperor Franz Joseph, has joined the party of young liberals. His best friend Maurice Szeps, the editor of a radical newspaper, has just been arrested. The news is brought to Rudolph by his enemy Count Taafe, who spies upon him incessantly. Rudolph demands an audience with his father, hoping to intercede for his friend. That afternoon he goes for a walk in the Prater where he meets a lonely girl who is embarrassed by the importunate stranger. The prince comes to her rescue. After they spend some time together, the girl returns to her mother and sister. That night Rudolph attends a gala performance at the Opera accompanied by his wife, the Archduchess Stephanie. In the loge opposite he sees the young girl. He learns that she is Marie Vetsera, who is making her first appearance in society. Marie recognizes His Royal Highness as the mysterious stranger of the Prater. Rudolph's aunt, the Countess Larish, arranges a meeting for the two. Rudolph is so charmed by the sincerity of Marie that for the first time he falls deeply in love. Taafe and his spies inform the emperor of the clandestine meetings and an anonymous note is sent to Marie's mother telling her daughter's secret. Marie refuses to divulge the name of the man she loves; she is sent away from Vienna for six weeks. Rudolph, in desperation, sinks back into his old life of debauchery. When Marie returns she is confronted by a changed Rudolph; her gentle pity subdues him. Rudolph realizes that his sole salvation lies in Marie. He writes to the Pope and asks him to grant a divorce from the archduchess. When the emperor hears from the Pope his son's wish, he threatens to send Marie Vetsera to a convent from which there is no return, if the prince fails to renounce her. Rudolph begs for twenty-four hours alone with her before acceding to his father's wishes. The two lovers flee to Mayerling, the prince's hunting lodge. For one grand and glorious day the lovers enjoy their final tryst. As night falls they make a death pact. At dawn a pistol shot is heard by Rudolph's faithful valet Loschek, followed a few minutes later by a second one. Then all is silence.

REVIEWS:

"*Mayerling* is as good a picture as Hollywood could produce, plus some local touches that are inaccessible to Hollywood."—*Variety*, February 19, 1936

"It is not in any matter of revelation, novelty, or shock that the film is superior. Its distinction lies in its charm."—*The New Yorker*, September 18, 1937

"[The film] is a poem to the proposition that the world's well lost for love.... *Mayerling* is a restrained, delicate and sensitive picture. The screen has never shown a more beautiful or sadder love story."—*New York Post*, September 14, 1937

REVIEWS FOR ANATOLE LITVAK:
"Particularly laudable, considering the lack of so-called action, is the fine direction which does not allow the simple story to lag."—*Hollywood Reporter*, March 4, 1936

"Technically, the direction is sometimes mannered, particularly in its use of the superimposition and the long (and not very significant) dissolve...."—*Monthly Film Bulletin*, November 30, 1936

"Here, through Anatol Litvak's superb assembling of scenes and through the matchless performances ... we are carried breathlessly along emotional millrace.... There is no resisting the fire that players, writer and director have struck from the screen."—*New York Times*, September 14, 1937

ADDITIONAL REVIEWS AND ARTICLES:
Cinémonde October 3, 1935; *Cinémonde* December 19, 1935; *Pour Vous* February 6, 1936; *Cinémonde* February 6, 1936; *La Cinématographie française* February 8, 1936; *Pour Vous* February 13, 1936; *Pour Vous* February 27, 1936; *Cinémonde* February 27, 1936; *Cinémonde* April 2, 1936; *La Gazzetta di Venezia* August 12, 1936; *Kinematograph Weekly* October 22, 1936; *Film Weekly* November 28, 1936; *Sight and Sound* December 1936; *Film Art* Spring 1937; *Daily News* September 13, 1937; *Stage* September 14, 1937; *New York Post* September 14, 1937; *New York Telegram* September 14, 1937; *The New Republic* September 15, 1937; *Daily Mirror* September 15, 1937; *Literary Digest* September 18, 1937; *New York Sun* September 19, 1937; *New York Sun* September 19, 1937; *Time Magazine* September 20, 1937; *Nation* September 25, 1937; *New York Times* September 26, 1937; *Stage* November 15, 1937; *New Yorker* December 18, 1937; *New York Times* December 31, 1937; *New York Times* January 9, 1938; *The Times* January 11, 1938; *NY World-Telegram* August 5, 1938; *Télérama* April 3, 1985; *New York Times* June 21, 1987; *Video Review* September 1987

AWARDS AND HONORS:
Venice Film Festival Nomination as Best Director for the Mussolini Cup Italy 1936; National Board of Review, Top Foreign Film, USA 1937; New York Film Critics Circle Awards, Best Foreign Language Film, USA 1937

NOTES: In pre-production the original title was *Meyerling*. This moving story was already filmed in Russia in 1915, in Germany as *Tragödie im House Habsburg* in 1924, and as *Das Schicksal derer von Habsburg* aka *Die Vetsera* in 1928. In 1957 Litvak directed a new version of *Mayerling*, as an episode of the NBC-TV series *Producer's Showcase* starring Mel Ferrer and Audrey Hepburn.

The Woman I Love

(Released in the U.K. as *The Woman Between*)

RKO Radio Pictures; B&W; 85 minutes; Released in New York City on April 15, 1937

CREDITS: *Producers*: Albert Lewis, Samuel J. Briskin; *Director*: Anatole Litvak; *Screenplay*: Ethel Borden; *Based on the Novel* L'Équipage *by* Joseph Kessel; *Contributing Writers*:

Frank Wead, Sascha Laurence; *Photography:* Charles Rosher; *Art Directors:* Van Nest Polglase, Perry Ferguson; *Editor:* Henri Rust; *Set Decorator:* Darrell Silvera; *Costumes:* Walter Plunkett; *Music Director:* Roy Webb; *Musical Score:* Arthur Honegger, Maurice Thiriet; *Recording:* John E. Tribby; *Special Effects* Vernon L. Walker, Russell A. Cully; *Stunts*: Paul Mantz

CAST: Paul Muni (Lieutenant Claude Maury), Miriam Hopkins (Denise LaValle/Hélène Maury), Louis Hayward (Lieutenant Jean Herbillion), Colin Clive (Capt. Thelis), Minor Watson (Deschamps), Elisabeth Risdon (Mother Herbillion), Paul Guilfoyle (Berthier), Wally Albright (Georges Herbillion), Mady Christians (Florence), Alec Craig (Doctor), Owen Davis, Jr. (Mezziers), Sterling Holloway (Duprez), Vince Barnett (Mathieu), Adrian Morris (Lieutenant Marbot), Donald Barry (Michel), Joe Twerp (Narbonne), William Stelling (Pianist), Richard Lane (Florence's Boyfriend), Richard Tucker (General), Doodles Weaver ("Chopin" Pianist), Dudley Clements, William Corson, Alan Curtis, Otto Hoffman, Maxine Jennings, Leonid Kinskey, Art Lewis, Mary Maclaren, Roland Varno

PLOT: In October 1917, Lieutenant Jean Herbillion meets Denise LaValle at an operetta in Paris and, taken with her beauty, insists that they dine together at a cafe. Although he spends only a short time with Denise, Jean, who is about to leave for the French front, falls in love with her and vows to write to her. Shortly after arriving in Jonchery, where he is to serve with the prestigious "Escadrille" flying unit, Jean meets Lt. Claude Maury, a pilot. Because two of his "observers" died while flying missions with him, Maury has been labeled a jinx by his superstitious fellows and is ostracized by the unit. Jean befriends Maury and, after encouraging him to continue his flying career, listens with respect as he describes his love for his wife Hélène. Capt. Thelis orders his men to choose a new flying partner with whom they can form equipage. Jean gladly teams with Maury and, inspired by their equipage (they "feel alike and think alike"), the two men down many German crafts, including a zeppelin. Six months later, Jean heads for Paris on leave, having promised Maury that he would deliver a letter to Hélène in person. As soon as Jean arrives in Paris, he meets Denise who, while happy to be reunited with him, acts nervous and evasive. When Jean delivers Maury's letter, he discovers that Hélène and Denise are the same person. In spite of her declaration of love, he is stricken with guilt and anger. Heartbroken, Jean returns to the front but is unable to tell Maury the truth about Denise. Weeks later, Denise, anxious for news about Jean, visits his mother and learns that he has been shipped to Château Neuf in Champagne. There Jean, who has been drinking heavily, snubs Maury and spends his free time with Florence, a local cafe owner. When Denise shows up in Champagne on the eve of the Château-Thierry battle, Jean tries to avoid her, but she eventually finds him in a church. Again Denise tries to convince Jean of the purity of her love, and again Jean rejects her. Maury, who is acting as a temporary captain, receives notice that a volunteer is needed to go to Paris as an instructor, Jean approaches him and Capt. Thelis about the assignment. Before signing his transfer, Jean has a change of heart and, on the advice of a knowing Thelis, decides to stay for the fateful battle. Just before their flight, Maury, who has deduced that Jean found out about the Paris assignment from his wife, accuses his partner of romantic betrayal, a charge Jean denies. Although wounded during the heated battle, Jean and Maury rely on their equipage to defeat the enemy. On their way back to the base, Jean pulls a photograph of Denise from his flight jacket and, while dying, tears it in two. Maury later finds the ripped photograph on the airplane floor but, while being nursed back to health by Denise in Paris, feigns ignorance of her illicit love and remembers his friend with only respect and love.

REVIEWS:

"Not that the picture is offensively bad. It is merely without distinction, and thus becomes a disappointment and boring."—*New York Post,* April 16, 1937

"All the clichés of the screen march in an orderly and somber fashion through *The Woman I Love....*"—*Daily News,* April 16, 1937

"*The Woman I Love,* in spite of its excellent acting and some honest writing, is an astonishingly insignificant entertainment."—*New York World-Telegram,* April 16, 1937

REVIEWS FOR ANATOLE LITVAK:

"The direction of the picture by Anatole Litvak is brilliant indeed."—*Hollywood Reporter,* April 14, 1937

"It was directed by Anatole Litvak, which should have recommended it, but it does not...."—*New York Times,* April 16, 1937

"Anatole Litvak ... has a nice touch and a sense of pace."—*Variety,* April 21, 1937

"The director has a number of individual tricks—long dissolves, swift camera-movements linking two shots of the same characters at different moments, and so forth—which are sometimes effective, sometimes no more than mannerisms."—*Monthly Film Bulletin,* May 31,1937

ADDITIONAL REVIEWS AND ARTICLES:

Hollywood Reporter December 12, 1936; *Hollywood Reporter* December 14, 1936; *Hollywood Reporter* December 16, 1936; *Hollywood Reporter* December 21, 1936; *Hollywood Reporter* December 28, 1936; *Hollywood Reporter* January 18, 1937; *Hollywood Reporter* January 22, 1937; *Hollywood Reporter* February 5, 1937; *Hollywood Reporter* February 22, 1937; *Washington Post* March 21, 1937; *Hollywood Now* April 1937; *Motion Picture Daily* April 14, 1937; *Film Daily* April 16, 1937; *New York Journal-American,* April 16, 1937; *New York Herald Tribune* April 16, 1937; *The New York Sun* April 16, 1937; *Motion Picture Herald* April 24, 1937; *Harrison's Reports* April 24, 1937; *Time Magazine* April 26, 1937; *The Times* May 1, 1937; *Kinematograph Weekly* May 6, 1937; *Canadian Magazine* June 1937; *Film Weekly* June 26, 1937; *Picturegoer* September 18, 1937; *Hollywood Reporter* February 9, 1939

NOTES: For this American version of *L'Équipage,* Litvak convinced RKO to hire his French editor Henri Rust. He also used Arthur Honegger's original musical score.

Tovarich

Warner Brothers; An Anatole Litvak Production; B&W; 94 minutes; Released in New York City on December 25, 1937

CREDITS: *Producer-Director:* Anatole Litvak; *Executive Producer:* Hal B. Wallis; *Associate Producer:* Robert Lord; *Assistant Director:* Chuck Hansen; *Screenplay:* Casey Robinson; *Based on the Play by* Jacques Deval, *adapted into English by* Robert E. Sherwood; *Dialogue Director:* Rowland Leigh; *Photography:* Charles Lang; *Art Director:* Anton Grot; *Editor:* Henri Rust; *Costumes:* Travis Banton, Orry-Kelly; *Music Director:* Leo F. Forbstein; *Music:* Max Steiner; *Sound:* Dolph Thomas; *Technical Advisor:* Bernard Deroux; *Unit Manager:* Robert Fellows; *Special Effects:* Byron Haskin

CAST: Claudette Colbert (Tatiana the Grand Duchess Petrovna aka Tina Dubrovsky), Charles Boyer (Mikail Prince Ouratieff aka Michael Dubrovsky), Basil Rathbone

(Gorotchenko), Anita Louise (Helene Dupont), Melville Cooper (Charles Dupont), Isabel Jeans (Fernande Dupont), Morris Carnovsky (Chauffourier-Dubieff), Victor Kilian (Gendarme), Maurice Murphy (Georges Dupont), Gregory Gaye (Count Frederik Brekenski), Montagu Love (M. Courtois), Renie Riano (Mme. Courtois), Fritz Feld (Martelleau), Heather Thatcher (Lady Kartegann), May Boley (Louise), Doris Lloyd (Mme. Chauffourier-Dubieff), Curt Bois (Alfonse), Ferdinand Munier (Mr. Van Hemert), Grace Hayle (Mrs. Van Hemert), Cliff Soubier (Grocer), Christian Rub (Trombone Player), Tommy Bupp, Delmar Watson, Jerry Tucker (Urchins), Torben Meyer (Servant), Alphonse Martell (Hairdresser), Leo White (Assistant hairdresser)

PLOT: Two Russian exiles, the Grand Duchess Tatiana Petrovna and Mikail, Prince Ouratieff, settle in Paris, bringing with them forty million francs smuggled out of Russia. They intend to use the money to finance the counter-revolution. Both the French government and the Soviets are eager to gain access to the money, but Mikail refuses to spend it, even though he and Tatiana are living in poverty. Finally, having spent their last cent, they decide to find work as servants, since as Russian nobility, their job was to wait on the Czar and his wife. Using the names Michel and Tina Dubrovsky, they obtain jobs in the household of banker Charles Dupont. When they arrive, the household is in total chaos, but Mikail and Tatiana totally charm the family, teach them Russian folk songs, and put things in order. On the night of a big dinner party in honor of Soviet commissar Gorotchenko, their noble background is revealed. After dinner, Gorotchenko visits Tatiana and Mikail in the kitchen. He confesses that although he had tortured them in Russia, he was so impressed by Tatiana that he allowed them to escape. Now, he begs Mikail to sign the czar's money over to the Soviets, so that Soviet oil fields will not have to be leased to foreigners. Surprisingly, Tatiana agrees, convincing Mikail that, at least this way, the money will benefit the Russian people and the country that they love.

REVIEWS:
"It is neither high comedy nor the low, but something in a pleasant middle ground...."—*The New York Times,* December 31, 1937

"Tender, gay, smart and sentimental, it is a graceful vehicle for Claudette Colbert and Charles Boyer...."—*Daily Mirror,* December 31, 1937

"The best way to describe the screen version of *Tovarich* ... is to say simply that it is every bit as delightful and entertaining as it was on the stage."—*The Telegraph,* December 31, 1937

REVIEWS FOR ANATOLE LITVAK:
"Anatole Litvak's direction keeps the comedy on a high plane of polished nonchalance and effervescent spirits in a way to delight picture audiences...."—*Hollywood Reporter,* December 1, 1937

"Litvak seems imbued with the idea that he had to make *Tovarich* look like a big picture whereas the story of the royal refugee couple ... is a yarn of charming and finely shaded characterizations."—*Variety,* December 8, 1937

"Anatole Litvak ... displays great versatility in the deftness and lightness of his handlings of the comedy lines and situations in his direction of *Tovarich*."—*Daily News,* December 26, 1937

"While Mr. Litvak has scarcely succeeded in giving *Tovarich* film contour, he has staged the offering handsomely and tastefully."—*New York Herald Tribune,* December 30, 1937

ADDITIONAL REVIEWS AND ARTICLES:
Literary Digest October 31, 1936; *Newsweek* October 24, 1936; *The New Republic* November 4, 1936; *Stage* November 1936; *Theatre Arts* December 1936; *New York World-Telegram* April 27, 1937; *Hollywood Reporter* July 1, 1937; *Hollywood Reporter* July 3, 1937; *The New York Times* July 25, 1937; *Hollywood Reporter* August 9, 1937; *Hollywood Reporter* September 15, 1937; *Stage* October 1937; *Motion Picture Herald* October 16, 1937; *The Cinema* October 20, 1937; *Daily Variety* December 1, 1937; *Motion Picture Daily* December 2, 1937; *Motion Picture Herald* December 4, 1937; *Film Daily* December 4, 1937; *The New York Times* December 5, 1937; *Commonweal* December 17, 1937; *Newsweek* December 20, 1937; *Life* December 20, 1937; *New York Post* December 31, 1937; *Brooklyn Daily Eagle* December 31, 1937; *Photoplay* January 1938; *Harrison's Report*s January 1, 1938; *Time* January 3, 1938; *Pour Vous* January 12, 1938; *Cinémonde* January 13, 1938; *Scholastic* January 22, 1938; *London Times* January 24, 1938; *Pour Vous* January 26, 1938; *Monthly Film Bulletin* January 31, 1938; *Canadian Magazine* February 1938

NOTES: The picture's pre-release title was *Tonight's Our Night*. The story was previously filmed in France in 1935 by director Jacques Deval, author of the original play. That cast included Irene de Zlahy as the Grand Duchess Tatiana and Andre Lefaur as Prince Mikail.

The Amazing Dr. Clitterhouse

Warner Brothers; An Anatole Litvak Production; B&W; 87 minutes; Released in New York City on July 30, 1938

CREDITS: *Director*: Anatole Litvak; *Producer*: Gilbert Miller; *Executive Producer*: Jack L. Warner, Hal. B Wallis; *Associate Producer:* Robert Lord; *Screenplay*: John Wexley, John Huston. *Based on the play by* Barré Lyndon; *Dialogue Director*: Jo Graham; *Photography:* Tony Gaudio; *Art Director*: Carl Jules Weyl; *Editor*: Warren Low; *Wardrobe:* Milo Anderson; *Music Director:* Leo F. Forbstein; *Orchestra:* George Parrish; *Sound*: C. A. Riggs; *Technical Advisor:* Dr. Leo Schulman; *Assistant Director:* Jack Sullivan

CAST: Edward G. Robinson (Dr. Clitterhouse), Claire Trevor (Jo Keller), Humphrey Bogart ("Rocks" Valentine), Allen Jenkins (Okay), Donald Crisp (Inspector Lane), Gale Page (Nurse Randolph), Henry O'Neill (Judge), John Litel (Prosecuting Attorney), Thurston Hall (Grant), Maxie Rosenbloom (Butch), Bert Hanlon (Pat), Curt Bois (Rabbit), Ward Bond (Tug), Vladimir Sokoloff (Popus), Billy Wayne (Candy), Robert Homans (Lt. Johnson), Irving Bacon (Foreman of Jury), Georgia Caine (Mrs. Updyke), Romaine Callender (Butler), Mary Field (Maid), William Worthington, Ed Mortimer, Larry Steers (Guests), William Haade (Watchman), Thomas Jackson (Connors), Edward Gargan (Sergeant), Ray Dawe, Bob Reeves, Ky Robinson (Policemen), Winifred Harris (Mrs. Ganswoort), Eric Stanley (Dr. Ames), Loia Cheaney (Nurse Donor), Wade Boteler (Capt. MacLevy), Mike Lally, Frank Anthony (Gamblers), Libby Taylor (Mrs. Jefferson), Joyce Williams (Patricia), Edgar Dearing (Patrolman), John Harron (Operator), Hal K. Dawson (Pedestrian), Sidney Bracy (Chemist), Earl Dwire (Surgeon), Monte Vandergrift, Jack Mower (Detectives), Frank Reicher (Professor Ludwig), Vera Lewis (Juror), Bruce Mitchell (Bailiff), Hal Craig

PLOT: Dr. Clitterhouse, a highly respected surgeon, is intensely interested in the mental and physical reactions of criminals at the moment when they engage in their illegal activities. Deciding that the best way to settle the question is to use himself for his own experiments, he embarks upon a career of crime. Keeping a record of his reactions, Dr. Clitterhouse pulls four robberies. His nurse discovers a pile of jewelry in his bag and he admits that they are stolen, explaining he is doing it as a means of furthering his scientific research into crime. Her loyalty to him keeps her mouth closed. Through his police connections, Dr. Clitterhouse learns the names of the best "fences" and invades the strongholds of the principal one, Jo Keller, who leads a gang of jewel robbers. He meets "Rocks" Valentine; Butch (Jo's bodyguard), Okay and other gang members and assumes command. Under Clitterhouse's direction they carry out numerous raids. He scrupulously divides the profits of the crimes and keeps in touch with his nurse, who has announced to his patients that he is in Europe. His research virtually completed, he plans one last robbery. But "Rocks," who is jealous of Clitterhouse, sees a chance to regain control of the gang and pushes the doctor into a vault and slams the door. Butch, who has been assigned by Joe to keep an eye on Clitterhouse, rushes back to the vault and succeeds in releasing the prisoner. Clitterhouse then bids goodbye to Jo since his research is completed. Meanwhile, "Rocks" has learned the doctor's true identity and visits his home to do a spot of blackmail. Cornered, Clitterhouse poisons "Rocks"' drink. That leads to the unmasking of the doctor's double life and he is placed on trial. Clitterhouse is advised to plead insanity. The foreman of the jury asks him if he thinks he was insane when he committed the crime. When Clitterhouse honestly says he was not, the jury promptly acquits him on the grounds of insanity, not because of his criminal actions, but because when he is put on the witness stand he undermines his own defense.

REVIEWS:

"The picture retains the jocular, impudent tone of the Barré Lyndon play...."—*New York Times*, July 21, 1938

"Brilliantly amusing version of the famous stage play.... Clever direction makes it an unusual and outstanding film."—*Monthly Film Bulletin*, September 30, 1938

"Here is an unusual and excellently acted crime story.... There are certain additions to the play, but on the whole it has been translated very literally into its medium."—*Picturegoer*, January 14, 1939

REVIEWS FOR ANATOLE LITVAK:

"Anatole Litvak's direction opens at a nice clip and holds a steady pace, with suspense well developed and light comedy relief adequately spotted."—*Variety*, June 22, 1938

"In *The Amazing Dr. Clitterhouse* the play was the thing. It made the picture and overshadowed some rather bad direction in the early sequences on the part of Anatole Litvak, which slowed the start down to a crawl."—*Hollywood Reporter*, June 28, 1938

"[Litvak] has accomplished his task very skillfully, early securing interest and sustaining it at a very high level until the hilarious finale."—*Today's Cinema*, August 27, 1938

"[Litvak] knows little about the mysteries of the mind and cares less, but he does know the abilities of Mr. Edward G. Robinson, and he realizes how suitable for exploiting them are the materials he has to hand."—*The Times*, November 21, 1938

ADDITIONAL REVIEWS AND ARTICLES:

Hollywood Reporter October 24, 1936; *Los Angeles Times* April 6, 1937; *Variety* April 7, 1937; *Los Angeles Examiner* August 20, 1937; *Hollywood Reporter* February 28, 1938; *Hollywood Reporter* April 4, 1938; *Motion Picture Herald* April 9, 1938; *Film Daily* June 21, 1938; *Motion Picture Herald* June 25, 1938; *Motion Picture Daily* June 29, 1938; *Newsweek* July 4, 1938; *Time* July 18, 1938; *New York Herald-Tribune* July 21, 1938; *Har-*

rison's Reports July 16, 1938; *Commonweal* August 5, 1938; *The New Republic* August 10, 1938; *Today's Cinema* August 31, 1938; *Pour Vous* November 9, 1938; *Cinémonde* November 10, 1938; *Film Weekly* November 19, 1938; *Positif* May 1970; *Cinématographe* August 1979; *American Cinemeditor* Summer/Fall 1982; *Favorite Westerns and Serial World* July 1989

NOTES: Ronald Colman was producer Robert Lord's first choice for the role of Clitterhouse. *The Amazing Dr. Clitterhouse* was adapted for radio by CBS's *Gulf Screen Guild Theatre* on November 2, 1941, featuring Robinson and Bogart, and by NBC's *Lady Esther's Screen Guild Theatre* on June 5, 1944, featuring Robinson and Lloyd Nolan.

The Sisters

Warner Brothers; An Anatole Litvak Production; B&W; 99 minutes; Released in New York City on October 14, 1938

CREDITS: *Executive Producers*: Jack L. Warner, Hal B. Wallis; *Associate Producer*: David Lewis; *Director:* Anatole Litvak; *Dialogue Director*: Irving Rapper; *Assistant Director*: Jack Sullivan; *Screenplay:* Milton Krims, Julius J. Epstein. *Based on the novel by* Myron Brinig; *Photography*: Tony Gaudio; *Art Director*: Carl Jules Weyl; *Editor*: Warren Low; *Gowns:* Orry-Kelly; *Music Director*: Leo F. Forbstein; *Music:* Max Steiner; *Sound:* C. A. Riggs; *Makeup*: William Phillips; *Hairdresser*: Margaret Donovan; *Grip*: Glen Harris; *Props*: Pat Patterson; *Still Photography*: Bert Six

CAST: Errol Flynn (Frank Medlin), Bette Davis (Louise Elliott), Anita Louise (Helen Elliott), Ian Hunter (William Benson), Donald Crisp (Tim Hazelton), Beulah Bondi (Rose Elliott), Jane Bryan (Grace Elliott), Alan Hale (Sam Johnson), Dick Foran (Tom Knivel), Henry Travers (Ned Elliott), Patric Knowles (Norman French), Lee Patrick (Flora Gibbon), Laura Hope Crews (Flora's Mother), Janet Shaw (Stella Johnson), Harry Davenport (Doc Moore), Ruth Garland (Laura Bennett), John Warburton (Anthony Bittick), Paul Harvey (Caleb Ammon), Mayo Methot (Blonde), Irving Bacon (Robert Forbes), Arthur Hoyt (Tom Selig), Stanley Fields (Ship Captain), Larry Williams (Young Man), Dudley Dickerson (Porter), Eddie Brian (Newsboy), Jessie Perry (Maid), Mildred Gover, Loia Cheaney (Maids), Lee Phelps, Granville Bates (Announcers), Bob Perry (Referee), Ed Stanley (Doctor), Robert Homans (Editor), Stuart Holmes, Glen Cavender (Bartenders), Russell Simpson, Elliott Sullivan, Frank Otto (Sailors), John Kelly (Drunken Sailor), Monte Vandergrift (Policeman), Jack Mower (Ship's Officer), Frank Puglia (Wireless Operator), Rosella Towne, Susan Hayward, Paulette Evans, Frances Morris (Telephone Operators), Edgar Edwards (Soldier), Jan Holm (Secretary), Charles Sullivan (Pug), Frank Meredith (Conductor), Joseph Crehan (Man Announcing Election Results), Vera Lewis, Lottie Williams, John Harron, Bessie Wade, Lew Harvey, Harry Semels, Jang Lim, Peggy Moran, Richard Bond, Mira McKinney, Georgie Cooper

PLOT: In the small town of Silver Bow live Louise, Helen and Grace, the daughters of Ned and Rose Elliott. For Louise (attractive, intelligent) and Helen (frivolous), the town of Silver Bow seems somehow never big enough. To Silver Bow comes a handsome "hail-fellow-well-met" journalist from San Francisco, Frank Medlin. Meeting Louise at the Eleventh Night Ball, he sweeps her off her feet and within a week they are married and on their way to San Francisco. The lighthearted Helen, looking more toward material happiness, marries Sam Johnson, a millionaire widower, who takes her off to New York and a life of ease. Grace, like her mother a stolid, home-loving person, marries Tom

Knivel, son of the town banker and Louise's rejected suitor. Both sisters seem happy in their different lives. But for Louise alone, desperately in love with Frank, married life has gone awry. Discouraged because he cannot give his loving wife a better home and because his book, inspired by Louise, has not come up to the expectations of his good friend Tom Hazelton, Frank deteriorates as a man and takes to drink. Frank leaves Louise and signs on as seaman on a Singapore-bound boat. The next day, at sea, he learns of the great San Francisco earthquake. But it is too late to return to Louise, and he continues on to Singapore. After the earthquake, Louise finally finds refuge in the home of a friend, where she is found by the store owner for whom Louise has been working, William Benson. He sends her back to Silver Bow for a time. Frank returns, upbraiding himself as a "tramp" but at the same time determined to see his wife whom he loves. Tim accompanies him to Silver Bow. It is again the night of the Presidential Ball, where Frank first saw Louise, and the three sisters are once more attending the dance together, Frank looks down from the balcony and sees the three beautiful sisters, the again happy, mother and father, and William Benson, looking like a man waiting for an answer. Tim brings Louise up to the balcony and seats her so that she cannot see Frank. She tells Tim that she still loves Frank, and that if he came back, she'd go to him, work and starve for him, but she feels that alone he might find what he was looking for. Frank suddenly steps out from where he is concealed. Bedlam breaks loose in the hall as election results are announced, but Frank and Louise are happy in each other's arms, because they've found each other again. Louise's two sisters, looking on, are happy too, at their sister's rediscovered joy.

REVIEWS:

"This film has the sweep of a virtual cavalcade of early 20th Century American history. Just how much this superbly made production does will depend largely on the campaign given it by individual exhibitors."—*Variety,* October 5, 1938

"*The Sisters* is still a credit to the Brothers having a fine cast and a not-too implausible story, and particularly lovely performance by Bette Davis...."—*New York Times,* October 15, 1938

"[The] history of an era still within memory, yet curiously closed and sealed, is reflected in Warner Bros.'s *The Sisters....* Bette Davis acts with such extraordinary grace, sensitivity and distinction that hers is already being acclaimed the movie performance of the year."—*Life,* October 31, 1938

REVIEWS FOR ANATOLE LITVAK:

"Anatole Litvak really comes into his own as a director, here. It is amazing the constancy of the pace he maintains. He too gets full value for value received, and the flow of the story in his capable hands is without a false move. He has gotten performances from every last member of the cast and what performances,"—*Hollywood Reporter,* October 4, 1938

"Anatole Litvak directed *The Sisters* and extracts very high realism at times for his characters."—*Los Angeles Times,* October 14, 1938

"The direction necessarily suffers from the limitations of the script."—*Monthly Film Bulletin,* January 31, 1939

ADDITIONAL REVIEWS AND ARTICLES:

Film Daily June 6, 1938; *Motion Picture Herald* July 2, 1938; *Hollywood Reporter* August 6, 1938; *Motion Picture Daily* October 4, 1938; *Motion Picture Herald* October 8, 1938; *Film Daily* October 10, 1938; *Harrison's Reports* October 15, 1938; *Sunday Mirror Magazine* October 16, 1938; *Time Magazine* October 17, 1938; *Commonweal* October

21, 1938; *Kinematograph Weekly* February 9, 1939; *Pour Vous* April 5, 1939; *Cinémonde* April 5, 1939; *Catholic Film News* June 1939; *The Spectator* June 28, 1939; *Today's Cinema* August 24, 1943; *Kinematograph Weekly* August 26, 1943

NOTES: In *The Sisters*, Susan Hayward's second film, she has an uncredited bit as a telephone operator. Humphrey Bogart's third wife Mayo Methot makes an appearance as a blonde at the boxing match. Dialogue coach Irving Rapper went on to direct Bette Davis in two very successful films, *Now, Voyager* (1942) and *The Corn Is Green* (1945).

Confessions of a Nazi Spy

Warner Brothers; B&W; 104 minutes; Premiered in Beverly Hills on April 27, 1939

CREDITS: *Executive Producers*: Jack L. Warner, Hal B. Wallis; *Associate Producer* Robert Lord; *Director*: Anatole Litvak; *Second Unit Director*: Claude E. Archer; *Dialogue Director*: Ted Thomas; *Assistant Director*: Chuck Hansen; *Screenplay*: Milton Krims, John Wexley; *Based on the articles by* Leon G. Turrou *as told to* David G. Wittels *in* The New York Post (December 5, 1938–January 4, 1939); *Photography*: Sol Polito, Ernest Hall; *Camera Assistant*: John Polito, Frank Evans; *Gaffer*: Frank Flanagan; *Art Director*: Carl Jules Weyl; *Editor*: Owen Marks; *Gowns*: Milo Anderson; *Wardrobe*: Dick Moder, Cora Lobb; *Music Director*: Leo F. Forbstein; *Sound*: Robert B. Lee; *Hairdresser*: Ruby Felker; *Makeup*: Joe Stinton, Bob Cowan; *Technical Advisor*: Leon G. Turrou; *Unit Manager*: Louis Baum; *Grip*: Harold Noyes; *Props*: M. Goldman; *Assistant Props*: H. Goldman; *Best Boy*: Bill Conger; *Still Photographer*: Mack Elliott; *Publicity*: Frank Heacock

CAST: Edward G. Robinson (Edward J. Renard), Francis Lederer (Kurt Schneider), George Sanders (Franz Schlager), Paul Lukas (Dr. Karl F. Kassell), Henry O'Neill (Attorney Kellogg), Dorothy Tree (Hilda Keinhauer), Lya Lys (Erika Wolf), Grace Stafford (Mrs. Schneider), James Stephenson (British military intelligence agent), Celia Sibelius (Mrs. Liza Kassell), Joe Sawyer (Werner Renz), Sig Rumann (Dr. Julius Gustav Krogman), Lionel Royce (Hintze), Henry Victor (Wildebrandt), Hans von Twardowsky (Max Helldorf), John Voigt (Johann Westphal), Frederick Vogeding (Capt. Richter), Willy Kaufman (Greutzwald), Robert O. Davis (Capt. Straubel), William Vaughn (Capt. von Eichen), George Rosener (Klauber), Frederick Burton (U.S. District Court Judge), Eily Malyon (Mrs. Mary MacLaughlin), Bodil Rosing (Boat Passenger), John Deering (Narrator), Fred Tozere (Phillips), Frank Mayo (Staunton), Lucien Prival (Kranz), Martin Kosleck (Goebbels), Ward Bond (American Legionnaire), Alec Craig (Postman), Jack Mower (McDonald), Jean Brooks (Kassell's Nurse), Robert Emmett Keane (Harrison), Charles Sherlock (Young), Edward Keane, William Gould, John Hamilton (F.B.I. Men), Selmer Jackson (Customs Official), Emmett Vogan (Hotel Clerk), John Ridgely (Army Hospital Clerk), Egon Brecher (Nazi Agent), Edwin Stanley (U.S. Official), Niccolai Yoshkin (The Man), John Conte (Announcer's Voice), Charles Trowbridge (Major Williams), Tommy Bupp (Shoeshine Boy), Ferdinand Schumann-Heink

PLOT: In a little Scottish village, a reclusive woman begins receiving mail from all points of the world. When a resident philatelist asks if she will give him the foreign stamps for his collection, the woman refuses explosively and slams her door in his face. He reports this strange behavior to Scotland Yard. British Intelligence agents soon discover that she is part of a Nazi spy ring. One of her letters from Kurt Schneider is intercepted, and it mentions a Nazi spy network in America and its plans to kidnap an American Air Corps general. British Intelligence contacts the U.S. government, and FBI man Edward J. Renard enters the investigation. Systematically, Renard pinpoints key spies, concentrating on Schneider, the weak link in the Nazi network. Taken into custody and interrogated by Renard, he admits that he was recruited by the Nazis to obtain secret government information. He explains that he is a reluctant spy, nagged by a wife wanting the "good life," and ridiculed for not being "a big shot." He admits impersonating a medical official and calling hospitals for military personnel figures in order to figure out the strength of garrisons in the New York area. Franz Schlager is the superior who pays him miserably, about $50 per report. Schneider also names Dr. Karl F. Kassell, head of the Nazi Bund, who is recruiting American youth into Hitler Jugend legions and is in league with Schlager. Kassel agrees to inform on the ruthless Schlager, but he is kidnapped by German agents and smuggled out of the country on a German ocean liner where Erika Wolf, posing as a hairdresser, orders him beaten senseless and held prisoner until he can be turned over to the Gestapo. Renard has enough information and rounds up the key Nazis before they can do further harm.

REVIEWS:

"This one is a wartime propaganda picture in flavor and essence. It must stand as a living document of how little words now mean."—*Variety,* May 3, 1939

"An excellent production.... There is realism in the action, as a result of an excellent direction and artistic acting."—*Harrison's Reports,* May 6, 1939

"The film represent[ed] a vital technical contribution to the esthetics of the motion picture: the use of a new method of interweaving documentary and dramatic material."—*Film News,* March 1939

REVIEWS FOR ANATOLE LITVAK:

"Anatole Litvak's direction under the astute supervision of Hal Wallis and Robert Lord is invariably starkly vital."—*Hollywood Reporter,* April 28, 1939

"As melodrama, the film isn't bad at all. Anatole Litvak has paced it well, and the performances ... are thoroughly satisfactory."—*New York Times,* April 29, 1939

"Direction and acting are excellent"—*Monthly Film Bulletin,* June 30, 1939

ADDITIONAL REVIEWS AND ARTICLES:

Hollywood Reporter December 6, 1938; *Hollywood Reporter* December 8, 1938; *Hollywood Reporter* December 30, 1938; *Hollywood Reporter* January 4, 1939; *Hollywood Reporter* January 13, 1939; *Hollywood Reporter* January 17, 1939; *New York Times* January 22, 1939; *New York Times* February 5, 1939; *New York Times* February 19, 1939; *Hollywood Reporter* March 7, 1939; *New York Times* April 2, 1939; *Hollywood Reporter* April 18, 1939; *New York Times* April 23, 1939; *Hollywood Reporter* April 28, 1939; *Motion Picture Daily* April 28, 1939; *Daily Variety* April 28, 1939; *Film Daily* April 28, 1939; *Motion Picture Herald* April 29, 1939; *The Examiner* May 5, 1939; *New York Times* May 7, 1939; *The New Republic* May 10, 1939; *Commonweal* May 19, 1939; *Hollywood Reporter* May 13, 1939; *The Nation* May 20, 1939; *New Theatre* June 1939; *Hollywood Reporter* June 6, 1939; *Los Angeles Examiner* June 6, 1939; *Pour Vous* June 21, 1939; *London Spectator* June 23, 1939; *Film Weekly* June 24, 1939; *Hollywood Reporter* July 1, 1939; *Hollywood Reporter* July 10, 1939; *Pour Vous* July 12, 1939; *Hollywood Reporter* July 14, 1939; *Hollywood Reporter* July 15, 1939; *Cinémonde* July 19, 1939; *Hollywood Reporter* July 20, 1939; *Hollywood Reporter* August 10, 1939; *Hollywood Reporter* August 22, 1939; *Hollywood Reporter* August 30, 1939; *Hollywood Reporter* September 6, 1939; *Pour Vous* September 13, 1939; *Hollywood Reporter* October 5, 1939; *Films* November 1939; *New York Times* December 25, 1939; *New York Times* May 26, 1940; *New York Times* June 2, 1940;

New York Times June 3, 1940; *Hollywood Reporter* June 11, 1940; *New York Times* June 16, 1940; *Hollywood Reporter* July 19, 1940; *New York Times* September 26, 1941; *Cinématographe* May 1983; *Historical Journal of Film Radio and Television* June 1991; *Film Comment* July/August 1991; *Positif* October 1993; *Historical Journal of Film, Radio and Television* September 2009

AWARDS AND HONORS:
National Board of Review, Best Film and Top Ten Films USA 1939

NOTES: The working title of *Confessions of a Nazi Spy* was *Storm Over America*. The FBI character Edward Renard played by Edward G. Robinson is not introduced until midway through the film. The picture was banned in Germany, Italy, Yugoslavia, Holland, Norway, Sweden, Japan and several Latin American countries. It was re-released in 1941 with additional documentary footage.

Castle on the Hudson

(Released in the U.K. as *Years Without Days*)
Warner Brothers; An Anatole Litvak Production; B&W; 77 minutes; Premiered in New York City on February 17, 1940

CREDITS: *Producers*: Jack L. Warner, Anatole Litvak; *Executive Producer*: Hal B. Wallis; *Associate Producer*: Samuel Bischoff; *Director*: Anatole Litvak; *Screenplay:* Seton I. Miller, Brown Holmes, Courtney Terrett; *Based on the Book* Twenty Thousand Years in Sing Sing *by* Lewis E. Lawes; *Assistant Director*: Chuck Hansen; *Photography*: Arthur Edeson; *Art Director*: John Hughes; *Editor*: Thomas Richards; *Gowns*: Howard Shoup; *Music Director*: Leo F. Forbstein; *Music:* Adolph Deutsch; *Orchestral Arrangements*: Ray Heindorf; *Sound:* Robert B. Lee; *Special Effects:* Byron Haskin, Edwin B. DuPar; *Makeup:* Perc Westmore; *Unit Manager*: Al Alleborn

CAST: John Garfield (Tommy Gordon), Ann Sheridan (Kay Manners), Pat O'Brien (Warden Long), Burgess Meredith (Steve Rockford), Henry O'Neill (District Attorney), Jerome Cowan (Ed Crowley), Guinn "Big Boy" Williams (Mike Cagle), John Litel (Chaplin), Margot Stevenson (Ann Rockford), Willard Robertson (Ragan), Edward Pawley (Black Jack), Billy Wayne (Pete), Nedda Harrigan (Mrs. Long), Wade Boteler (Principal Keeper), Barbara Pepper (Goldie), Robert Strange (Joe Morris), Grant Mitchell (Dr. Ames), Robert Homans (Clyde Burton), Joseph Downing, Sol Gorss (Gangster), Charles Sherlock, Mike Lally, Jack Mower, Frank Mayo, Pat O'Malley, Walter Miller, Pat Flaherty, James Richard, Eddy Chandler, Harry Strang, Ed Gargan, James Flavin, Lee Phelps, Cliff Saum, Alan Davis (Guards), Ed Kane (Manager), George Sorel (Waiter), Claude Wisberg (Newsboy), Michael Conroy (Newsboy), Howard Hickman (Judge), Stuart Holmes (Foreman), Ralph Dunn (Court Clerk), Thomas Jackson (First reporter), Emmett Vogan (Second reporter), Howard Mitchell (Officer), Clyde Courtwright (Conductor), John Ridgely, Eddie Acuff, Frank Faylen, Alan Davis (Clerks), Cliff Clark (Sergeant), Dutch Hendrian, Frank Sully, Adrian Morris, Max Marx, Jack Richardson, Charles Sullivan, John Lester Johnson (Prisoners), Ernest Whitman (Alexander "8 Ball" Hamilton, John Kelly (Convict), Ernie Adams (Kelner), Dick Wessel (Trusty), Philip Morris (Joe—Detective), Julie Stevens (Operator), Brenda Fowler (Nurse), Richard Clayton (Elevator Boy), William Telaak, Nat Carr, William Hopper (Reporters), Max Hoffman, Jr. (Warden's Clerk), Robert Stevenson (Sailor), Frank Puglia (Tony), Sugar Willie Keeler (Joe), Loia Cheaney (Lady in Room 611)

PLOT: Tommy Gordon, a cocky and arrogant young racketeer, takes what he wants from the world. His one weakness is Kay, whom he adores. They are dancing one evening in a nightclub when the police apprehend him for his most recent robbery, and despite his "connections" he is sent to Sing Sing Prison. He makes little attempt to adjust himself to his life there, and is constantly in trouble despite the efforts of Warden Long to rehabilitate him. During a prison break led by Steve Rockford, Tommy makes no attempt to escape. This leads the warden to trust him when he begs permission soon after to go and see Kay, who was seriously injured in an accident. He gives the warden his word that he will return, and hurries to her apartment. There he learns that his lawyer Ed Crowley was responsible for the accident. When Crowley turns up at the apartment, Tommy goes for him. They fight, and to save Tommy's life, Kay shoots Crowley, and then persuades Tommy to run away. Tommy is wanted for murder, and although he has a chance to escape, he goes back to prison to save the warden from public humiliation. He is sentenced to the electric chair.

REVIEWS:
"The cast is good—so good that a player like Burgess Meredith appears satisfied with fourth billing—but the plot, the dialogue and the scenery are the same as ever."—*New York Times*, March 4, 1940

"It is a strong prison melodrama, unpleasant in some respects, but gripping for the most part."—*Harrison's Reports*, March 2, 1940

"Although much of the prison scene is familiar the acting is excellent, particularly that of John Garfield, who mingles fierce arrogant willfulness with charm."—*Monthly Film Bulletin*, April 6, 1940

REVIEWS FOR ANATOLE LITVAK:
"Anatole Litvak's direction is smoothly effective and makes the most of the well-constructed script...."—*Hollywood Reporter*, February 22, 1940

"Nothing unusual about Anatole Litvak's direction, except that he keeps the yearn moving at a speedy pace."—*Variety*, February 28, 1940

ADDITIONAL REVIEWS AND ARTICLES:
Hollywood Reporter June 5, 1939; *Hollywood Reporter* June 9, 1939; *Hollywood Reporter* July 10, 1939; *Hollywood Reporter* August 11, 1939; *Motion Picture Herald* October 28, 1939; *Hollywood Reporter* February 22, 1940; *Motion Picture Daily* February 27, 1940; *Motion Picture Herald* March 2, 1940; *Film Daily* March 8, 1940; *Today's Cinema* March 20, 1940; *Kinematograph Weekly* March 21, 1940; *Movie-Radio Guide* April 27, 1940; *Favorite Western and Serial World* n.32, 1989

NOTES: The character's last name, played by Garfield, is spelled Gordan in the headlines in the film, but Gordon in the credits. The working titles for the film were *City of Lost Men* and *Years Without Days*. The latter became the release titled in the United Kingdom). *Castle on the Hudson* was a remake of the 1933 Warner Bros. film *20,000 Years in Sing Sing* starring Spencer Tracy and Bette Davis.

All This, and Heaven Too

Warner Brothers; An Anatole Litvak Production; B&W; 143 minutes; Premiered in Los Angeles on June 13, 1940

CREDITS: *Producer*: Jack Warner; *Executive Producer*: Hal B. Wallis; *Associate Producer*: David Lewis; *Director*: Anatole Litvak; *Dialogue Director*: Irving Rapper; *Assistant*

Director: Sherry Shourds; *Screenplay:* Casey Robinson. *Based on the novel* All This, and Heaven Too *by* Rachel Field; *Photography*: Ernie Haller; *Art Director*: Carl Jules Weyl; *Editor:* Warren Low; *Costumes:* Orry-Kelly; *Music Director*: Leo F. Forbstein; *Music*: Max Steiner; *Orchestral Arrangements*: Hugo Friedhofer; *Sound*: Robert B. Lee; *Special Effects:* Byron Haskin, Rex Wimpy; *Makeup:* Perc Westmore; *Technical Advisor*: Bernard Deroux; *Unit Manager*: Al Alleborn

CAST: Bette Davis (Henriette Deluzy-Desportes), Charles Boyer (Duc de Praslin), Jeffrey Lynn (Henry Martyn Field), Barbara O'Neil (Duchesse Francis de Praslin), Virginia Weidler (Louise), Helen Westley (Madame LeMaire), Walter Hampden (Pasquier), Henry Daniell (Broussais), Harry Davenport (Pierre), George Coulouris (Charpentier), Montagu Love (Marechal Sabastiani), Janet Beecher (Miss Haines), June Lockhart (Isabelle), Ann Todd (Berthe), Richard Nichols (Raynald), Fritz Leiber (Abbe Gallard), Ian Keith (DeLangle), Sibyl Harris (Mlle. Maillard), Edward Fielding (Dr. Louis), Mary Anderson (Rebecca Jay), Ann Gillis (Emily Schuyler), Peggy Stewart (Helen Lexington), Victor Kilian (Gendarme), Mrs. Gardner Crane (Madame Gauthier), Christian Rub (Loti), Frank Reicher (Police Official), Egon Brecher (Doctor), Betty Jean Hainey (Elizabeth Ward), Cora Sue Collins (Louise de Rham), Betty Jane Graham (Clara Parker), Doris Bren (Agnes Brevoort), Marilyn Knowlden (Marianna Van Horn), Ann Howard (Isabelle Loullard), Gloria Fisher (Kate Delancey), Jeanne Wells (Mary Simpson), Susanne Ransom (Dora Vanderbilt), Creighton Hale (Officer), Carmen Bretta (Maxine)

PLOT: The apprehensions of Mlle. Henriette Deluzy-Desportes, newly arrived in New York from Europe to start life anew teaching French at Miss Haines School for Young Ladies in the year 1849, turn to panic as she finds her pupils recognize her as the notorious "Mlle. D," the talk of Europe. She rushes blindly from the classes to the office of Miss Haines, where she finds sympathy she dared not to expect and a friend she had not hoped to see: Henry Field. Field had known Henriette briefly in Europe the year before. Her two friends prevail on her to return to her class. Summoning every ounce of courage, she re-enters the classroom restores order, and starts to tell a true story. It commences with her meeting Field aboard an English Channel steamer bound for France. Upon their arrival, they part, never expecting to meet again. Henriette proceeds to the household of the Duc and Duchesse de Praslin, where she is to have the position of the children's governess. She is interviewed by the Duc and the Duchesse, finally accepted and introduced to the children, Isabelle, Louise, Berthe and Raynald. During the weeks that follow, she gains their love and the respect of the Duc. In so doing, she arouses the jealousy of the neurotic Duchess, who has a spy in every servant, and the Abbe, her confessor. Tenseness grows through the following months, while the Duchesse spreads malicious gossip. The result of this groundless whispering is Henriette's resignation. Weeks of near poverty pass, while Henriette awaits the indispensible letter of reference from the Duchesse. The Duc, hearing of her plight, is determined to force his wife to write the much-needed letter. When the Duchesse is found murdered. Henriette and the Duc are taken into custody. Henriette proves her innocence. The Duc is silent, and before he can be tried, takes poison and dies, telling old Pierre, a trusted servant, of his love for Henriette. As Henriette finishes her story, the children profess their sorrow, and promise never to mention "Mlle. D" again. Field is waiting in the doorway, and as she takes his arm their mutual regard is evident.

REVIEWS:

"[Viewers] will find the film a source of much emotional satisfaction; others ... will certainly protest that it wears out their patience in the telling of a comparatively uncomplicated tale."—*New York Times,* July 5, 1940

"The production is lavish, and the direction and performances are of the highest order."—*Harrison's Reports,* June 22, 1940

"The substance of this film is impersonal. The careful detailing brought to some scenes, however, reminds us that Anatole Litvak once made *Mayerling*."—*L'Écran Français,* November 26, 1946

REVIEWS FOR ANATOLE LITVAK:

"Anatole Litvak's direction is outstanding."—*Variety,* June 12, 1940

"[U]nder the sensitive direction of Anatole Litvak, the production ... is of striking beauty."—*Hollywood Reporter,* June 14, 1940

"I do not know how many of you saw *Mayerling,* one of the outstanding pictures of the past few years, but those of you did will be quite prepared to find that [Litvak] would do justice to Rachel Field's best seller *All This, and Heaven Too.* He certainly has."—*Picturegoer,* January 11, 1941

ADDITIONAL REVIEWS AND ARTICLES:

Hollywood Reporter August 10, 1939; *Hollywood Reporter* January 10, 1940; *Hollywood Reporter* February 7, 1940; *New York Times* March 17, 1940; *New York Times* May 5, 1940; *Film Daily* June 17, 1940; *Life* June 1, 1940; *Motion Picture Daily* June 17, 1940; *Motion Picture Herald* June 22, 1940; *The Hartford Daily Courant* June 19, 1940; *Newsweek* June 24, 1940; *Time* 24 June 1940; *Photoplay* July 1940; *Today's Cinema* November 20, 1940; *Monthly Film Bulletin* January 1941; *Picturegoer* March 15, 1941; *La Revue du Cinéma* March 1983; *Cinema Journal* Winter 2008

AWARDS AND HONORS:

Academy Awards, USA 1941. Nominated: Best Picture, Best Actress in a Supporting Role: Barbara O'Neil, Best Cinematography, Black-and-white: Ernie Haller

NOTES: For the role of Henriette Warner Bros originally wanted Helen Hayes or Miriam Hopkins, while associate producer David Lewis' first choice was Greta Garbo.

City for Conquest

Warner Brothers; An Anatole Litvak Production; B&W; 103 minutes; Released in New York City on September 21, 1940

CREDITS: *Producer-Director*: Anatole Litvak; *Executive Producer*: Hal B. Wallis; *Associate Producer*: William Cagney; *Dialogue Director*: Irving Rapper; *Assistant Directors*: Sherry Shourds, Chuck Hansen; *Screenplay:* John Wexley, Robert Rossen; *Based on the novel by* Aben Kandel; *Photography:* James Wong Howe, Sol Polito; *Art Director:* Robert Haas; *Editor*: William Holmes; *Gowns*: Howard Shoup; *Music*: Max Steiner; *Music Director*: Leo F. Forbstein; *Orchestral Arrangements*: Ray Heindorf, Hugo Friedhofer; *Sound*: E.A. Brown; *Special Effects:* Byron Haskin, Rex Wimpy; *Dance Director:* Robert Vreeland; *Makeup:* Perc Westmore; *Unit Manager*: Frank Mattison

CAST: James Cagney (Danny Kenny), Ann Sheridan (Peggy Nash), Frank Craven ("Old Timer"), Arthur Kennedy (Eddie Kenny), Donald Crisp (Scotty MacPherson), Frank McHugh ("Mutt"), George Tobias ("Pinky"), Elia Kazan ("Googi"), Anthony Quinn (Murray Burns), Jerome Cowan ("Dutch"), Lee Patrick (Gladys), Blanche Yurka (Mrs. Nash), George Lloyd ("Goldie"), Joyce Compton (Lilly), Thurston Hall (Max Leonard), Ben Welden (Cobb), John Arledge (Salesman), Ed Keane (Gaul), Selmer Jackson, Joseph Crehan (Doctors), Murray Alper (Taxi Driver), Ward Bond (First Policeman), Wade Boteler (New York Policeman), James Conaty, Carl M. Leviness, Dale Van Sickel (Championship Fight Spectators), Dudley Dickerson (Doorman), John Dilson (Mr. Cahn—Man Buying Newspaper), James Dime (Gym Rat), Warren Douglas (Elevator Operator), Frank Faylen (Band Conductor and Emcee), Pat Flaherty (Dance Floor Guard), Edward Gargan (Joe—Foreman), Harris Berger, David Gorcey (Ticket Takers), Joe Gray (Cannonball Wales), Harrison Greene (Dance Judge), Kit Guard (Mickey Miller), Margaret Hayes (Sally—Irene's Friend), Sam Hayes (Sam Hayes—Radio Announcer), Oscar "Dutch" Hendrian (Gym Trainer), Arthur Housman, Frank Sully (Radio Listeners), George Humbert (Organ Grinder's Shill), John Indrisano (Referee in Wales Fight), Thomas E. Jackson (Pep-Sportswriter), Payne B. Johnson (Boy), Colin Kenny (Al's Pal), Victor Kilian (Sign Painter), Mike Lally (Fight Ringsider/Party Guest), Charles Lane (Al—Dance Team Manager), Ethelreda Leopold (Irene—Dressing Room Blonde), Michael Mark (Tombstone Painter), William Marshall (Man in Peggy's Dressing Room), Pat McKee (Danny's Trainer), Sidney Miller (Band Conductor and Emcee), Bert Moorhouse (Nightclub Patron), Jack Mower (Man Next to MacPherson at Fight), William Newell (Max's Lyricist), William H. O'Brien (Waiter), George O'Hanlon (Newsboy), Garry Owen (Reporter), Paul Panzer (Dance Contest Observer), Sally Payne (Singer), Jack Perry (Wales' Handler), Lee Phelps (Ring Announcer), William "Bill" Phillips (Sailor-Sparring Partner), Bernice Pilot (Della—Peggy's Maid), Alexander Pollard (Waiter), John Sheehan (Man Yelling at Ringside), Charles Sherlock (Dance Judge), Buster Slaven (Sidney—Pupil), Bob Steele (Kid Callahan), Jay Eaton, Larry Steers, Frank Wilcox (Party Guests), Charles Sullivan (Dance Floor Guard #2), Elliott Sullivan (Photographer), Billy Wayne (Happy—Googi's Henchman), Dick Wessel (Cab Driver by Fire), Leo White (Dance Contest Observer), Charles C. Wilson (Bill—Man Behind MacPherson at Fight), Tom Wilson (Man on Fire Escape), Robert Winkler (Mush)

PLOT: Closely watched by the philosophic "Old Timer," personification of the wisdom of the curbstones of New York's alleys and side streets, tough Danny Kenny and cheerful Peggy Nash grow up with the promise to be sweethearts always. Danny dominates his "gang," which includes the Italian "Googi" and the slow thinking "Muttface." Danny declines to turn professional boxer after winning the Golden Gloves title at the age of seventeen. He has the "Old Timer's" approval for preferring a truck driver's job, for it spells a steady salary, a musical education for his talented brother Eddie, and a happy married life with his sweetheart, Peggy. But Peggy nearly breaks Danny's heart when she dances out of his circle into that of a black-haired youth named Murray Burns. At first they are Murray Burns and Company, a dance team of the side street nightclubs, but soon they become "Maurice and Margalo," of the bright lights of the key cities. Danny tries to match Peggy's new celebrity with his own. He turns back to the boxing arena he had spurned, and with the new name Young Samson rises rapidly in his new profession. But although shrewd, square-dealing Scotty MacPherson, Danny's fight manager, knows he is no match for the experienced, unscrupulous boxer Cannonball Wales, he gives way to Danny's insistence and arranges the fight. By the time the fight takes place, Peggy is already regretting her faith in Burns. The loyal "Muttface" is Danny's second, and "Googi," now the prosperous boss of a "racket," lays heavy bets against the hard-eyed backers of Cannonball. Danny fights gamely, but rosin on the tips of the Cannonball's gloves is deliberately rubbed

Filmography (As Director) 145

into his eyes to blind him. He loses the fight, and his sight is only just saved. "Googi's" bid for vengeance takes the life one of the Cannonball's backers, but costs "Googi" his own life. Heartbroken, Peggy leaves Burns and returns to New York, but Scotty, blaming her apparent jilting of Danny for the tragedy, refuses to let her see him. While Danny, backed by Scotty's savings after his own funds have been exhausted, sits at his newspaper stand and listens on a small radio to the ovation accorded his brother Eddie's new "Symphony of a Great City," he seems to hear the sage words of the "Old Timer"—all the blending noises of the city itself, and the little song of his own resigned heart. Suddenly his name is called, and he turns to see, dimly, that Peggy has come back to be his girl, always.

REVIEWS:
"Very good mass entertainment! It is a mixture of melodrama with comedy, pathos and romance, and it has just enough music and dancing to give it an extra added flavor."—*Harrison's Reports,* September 28, 1940

"[It's] unevenly paced, mounts slowly to a sizzling prizefight sequence, which comes somewhere about the middle, then sags off to a long-drawn, agonized finish."—*New York Times,* September 28, 1940

"The production is of a high standard, the direction is capable and the cast a strong one."—*Monthly Film Bulletin,* March 31, 1941

REVIEWS FOR ANATOLE LITVAK:
"To this reviewer the work of Anatole Litvak is the outstanding credit. He seems to have topped every other effort in his direction of each and every sequence of this picture. His fight scenes are terrific; his love scenes give you creeps of joy; his pacing of the yarn, because it told so much, was perfection.... Litvak is definitely at the top of the heap with this contribution. It was no easy task."—*Hollywood Reporter,* September 10, 1940

"...deftly directed by Anatole Litvak.... Picture carries plenty of dramatic punch and interesting entertainment...."—*Variety,* September 11, 1940

"Some critics also noticed that Anatole Litvak and primarily the directors of photography Sol Polito and James Wong Howe did their job responsibly, but we must admit, without much faith in it."—*L'Écran Français,* May 13, 1947

ADDITIONAL REVIEWS AND ARTICLES:
Film Daily September 13, 1940; *Hollywood Reporter* April 12, 1940; *New York Times,* May 19, 1940; *Hollywood Reporter* May 31, 1940; *Hollywood Reporter* July 30, 1940; *Motion Picture Daily* September 13, 1940; *Motion Picture Herald* September 14, 1940; *Daily Worker* September 28, 1940; *New York World-Telegram* September 28, 1940; New York Post September 28, 1940; *New York Daily News* September 28, 1940; *Morning Telegraph* September 28, 1940; *New York Post* September 28, 1940; *New York Herald Tribune* September 28, 1940; *Commonweal* October 4, 1940; *Pittsburgh Post-Gazette* October 4, 1940; *Liberty* November 2, 1940; *Modern Screen* December 1940; *Today's Cinema* February 26, 1941; *Kinematograph Weekly* February 27, 1941; *Today's Cinema* March 10, 1948; *Kinematograph Weekly* March 11, 1948; *La Revue du Cinéma* March 1983; *Films of the Golden Age* Summer 2005

NOTES: The film was originally titled *The World Moves On.* Jean Negulesco assumed the direction of the film for a few days when Litvak suffered an eye injury. Ginger Rogers was Warners' first choice for the role of Peggy Nash. *City for Conquest* marked Arthur Kennedy's film debut and one of Elia Kazan's first roles on screen. It was reported that screenwriter Aben Kandel was working on a sequel, continuing the saga of all his characters; the project never materialized.

Out of the Fog

Warner Brothers; B&W; 85 minutes; Released in New York City on June 14, 1941

CREDITS: *Executive Producer*: Hal B. Wallis; *Associate Producer*: Henry Blanke; *Director*: Anatole Litvak; *Dialogue Director*: Jo Graham; *Assistant Directors:* Lee Katz, Chuck Hansen; *Screenplay:* Robert Rossen, Jerry Wald, Richard Macaulay; *Based on the Play* The Gentle People *by* Irwin Shaw; *Screenplay*; *Photography*: James Wong Howe; *Art Director*: Carl Jules Weyl; *Editor*: Warren Low; *Gowns*: Howard Shoup; *Music Director*: Leo F. Forbstein; *Music*: Max Steiner, Heinz Roemheld; *Sound*: Everett A. Brown; *Special Effects*: Rex Wimpy; *Makeup:* Perc Westmore; *Unit Manager:* Chuck Hansen

CAST: John Garfield (Harold Goff), Ida Lupino (Stella Goodwin), Thomas Mitchell (Jonah Goodwin), Eddie Albert (George Watkins), George Tobias (Gregor Propotkin), John Qualen (Olaf Johnson), Aline MacMahon (Florence Goodwin), Jerome Cowan (Assistant District Attorney), Odette Myrtil (Caroline Pomponette), Leo Gorcey (Eddie), Robert Homans (Officer Magruder), Bernard Gorcey (Sam Pepper), Paul Harvey (Judge Moriarity), Charles C. Wilson (Detective), Jack Mower (Detective), Konstantin Sankar (Bublitchki), Ben Welden (Boss), James Conlin (Kibitzer), Walter Tetley (Buddy), Murray Alper (Clerk), Danny Jackson (Boy), David Willock (Elevator Boy), Barbara Pepper (Cigarette Girl), Mayta Palmera (Dancer), Max Hoffman, Jr. (Taxi Driver), Billy Wayne (Joe), Frank Darien (Newspaper Vendor), Frank Coghlan, Jr. (Newsboy), Herbert Heywood (Morgue Attendant), Frank Mayo, Charles Drake, Richard Kipling, Jack Wise, Eddie Graham, Alexander Leftwich (Reporters), Alec Craig, Ed Keane, Garland Smith, Charles Sherlock

PLOT: Brooklyn's Sheepshead Bay is lonely and isolated, but two who love its peace are Jonah Goodwin, a gentle, frustrated tailor, and his friend Olaf Johnson, a timid chef. Jonah's wife Florence is a nagging hypochondriac, and his pretty daughter Stella is resentful of her drab life and the uninspired love-making of her plodding boyfriend George Watkins. Olaf has to dodge the unwanted attentions of his employer, Caroline Pomponette. Jonah and Olaf have a little boat from which they fish four nights a week. Towards the bigger boat they hope to own some day they have saved $190. One night Harold Goff, self-appointed "Admiral of the Sheepshead Bay," threatens them into agreeing to pay five dollars a week for "protection" of their boat. To establish legal claim for the payments, he makes them sign a $1,000 note. Unaware of her father's connection with him, Stella meets Goff and is fascinated by his daring recklessness. Alarmed when he discovers the friendship, Jonah offers Stella the money for a trip to Cuba, which would take all his savings. Stella refuses the sacrifice, but inadvertently mention it to Goff. When Goff demands the $190, Jonah rebels and has him arrested but in court the $1,000 note establishes Goff's claim. That night Goff beats Jonah brutally with a rubber hose. After this, Jonah and Olaf plan his murder. Pretending they have a message from Stella for him, the friends take the racketeer on their little boat. Olaf is unable to attack Goff, who discovers the plot. After knocking both men to the bottom of the boat, he loses his balance, falls overboard and drowns. It is several days before Goff's body is recovered by the police, and a day or two longer before their investigation leads them to Sheepshead Bay. Defiant and bewildered, Stella is taken to the morgue to identify

Goff's body. The police learn that she and the racketeer had planned to go to Cuba together. They know, too, of the extortion charge that had been brought by Jonah and Olaf. All through her ordeal of questioning by the assistant district attorney, George is there to be supportive of Stella. The police go to Sheepshead to question Jonah and Olaf, just returned from a night of fishing. They have found Goff's wallet in the bottom of their boat. Jonah has the presence of mind to hook the wallet on a fishing line and throw it into the water before he is searched and questioned by the police. It is a mighty relief to Olaf and Jonah when the brusque inspector leaves. Happy as children, they retrieve the wallet, extract their $190 plus $5 for every week they had to pay protection, earmark the rest of the money for a children's charity, and throw the empty wallet into the sea. To add to Jonah's contentment, Stella recognizes the true worth of the commonplace but faithful George and is reconciled with him.

REVIEWS:
"*Out of the Fog* ... is a heavy and dreary recital of largely synthetic woes, laced with moderate suspense and spotted here and there with humor. It doesn't even come close to being a really good film, and if you want the honest truth it is literally as old-fashioned as sin.—*New York Times,* June 21, 1941

"It is cheering news ... that *Out of the Fog* ... is a work of distinction.... [It] has succeeded in converting a disappointing stage work into a vastly entertaining motion picture."—*New York Herald Tribune,* June 21, 1941

"From the standpoint of direction, acting and writing, this drama is very good. But it is somber entertainment, and since it is a study in characterizations and moods its appeal will mostly likely be directed to the class trade rather than to the masses."—*Harrison's Reports,* June 21, 1941

REVIEWS FOR ANATOLE LITVAK:
"Litvak did a workmanlike job in handling the assignment of keeping things going mainly on incident and human reactions to problems that arise."—*Variety,* June 6, 1941

"Expertly directed by Anatole Litvak ... [his] direction is at its best in the steam-room scene...."—*Hollywood Reporter,* June 6, 1941

"This is a very strong story well worked out and directed most admirably by Anatole Litvak."—*Monthly Film Bulletin,* March 31, 1942

ADDITIONAL REVIEWS AND ARTICLES:
Hollywood Reporter October 10, 1940; *Hollywood Reporter* January 27, 1941; *Hollywood Reporter* February 14, 1941; *Hollywood Reporter* March 19, 1941; *Hollywood Reporter* May 12, 1941; *Motion Picture Herald Product Digest* May 31, 1941; *Film Daily* June 11, 1941; *Motion Picture Herald* June 14, 1941; *Box Office* June 14, 1941; *New Yorker* July 21, 1941; *Nation* June 21, 1941; *Newsweek* June 23, 1941; *Commonweal* July 4, 1941; *Kinematograph Weekly* February 26, 1942

NOTES: The film's working titles were *The Gentle People* and *Danger Harbor*. Ann Sheridan was originally cast as Stella. Louis Hayward was considered for the part of Harold Goff and Humphrey Bogart was to have a shot at it if Hayward turned it down.

Blues in the Night

Warner Brothers; B&W; 88 minutes; Released in New York City on November 15, 1941

FILMOGRAPHY (AS DIRECTOR)

CREDITS: *Executive Producer*: Hal B. Wallis; *Associate Producer*: Henry Blanke; *Director*: Anatole Litvak; *Dialogue Director*: Harold Winston; *Assistant Director*: Lee Katz; *Screenplay*: Robert Rossen with contributions by Edwin Gilbert; *Based on the Play* Hot Nocturne *by* Edwin Gilbert; *Photography*: Ernie Haller; *Art Director*: Max Parker; *Editor*: Owen Marks; *Gowns*: Damon Giffard; *Music*: Heinz Roemheld; *Songs*: Harold Arlen; *Lyrics*: Johnny Mercer; *Orchestral Arrangements*: Ray Heindorf; *Music Director*: Leo F. Forbstein; *Sound*: Everett A. Brown; *Montages*: Don Siegel; *Makeup*: Perc Westmore; *Trumpet playing for Jack Carson*: "Snookie" Young, Frankie Zinzer; *Pianist for Richard Whorf*: Stan Wrightsman; *Clarinet solos*: Archie Rosate

CAST: Priscilla Lane (Ginger "Character" Powell), Betty Field (Kay Grant), Richard Whorf (Jigger Pine), Lloyd Nolan (Del Davis), Jack Carson (Leo Powell), Wallace Ford (Brad Ames), Elia Kazan (Nickie Haroyan), Peter Whitney (Pete Bassett), Billy Halop (Peppi), Howard Da Silva (Sam Paryas), Herbert Heywood (Brakeman), George Lloyd (Joe), Charles Wilson (Barney), Matt McHugh (Drunk), Jimmy Lunceford ("A Barnstorming Band"), Will Osborne ("Guy Heisers Band"), Joyce Compton (Blonde), Mabel Todd (Singer), William Gillespie (Singer in Jail), Hank Mann, Cliff Saum (Prisoners), Jack Mower (Jailer), Lee Phelps (Guard), William Hopper (Pool Player), Billy Wayne, Pat McVey, Elliott Sullivan (Waiters), Louis Natheaux (Croupier), Fred Kelsey (Bartender), Anthony Warde (Del's Bodyguard), Sol Gorss (Del's Bodyguard), John Dilson, John Hamilton (Doctors), Emmett Vogan (Hotel Clerk), Robert Homans (Bill—Bartender), Faye Emerson, Leah Baird (Nurses), Faith Domergue, Juanita Stark, David Gorcey, George Offerman, Jr., Jean Ames (Jitterbugs), Ann Edmonds (Woman in Telephone Booth), Ernest Whitman, Napoleon Simpson, Dudley Dickerson (Black Prisoners), Ed Keane, Harrison Greene (Drunks), Cyril Ring, Creighton Hale, Eddie Graham, Frank Mayo, Roland Drew (Gamblers), Charles Irwin, Hal K. Dawson (Men Sitting with Kay)

PLOT: Pianist Jigger Pine, drummer Peppi, clarinet player Nickie Haroyan, bass player Pete Bassett and trumpeter Leo Powell are dedicated to playing jazz and blues. Together with Leo's wife "Character," a singer, the group plays throughout the South, hitchhiking and hopping trains to get around. Along the way, "Character" becomes pregnant, but refuses to tell Leo because she is afraid that he will leave her. One day, escaped convict Del Davis rides in the same railroad car and steals the band's meager funds. They do not turn him over to the authorities so Davis offers them a job at the New Jersey roadhouse that he owns. Also at the roadhouse are Davis' former accomplices, Sam Paryas, crippled Brad Ames and sultry Kay Grant. The three are not happy to see Davis, whom they set up to take the blame for their crimes. Working well together, the band draws a lively crowd to the roadhouse. Hoping to make Davis jealous, Kay flirts with Leo, and Jigger begs her not to break up the band. Kay ignores Jigger. When Leo learns he is to be a father, he happily devotes himself to "Character." Kay then transfers her attentions to Jigger, who tries to resist her. When a doctor tells "Character" that she must stop singing until after the baby is born, Jigger suggests that Kay take her place. Despite the protests of the band, Jigger works hard to improve Kay's singing. When she finally rebels, Jigger tells her that he loves her. Brad overhears and advises Jigger to keep away from Kay, adding that his own love for Kay resulted in the accident that crippled him. When Kay tries to win Davis back by revealing Sam's plan to turn him in to the police, he kills Sam and orders Kay to leave. Despite his loyalty to the band, Jigger takes a job playing piano for a more traditional band and leaves with Kay. Jigger longs to return, but when he begs

Kay to come with him, she laughs at him, saying that she has always been in love with Davis. The rejected Jigger goes on a drunken binge and is eventually found by his friends, who bring him back to the roadhouse to recover. Shortly afterward, Kay also returns to beg Davis to take her back. When he refuses, Kay angrily threatens to turn him in, forcing Davis to pull a gun on her. Jigger rushes to Kay's defense, and in the struggle, Davis drops the gun, which Kay then uses to kill him. Jigger is about to leave with Kay, but the band members intercede, telling him that the stress of the last separation caused "Character" to lose her baby. Not wanting Jigger to ruin his life, Brad drives Kay over a cliff, killing them both. Together again, the band goes back on the road.

REVIEWS:
"This melodrama with music may not be cheerful entertainment, but it has the ingredients for strong mass appeal. For one thing, the music which is of the blues variety is still popular; for another, the melodramatic action holds one in suspense; and for still another, the acting of some of the characters is superb."—*Harrison's Reports,* November 1, 1941

"It is a fast-action musical melodrama with a cast that gets in the groove and stays there."—*Los Angeles Times,* November 14, 1941

"*Blues in the Night* is anything like a masterpiece but … it is worthy of the attention of repertory cinemas and of inclusion in the Library of the British Film Institute, or even of revival by Warners."—*News Chronicle* (UK), April 5, 1946

REVIEWS FOR ANATOLE LITVAK:
"Despite the unoriginality of the script in the second half, picture is geared to swift tempo via Anatole Litvak's direction."—*Variety,* October 30, 1941

"The pounding forceful direction of Anatole Litvak and the performances of the principals are equally distinguished."—*Hollywood Reporter,* October 30, 1941

"Anatole Litvak has directed the musical sequences which happily are many, in showmanly fashion, employing montage shots most effectively to maintain fast tempi. But when he gets into the story of the ups and downs of his vagabond musical quintet, Mr. Litvak loses control. However, there probably wasn't much he could do anyway with the melodramatic material the script writers ask him to juggle about for an hour and half."—*New York Times,* December 12, 1941

ADDITIONAL REVIEWS AND ARTICLES:
Hollywood Reporter April 10, 1941; *Hollywood Reporter* May 27, 1941; *Daily Worker New* York June 17, 1941; *New York Times* October 26, 1941; *Film Daily* October 30, 1941; *Motion Picture Herald Product Digest* November 1, 1941; *Box Office* November 1, 1941; *Etude* December 1941; *New York Post* December 12, 1941; *Commonweal* December 12, 1941; *Monthly Film Bulletin* May 31, 1942; *Down Beat* June 15, 1943; *Down Beat* September 1, 1945; *Films in Review* March 1980; *Film Comment* November–December 2004; *Sight and Sound* October 2008

AWARDS AND HONORS:
Academy Awards, USA 1942. Nominated*: Best Music, Original Song.* Harold Arlen (music), Johnny Mercer (lyrics) for the song *Blues in the Night.*

NOTES: The film's title was changed from *Hot Nocturne* to *New Orleans Blues* and, just prior to its release, to *Blues in the Night.* John Garfield and James Cagney were both offered the part of Jigger Pine. Curtis Bernhardt was the first director attached to the project.

This Above All

20th Century–Fox; B&W; 110 minutes; World premiere in New York City on May 12, 1942

CREDITS: *Producer*: Darryl F. Zanuck; *Associate Producer:* Robert Bassler; *Director*: Anatole Litvak; *Assistant Director*: Aaron Rosenberg; *Screenplay*: R. C. Sherriff. *Based on the novel by* Eric M. Knight; *Photography:* Arthur Miller; *Art Directors*: Richard Day, Joseph C. Wright; *Editor*: Walter Thompson; *Set Decorator:* Thomas Little; *Costumes*: Gwen Wakeling; *Music*: Alfred Newman; *Sound:* Arthur von Kirbach, Roger Heman; *Makeup*: Guy Pearce; *Technical Advisors:* Section Officer Iris Houston, Flight Lieutenant Kathleen Hunt, Major Douglas Francis.

CAST: Tyrone Power (Clive Briggs), Joan Fontaine (Prudence Cathaway), Thomas Mitchell (Monty), Henry Stephenson (Gen. Cathaway), Nigel Bruce (Ramsbottom), Gladys Cooper (Iris Cathaway), Philip Merivale (Dr. Roger Cathaway), Sara Allgood (Waitress), Alexander Knox (Rector), Queenie Leonard (Violet Worthing), Melville Cooper (Wilbur), Jill Esmond (Nurse Emily), Holmes Herbert (Dr. Mathias), Denis Green (Dr. Ferris), Arthur Shields (Chaplain), Dennis Hoey (Parsons), Thomas Louden (Vicar), Miles Mander (Major), Rhys Williams (Sergeant), Doris Lloyd (Sergeant), John Abbott (Joe), Carol Curtis-Brown (Maid), Gwendolyn Logan (Maid), Mary Field (Maid), Mary Forbes (Vicar's Wife), Forrester Harvey (Proprietor), Olaf Hytten (Proprietor), Yorke Sherwood (Proprietor), Harold de Becker (Conductor), Alec Craig (Conductor), Jessica Newcombe (Matron), Billy Bevan (Farmer), Aubrey Mather, Lumsden Hare (Headwaiters), Heather Thatcher, Jean Prescott, Stella Rae, Cecil Weston (Nurses), Brenda Forbes (Mae, a Singer), Rita Page (Corporal), Clare Verdera (Corporal), Joyce Wynn, Valerie Cole, Stephanie Insall, Dorothy Daniels (WAAF Girls), Alan Edmiston, Gerald Hamer (Porters), Morton Lowry, Ernie Stanton (Soldiers), Wyndham Standing (Doctor), Mrs. Wilfrid North (Doctor's Wife), Clifford Severn (Lift Boy), David Clyde (Clerk), Lilyan Irene (Rosie), Sylvia Chaldecott (Counter Woman), Gordon Wallace (Airman), Anita Bolster, May Beatty (Customers), Donald Stuart (Messenger), Clyde Cook (Driver), Harry Allen (Waiter), Stuart Robinson (Officer), Charles Irwin (Captain), Will Stanton (Bartender), Cyril Thornton (Station Master), Leyland Hodgson (Policeman in Post Office), Herbert Clifton (Secretary), Val Stanton, Leonard Carey (Policemen), Virginia McDowall (Girl), Raymond Severn (Boy), Ottola Nesmith, David Thursby, John Rogers, Colin Campbell, Connie Leon

PLOT: Prudence Cathaway, determined daughter of a London surgeon, is a volunteer member of the Women's Auxiliary Air Force. Prudence's aunt Iris is not too happy with her niece's decision; Prudence lectures her on her outdated values. At the WAAF training camp, Prudence meets Violet Worthing, who soon fixes her up with Clive Briggs, an army friend of Violet's sweetheart Joe. Unaware that Prudence is from aristocracy, Clive declares his distaste for all of England's upper class, but Prudence falls in love with him anyway. As their romance flourishes, Clive and Prudence go on their first military leave together, taking a seven-day vacation at the Dover Grand Hotel. In Dover, Prudence runs into Aunt Iris, but the two merely exchange unfriendly glances. Fearing that her aunt will tell her family about her affair with Clive and that she will be further ostracized by them, Prudence becomes distraught. Clive begins to act strangely, yelling military orders in his sleep and becoming generally distracted. When Prudence reads the telegram that seemed to trigger Clive's unusual behavior, she learns only that his friend Monty is coming to visit him. Prudence later learns that Clive deserted the army after being wounded at Dunkerque, and that Monty has come to return Clive to his regiment before he is officially listed as a deserter. Clive eventually confides in Prudence that he left the service because he disliked defending England's aristocracy. Prudence responds by giving Clive an impassioned lecture about the glory of England—a speech that brings tears to her eyes and drives Clive away. Clive sets out on foot but does not get far before a farmer, mistaking him for a spy, assaults him. The bloodied Clive takes refuge at a nurse's home, but the nurse learns that he is a suspected spy and threatens to call the police. Clive then seeks help from a clergyman, who lectures Clive on faith and inspires him to return to his regiment. Before turning himself in, however, Clive sends Prudence a message to meet him in Central London so that they can be married. On his way, Clive is arrested by military police and taken to headquarters. After pleading with his commander, Clive manages to secure a two-hour leave so that he can meet Prudence one last time. Clive's second attempt to meet Prudence is obstructed when he is wounded while rescuing a woman and her child from a burning building. Clive is rushed to a hospital, and as his life hangs in the balance, Prudence arranges an improvised wedding. At Clive's bedside, a nurse, reading from Shakespeare's play *Hamlet*, says, "This above all: To thine own self be true." Following his recuperation, they are married and ready to face the uncertain future together.

REVIEWS:
"*This Above All* is not quite what it might very well have been. But the tension and pathos of love reaching hopefully for some fulfillment amid deep woe is expressively captured in it."—*New York Times*, May 13, 1942

"Beautiful ... stimulating and occasionally powerful...."—*New York Herald Tribune*, May 13, 1942

"An interesting and deeply moving romantic drama ... a class picture...."—*Harrison's Reports*, May 16, 1942

REVIEWS FOR ANATOLE LITVAK:
"Anatole Litvak does a job of direction he will be hard put to match, for perfectly selected players people each role and contribute peak performances under the painstaking piloting of Litvak."—*Hollywood Reporter*, May 13, 1942

"Anatole Litvak's direction is unmistakably expressive."—*Variety*, May 13, 1942

"This strong and moving story has been expertly handled by Darryl F. Zanuck and Anatole Litvak, producer and director respectively, so expertly that it seems niggling to comment on the un-English platform designations...."—*Monthly Film Bulletin*, June 30, 1942

ADDITIONAL REVIEWS AND ARTICLES:
Hollywood Reporter February 24, 1941; *Hollywood Reporter* July 8, 1941; *Los Angeles Times* July 8, 1941; *Hollywood Reporter* July 9, 1941; *Hollywood Reporter* August 14, 1941; *Hollywood Reporter* August 21, 1941; *Hollywood Reporter* September 12, 1941; *Hollywood Reporter* September 19, 1941; *Hollywood Reporter* September 23, 1941; *Hollywood Reporter* October 21, 1941; *Hollywood Reporter* November 12, 1941; *Hollywood Reporter* November 17, 1941; *Hollywood Reporter* November 26, 1941; *Hollywood Reporter* November 28, 1941; *Hollywood Reporter* December 1, 1941; *Hollywood Reporter* December 2, 1941; *Hollywood Reporter* December 5, 1941; *Hollywood Reporter* December 11, 1941; *Photoplay* February 1942; *Hollywood Reporter* February 24, 1942; *Hollywood Reporter* March 20, 1942; *New York Times* May 3, 1942; *Film Daily* May 13, 1942; *Motion*

Picture Herald Product Digest May 16, 1942; *Box Office* May 16, 1942; *New York Times* May 17, 1942; *Newsweek* May 18, 1942; *Motion Picture Exhibitor* May 20, 1942; *Hollywood Reporter* May 29, 1942; *Time* June 1, 1942; *The New Republic* June 1, 1942; *Commonweal* June 5, 1942; *Today's Cinema* July 3, 1942; *Kinematograph Weekly* July 9, 1942; *The London Times* September 16, 1942; *The Saturday Evening Post* June 27, 1946; *L'Écran Français* May 13, 1947; *Mon Film* July 16, 1947; *La Revue du Cinéma* March 1983

AWARDS AND HONORS:

Academy Awards, 1943; Winner: *Best Art Direction-Interior Decoration, Black-and-White*: Richard Day, Joseph C. Wright, Thomas Little; Academy Awards, 1943; Nominated: *Best Cinematography, Black-and-White* Arthur C. Miller *Best Sound Recording* Edmund H. Hansen *Best Editing* Walter Thompson

NOTES: The title of Eric Knight's novel and the film is derived from a quote by Polonius in William Shakespeare's play *Hamlet* (Act 1, Scene 3): "This above all: to thine own self be true. And it must follow, as the night the day/Thou canst not then be false to any man." Robert Donat, Laurence Olivier and Richard Greene were also considered for the role of Clive Briggs.

The Long Night

RKO Radio Pictures; B&W; 101 minutes; Released on September 16, 1947

CREDITS: *Producers*: Robert Hakim, Raymond Hakim, Anatole Litvak; *Director*: Anatole Litvak; *Assistant Director:* Aaron Rosenberg; *Screenplay:* John Wexley; *Based on the Story "Les Jour se Leve" by* Jacques Viot; *Photography:* Sol Polito; *Art Director:* Eugène Lourié; *Editor:* Robert Swink; *Set Decorator:* Darrell Silvera; *Costumes*: Renié; *Music*: Dimitri Tiomkin; *Music Director*: C. Bakaleinikoff; *Sound*: Richard Van Hessen, Clem Portman; *Special Effects:* Russell A. Cully; *Makeup:* Layne Britton; *Production Manager*: Sam Ruman; *Production Assistant:* H. de Schulthess

CAST: Henry Fonda (Joe Adams), Barbara Bel Geddes (Jo Ann), Vincent Price (Maximilian), Ann Dvorak (Charlene), Howard Freeman (Sheriff Ned Meade), Moroni Olsen (Police Chief Bob McManus), Elisha Cook, Jr. (Frank Dunlap), Queenie Smith (Mrs. Tully), David Clarke (Bill Pulanski), Charles McGraw (Policeman Ed Stevens), Patty King (Peggy), Robert A. Davis (Freddie), Will Wright (Mr. Tully—Janitor), Ray Teal (Mr. Hudson), Pat Flaherty (Police Sergeant), Dick Reeves (Cop), Jack Overman (Man in Crowd), Mary Gordon (Old Lady in Crowd), Murray Alper (Bartender), Byron Foulger (Man with Bike), Ida Moore (Lady with Birdcage), Garry Owen (Library Lecturer)

PLOT: In an Ohio mill town, blind veteran Frank Dunlap is walking to his tenement apartment when a wounded man tumbles down the stairs and dies at his feet. Soon after arriving on the scene, the police deduce that the man, Maximilian, must have been shot on the top floor, in a room occupied by Joe Adams. When they try to question Joe, he fires a shot through his door and refuses to talk. Ned Meade, a no-nonsense sheriff, orders his men to position themselves in a hotel room directly across the street so that they can shoot at Joe from their window. As the police open fire, Joe avoids the window and begins to recall the events that led him to commit murder: One day, while working as a sandblaster, Joe, a recently discharged veteran, meets Jo Ann, a sweet young woman from a flower shop. Joe flirts with Jo Ann and learns that she grew up in the same orphanage as he and now lives with an older couple who own the flower shop. Joe begins dating Jo Ann, and three weeks later, deeply in love, proposes to her. Jo Ann is unsure about her feelings for Joe and does not give him an answer. Suspicious, Joe follows her to a nightclub, where magician Maximilian the Great is performing his dog and magic act. As an entranced Jo Ann watches Max from her table, Charlene, known as "Charlie," who has just quit her job as Max's assistant, strikes up a conversation with Joe. After the embittered but resigned Charlie tells Joe that Max is a sadistic fraud, the middle-aged Max sends Jo Ann to his private table, then attempts to convince Charlie to return to the act. Angered by Max's patronizing attitude toward Charlie, Joe comes to her defense. Back in the present, as a crowd gathers outside Joe's apartment building, Bill Pulanski, Joe's neighbor, begs for a chance to talk to Joe, but Police Chief McManus refuses. Charlie asks to speak with Joe, but is forcibly kept away. McManus' men then shoot through Joe's door lock, but Joe blocks the door with his dresser before they can enter. After Meade orders tear gas brought in, Joe returns to his recollections: Joe is visiting Charlie, who has fallen in love with him, when Max shows up, anxious to talk to him. Max informs Joe that he is Jo Ann's long-lost father and cautions him to stay away from her, as he feels that Joe will tie her to a "life of drudgery." Indignant, Joe tells Max that he is marrying Jo Ann and goes to see her. When Joe states that he knows Max is her father, Jo Ann is stunned and insists that they are not related. Jo Ann then tells Joe how she met Max months before: While watching Max perform one night, the lonely, insecure Jo Ann is selected to participate in a portion of the act. Jo Ann is both frightened and excited by the charismatic magician and, a few days later, attends a concert with him. Max insists that he and Jo Ann are soulmates and are destined to become lifelong "companions." When Max later tries to force himself on her, Jo Ann slaps him, then runs home. Despite her anger, Jo Ann finds she is drawn to Max and after he sends her a dress he claims he bought for his sister, she sees him twice more before he departs for his winter tour. During Max's absence, Jo Ann meets Joe. After Jo Ann concludes her story, she assures Joe that she loves him and gives him a special Aztec brooch as a token. Later, as Joe is saying goodbye to Charlie, he sees a cardboard sheet with several of the Aztec brooches that Charlie explains Max gives to young women he likes. Seeing Joe's pained reaction, Charlie deduces that he is in love with Jo Ann. Knowing of Max's involvement with the younger woman, she unwittingly laughs. Back at Joe's apartment in the present, while deputies bring Jo Ann, McManus talks to Joe over a bullhorn, encouraging him to surrender. Joe comes to the window and refuses to give up, challenging the police and crowd below to "finish him off." When Frank, Bill, Charlie and various neighbors call out their support for Joe, however, he ignores them, turning away from the window. As Jo Ann runs through the crowd, desperate to reach Joe, she is knocked down by a man carrying a bicycle. More police arrive, and Joe recalls his final meeting with Max: When Max shows up, demanding that Joe stop seeing Jo Ann, an enraged Joe almost throws him out the window. Max calmly reveals that he came intending to shoot Joe, then sees Jo Ann's brooch on Joe's dresser and starts to tease him about it. Unable to endure Max's suggestive taunts, Joe grabs his gun and shoots him. Back outside the apartment, the police start throwing tear gas through Joe's window, just as Jo Ann sneaks up the stairs to his room. After Jo Ann pleads with Joe to believe in himself, as she and his friends do, Joe finally opens his door, and she helps him escape the tear gas. Joe then gives himself up, and Jo Ann vows to wait for him. (American Film Institute source)

REVIEWS:

"*Long Night* is a sullen brooding film.... There's some good, challenging writing."— *Variety*, May 28, 1947

"[A] first-class shocker.... [But] the motives, the behavior and interactions of the characters ... simply do not ring true."—*Los Angeles Times,* September 25, 1947

"It is impossible to view *The Long Night* without it bringing back strong memories of the emotions associated with *Le Jour se Lève,* and continually falling short of those memories because it dare not set out to be a film in the same class."—*Sight & Sound,* October 1947

"A highly effective dramatic offering, marked by skillful direction and first rate acting."—*Harrison's Reports,* May 31, 1947

REVIEWS FOR ANATOLE LITVAK:

"Litvak's direction is most notable throughout, and he wrings dry every emotions. Especially fine is the mass movements of the street crowds. It is Litvak's first picture since the war, and from the standpoint of his contribution rank with his finest."—*Hollywood Reporter,* May 28, 1947

"Litvak often makes up in violence of movement and ardor of feeling what the picture lacks in subtlety."—*Time,* August 18, 1947.

"Mr. Litvak's production is an obvious theatrical fake, exposed by its own pretentions and an over-talked John Wexler script. And a lay-out of flashy performances do not match the French originals."—*New York Times,* September 17, 1947

ADDITIONAL REVIEWS AND ARTICLES:

Hollywood Reporter May 22, 1946; *Hollywood Reporter* August 9, 1946; *Hollywood Reporter* August 22, 1946; *Hollywood Reporter* August 23, 1946; *Hollywood Reporter* August 26, 1946; *Hollywood Reporter* September 6, 1946; *Hollywood Reporter* September 1946; *Hollywood Reporter* September 25, 1946; *Hollywood Reporter* December 9, 1946; *Hollywood Reporter* December 18, 1946; *Life* May 19, 1947; *Film Daily* May 28, 1947; *Motion Picture Herald Product Digest* May 31, 1947; *Box Office* June 7, 1947; *Hollywood Reporter* July 25, 1947; *Today's Cinema* August 1, 1947; *The Nation* August 30, 1947; *Cosmopolitan* September 1947; *Theatre Arts* September 1947; *Photoplay* September 1947; *New York Times* September 14, 1947; *Commonweal* September 16, 1947; *Today's Cinema* September 17, 1947; *Kinematograph Weekly* September 18, 1947; *Newsweek* September 22, 1947; *New Yorker* September 27, 1947; *New Republic* October 6, 1947; *Life* October 6, 1947; *Monthly Film Bulletin* October 1947; *L'Écran Français* November 4, 1947; *Life* April 12, 1948; *Hollywood* (Italy) September 3, 1949; *Daily Worker* September 20, 1949; *Classic Images* December 2000; *Classic Images* January 2001

NOTES: The film's working title was *A Time to Kill.* It is a remake of the 1939 French classic *Le Jour se Lève* [Daybreak], directed by Marcel Carné and starring Jean Gabin, Jules Berry and Arletty.

The Snake Pit

20th Century–Fox; B&W; 108 minutes; World premiere in New York City on November 4, 1948

CREDITS: *Producers*: Darryl F. Zanuck, Anatole Litvak, Robert Bassler; *Director*: Anatole Litvak; *Assistant Director*: Henry Weinberger; *Screenplay*: Frank Partos, Millen Brand, Arthur Laurents; *Based on the novel by* Mary Jane Ward, *Dialogue Director*: Norman Stuart; *Photography:* Leo Tover; *Art Directors*: Lyle Wheeler, Joseph C. Wright; *Editor*: Dorothy Spencer; *Set Decorators*: Thomas Little, Ernest Lansing; *Wardrobe Director:* Charles Le Maire; *Costumes:* Bonnie Cashin; *Music:* Alfred Newman; *Orchestral*

Arrangements: Edward Powell; *Sound*: Arthur L. Kirbach, Harry M. Leonard, Thomas T. Moulton; *Special Photographic Effects*: Fred Sersen; *Makeup:* Ben Nye; *Production Manager:* R. A. Klune

CAST: Olivia de Havilland (Virginia Stuart Cunningham), Mark Stevens (Robert Cunningham), Leo Genn (Dr. Mark Kik), Celeste Holm (Grace), Glenn Langan (Dr. Terry), Helen Craig (Miss Davis), Leif Erickson (Gordon), Beulah Bondi (Mrs. Greer), Lee Patrick (Asylum Inmate), Howard Freeman (Dr. Curtis), Natalie Schafer (Mrs. Stuart), Ruth Donnelly (Ruth), Katherine Locke (Margaret), Frank Conroy (Dr. Jonathan Gifford), Minna Gombell (Miss Hart), June Storey (Miss Bixby), Lora Lee Michel (Virginia, age 6), Damian O'Flynn (Mr. Stuart), Ann Doran (Valerie), Esther Somers (Miss Vance), Jacqueline de Wit (Miss Celia Sommerville), Betsy Blair (Hester), Lela Bliss (Miss Greene), Queenie Smith (Lola), Virginia Brissac (Miss Seiffert), Grayce Hampton (Countess Marie Duvarre), Dorothy Neumann (Champion), Jan Clayton (Singing Inmate), Isabel Jewell, Victoria Horne, Tamara Shayne, Grace Poggi, Belle Mitchell, Claire Whitney (Asylum Inmates), Syd Saylor (Inmate Wearing Visor at Dance), Angela Clarke (Greek Patient), Mae Marsh (Boy's Mother), Marion Marshall (Young Girl), Ashley Cowan (Young Man), Minerva Urecal, Helen Servis, Celia Lovsky, Doris Kemper, Ruth Warren, Polly Bailey, Mabel Forrest, Jeri Jordan, Geraldine Garrick, Ellen Lowe, Donna Hamilton, Mira McKinney, Therese Lyon, Sylvia Andrew, Marie Blake, Mary Newton, Dorothy Vaughn, Frances Morris, Marjorie Eaton, Barbara Pepper, Mary Emery, Alvin Hammer, Nina Gilbert (Patients), Inez Palange (Italian Patient), Sally Shepherd, Ruth Clifford, Ann Staunton, Wanda Perry, Louise Lorimer, Mary Treen (Nurses), Ben Erway, Irene Dehn, Harry Hays Morgan, Jean Andren, Joel Friedkin, George Lynn, Ray Teal (Doctors), Lester Sharpe (Dr. Somer), Carol Savage (Maxine), Pat Marlowe (Practical Nurse), Bobby Barber, Phil Arnold (Bald Men), Margaret Brayton (Staff Room Nurse), Anne O'Neal (Waitress Patient), Janna de Loos (Stenographer Nurse), Bee Humphries (Emma), Isabel Withers (Miss Johnson), Mary Tarcai (Miss Jenkins), Louise Robinson, Edna Holland (Husky Attendants), Robert Williams, Eula Morgan, Jean Babe London, G. Pat Collins (Attendants), Kate Lawson (Cashier), Forrest Dickson (Counterwoman), Laura Treadwell (Mother), Leo Kaye (Hospital Attendant), Larry Johns (Minister), Cliff Clark (Barker), Victoria Albright (Virginia, age 2)

PLOT: At Jumper Hill Hospital, Virginia Stuart Cunningham, a writer suffering from a disease of the mind, is unaware of her surroundings, her past and the fact she is married. When her husband Robert visits, she fails to recognize him. Dr. Mark Kik takes a great interest in her case and he learns from Cunningham that he first met Virginia in Chicago and saw a great deal of her until suddenly she left him just before they were due to go to a concert. They met again in New York and were married. A few days later, Cunningham returned home to find that Virginia had lost her reason. Kik tries shock treatment and soon Virginia seems to be improving but she still does not remember her husband and is still frightened of something that happened in the past. Next, Kik experiments with injections and is eventually able to trace Virginia's history back to her childhood and he comes to appreciate the contributory factors of her past life which brought about her present mental condition. As Virginia improves, her husband is anxious to get her out of the hospital and to take her to convalescence at his parents' farm. This is against Kik's judgment as he thinks she is not yet ready to leave. Before a board of doctors, her mental fitness is tested. Stupidly handled by an examining doctor, she has a relapse and has to stay for further treatments. Sent to Ward I, where patients soon to be discharged are placed, she is badly treated by the nurse in charge, who is jealous of the interest Dr. Kik takes in her. At a moment of great mental stress provoked by the nurse, she loses control of herself and is sent to a ward where more violent patients are kept. Virginia continues to show improvement and, treated with great patience and understanding by Kik, she gradually loses her inhibitions, fears and doubts. It is not long before she effects a real recovery. As she says goodbye to Kik and leaves with her husband, she observes that sane people should be in the hospital to see what is like and feels that from outside she can do a lot to help people to help the pathetic patients within.

REVIEWS:

"A great picture! ... What is outstanding about the picture is the realistic manner in which life in an insane asylum is depicted ... with realism that is grim and frequently shocking but it is so dramatically powerful and profoundly moving that one's attention is gripped throughout every moment of its enfoldment. It is a masterpiece of picture-making, as well as a highly intelligent, sympathetic presentation of a most difficult subject."—*Harrison's Reports,* November 6, 1948

"As director, Litvak has given it hard, shocking reality in the filming. It is an adroit combination of realism and hokum, emotional but not maudlin."—*Variety,* November 3, 1948

"*The Snake Pit* ... is a mature sustained case history, more like a documentary than a drama."—*Theatre Arts,* March 1949

REVIEWS FOR ANATOLE LITVAK:

"The tempo Litvak achieves in his direction literally takes the spectator's breath away as he moves his story relentlessly from one dramatic peak to another one. It is an extraordinary directorial feat for which the greatest credit must be given."—*Hollywood Reporter,* November 4, 1948

"Litvak has guided the company surely through the maze of the action in a superior job of direction."—*Herald Tribune,* November 5, 1948

"Mr. Litvak's direction is sure and rhythmic throughout."—*New York Times,* November 5, 1948

ADDITIONAL REVIEWS AND ARTICLES:

New York Times April 26, 1946; *Hollywood Reporter* August 19, 1946; *Hollywood Reporter* August 28, 1946; *Hollywood Reporter* December 19, 1946; *Hollywood Reporter* June 12, 1947; *Hollywood Reporter* June 20, 1947; *Hollywood Reporter* July 17, 1947; *Hollywood Reporter* July 18, 1947; *New York Times* September 7, 1947; *Hollywood Reporter* September 10, 1947; *Hollywood Reporter* October 27, 1947; *Hollywood Reporter* October 29, 1947; *Motion Picture Herald Product Digest* January 31, 1948; *Good Housekeeping* October 1948; *Hollywood Reporter* October 22, 1948; *Hollywood Reporter* October 28, 1948; *Film Daily* November 3, 1948; *New Republic* November 8, 1948; *Newsweek* November 8, 1948; *Hollywood Reporter* November 9, 1948; *Commonweal* November 12, 1948; *New Yorker* November 13, 1948; *Box Office* November 13, 1948; *New York Times* November 14, 1948; *Life* November 19, 1948; *Nation* November 20, 1948; *Saturday Review* November 27, 1948; *Scholastic* December 1, 1948; *Hollywood Reporter* December 9, 1948; *Hollywood Reporter* December 16, 1948; *Daily Variety* December 20, 1948; *Time* December 20, 1948; *Hollywood Reporter* December 21, 1948; *Hollywood Reporter* December 29, 1948; *Photoplay* January 1949; *Rotarian* January 1949; *Hollywood Reporter* January 4, 1949; *Canadian Forum* February 1949; *American Cinematographer* February 1949; *Hollywood Reporter* February 28, 1949; *Hollywood Reporter* March 2, 1949; *Hollywood*

Reporter March 7, 1949; *Sight & Sound* Spring 1949; *Hollywood Reporter* April 6, 1949; *Hollywood Reporter* April 13, 1949; *Hollywood Reporter* April 19, 1949; *Hollywood Reporter* April 26, 1949; *Hollywood Reporter* May 17, 1949; *Hollywood Reporter* May 20, 1949; *Picture Post* May 21, 1949; *Hollywood Reporter* May 25, 1949; *Time* May 30, 1949; *Picture Post* June 4, 1949; *Hollywood Reporter* June 24, 1949; *Collier's*, June 25, 1949; *Hollywood* (Italy) July 2, 1949; *Picture Show* October 29, 1949; *Motion Picture Herald* April 23, 1950; *Daily Variety* September 5, 1952

AWARDS AND HONORS:
New York Film Critics Circle Awards, USA 1948; Winner: Best Actress: Olivia de Havilland; Best Film: 3rd place, NYFCC Award; National Board of Review, USA 1948; Winner: Best Actress: Olivia de Havilland; Top Ten Films; Italian National Syndicate of Film Journalists, Italy 1949; Winner: Silver Ribbon: Best Foreign Actress Olivia de Havilland; Academy Awards, USA 1949; Best Actress in a Leading Role: Olivia de Havilland; Best Sound, Recording: Thomas T Moulton 20th Century–Fox Studio Sound Department; *Nominated*: Best Picture Best Director: Anatole Litvak; Best Writing, Screenplay: Frank Partos, Millen Brand; Best Music: Scoring of a Dramatic or Comedy Picture: Alfred Newman; Directors Guild of America, USA 1949; Nominated: Outstanding Directorial Achievement in Motion Picture: Anatole Litvak; Writers Guild of America, USA 1949; Winner: Best Written American Drama: Frank Partos, Millen Brand The Robert Meltzer Award (Screenplay Dealing Most Ably with Problems of the American Scene): Frank Partos, Millen Brand; Venice Film Festival (Italy) 1949; Winner: International Award: Anatole Litvak Best Actress: Olivia de Havilland; Nominated for Golden Lion: Best Director: Anatole Litvak; Bodil Awards Denmark 1950; Winner: Best American Film, Anatole Litvak (director); Satellite Awards, USA 2005; Nominated: Best Classic DVD

NOTES: Although some sources state that Olivia de Havilland was the first choice to play Virginia, others indicate that Ingrid Bergman was Litvak's first choice. Some press in 1946 announced both Gene Tierney and Joan Fontaine, de Havilland's sister, as possible stars. Joseph Cotten and Richard Conte were considered for the part of Dr.Kik. The California Citizens Committee for Mental Hygiene gave *The Snake Pit* a scroll, honoring it for awakening "millions to a greater knowledge and appreciation of the causes of mental illness." Olivia de Havilland, Mark Stevens and Leo Genn reprised their roles on an April 10, 1950, *Lux Radio Theatre* broadcast.

Sorry, Wrong Number

Paramount Pictures; B&W; 89 minutes; World premiere in New York City on September 1, 1948

CREDITS: *Producers*: Hal Wallis, Anatole Litvak; *Director*: Anatole Litvak; *Assistant Directors*: Richard McWhorter, Dan McCauley; *Screenplay* Lucille Fletcher, *based on her radio play*; *Photography*: Sol Polito; *Art Directors:* Hans Dreier, Earl Hedrick; *Editor*: Warren Low; *Set Decorators:* Sam Comer, Bertram Granger; *Costumes:* Edith Head; *Music*: Franz Waxman; *Sound*: Gene Merritt, Walter Oberst; *Special Effects*: Gordon Jennings; *Process Photography*: Farciot Edouart; *Makeup*: Wally Westmore

CAST: Barbara Stanwyck (Leona Cotterell Stevenson), Burt Lancaster (Henry Stevenson), Ann Richards (Sally Hunt Lord), Wendell Corey (Dr. Alexander), Harold Vermilyea (Waldo Evans), Ed Begley (James Cotterell), Leif Erickson (Fred Lord), William

Conrad (Morano), John Bromfield (Joe—Detective), Jimmy Hunt (Peter Lord), Dorothy Neumann (Miss Jennings), Paul Fierro (Harpootlian), Kristine Miller (Dolly—Dr. Alexander's Girl Friend), Suzanne Dalbert (Cigarette Girl), George Stern (Drug Store Proprietor), Joyce Compton (Blonde), Tito Vuolo (Albert—Waiter), Garry Owen (Bingo Caller), Holmes Herbert (Wilkins—Butler), Neal Dodd (Minister), Louise Lorimer (Nurse), Yola d'Avril (Marie—Maid), Pepito Perez (Boat Operator), Ashley Cowan (Clam Digger), Igor Dega, Grace Poggi (Dancers), Cliff Clark (Sgt. Duffy)

PLOT: Leona Stevenson is a bedridden, neurotic woman alone on the top floor of her Manhattan townhouse. One night when she tries to phone her husband Henry at work, she overhears in a crossed-line connection two men planning the murder of a woman later that same evening. Her attempts to interest the police are frustrating since they take her story lightly. As she keeps making calls, Leona learns from Sally Lord that Henry was being investigated by Sally's husband Fred, a lawyer. Henry is in fact heavily in debt to a group of gangsters and had hired a man to kill his wife to collect her insurance money and pay his debts. Upon discovering Henry's plot over the phone, Leona frantically attempts to reach out for help, while her husband is waiting for the fateful moment listening on an extension. Henry suddenly realizes the mistake is about to make, but he can only save Leona's life by risking his own. Yet it is too late to stop the paid killer who is already in the house. On his next phone call home Henry implores his wife to go to the window and scream, but Leona is paralyzed by fear. She hangs up the phone just before she is murdered. Henry, who is about to be arrested, calls Leona back. The murderer picks up the phone and, when Henry asks for his wife, responds, "Sorry, wrong number."

REVIEWS:

"[T]his melodrama unfolds with considerable suspense and terror, yet is not more than mildly engrossing because of a plot that is frequently confusing and quite often obscure"—*Harrison's Reports,* July 31, 1948

"As a sheer exercise in melodrama and in cumulative suspense, this film has some highly vivid episodes and a grimly exciting final reel."—*New York Times,* September 2, 1948

"*Sorry, Wrong Number* is the screen version of a radio melodrama that made a pretty good name for itself.... [T]he film is less efficient. Radio scripter Lucille Fletcher has had to fill out her original script, and too much of what she has added is mere stuffing."—*Time,* September 20, 1948

REVIEWS FOR ANATOLE LITVAK:

"Litvak breathes action into monologues and long, narrative passages as he moves a restless camera through the empty apartment. He creates suspense with inanimate objects. Every move, every ring of the telephone, every sound of the city is utilized to keep his story moving steadily toward its shocking conclusion."—*Hollywood Reporter,* July 26, 1948

"Litvak's direction builds carefully constantly heightening the tension to the nerve-wracking finale."—*Variety,* July 28, 1948

"With Anatole Litvak's brilliant direction and taut performances by Barbara Stanwyck, Burt Lancaster and others, the show is calculated to scare the wits out of a spectator.... Litvak [builds] to a staccato and brutal climax."—*Herald Tribune,* September 2, 1948

ADDITIONAL REVIEWS AND ARTICLES:
New York Times May 26, 1946; *The Picturegoer* December 20, 1947; *Motion Picture Herald Product Digest* July 17, 1948; *Film Daily* July 27, 1948; *Motion Picture Herald Product Digest* July 31, 1948; *Box Office* July 31, 1948; *Life* August 23, 1948; *Newsweek* September 6, 1948; *Commonweal* September 10, 1948; *New Yorker* September 11, 1948; *New Republic* September 13, 1948; *Today's Cinema* September 28, 1948; *Cosmopolitan* October 1948; *Good Housekeeping* October 1948; *Photoplay* October 1948; *Woman's Home Company* October 1948; *Hollywood* (Italy) December 24, 1948; *Times* February 7, 1949; *Daily Express* February 4, 1949; *L'Écran Français* February 20, 1950; *Photoplay* May 1982; *Film Criticism* Spring 1986; *Quarterly Review of Film and Video* July 1995

AWARDS AND HONORS:
Academy Awards, 1949; *Nominated*: Best Actress in a Leading Role: Barbara Stanwyck; Writers Guild of America, USA 1949; *Nominated*: Best Written American Drama: Lucille Fletcher; Edgar Allan Poe Awards for Best Motion Picture USA 1949; *Nominated*: Best Written American Drama: Lucille Fletcher

NOTES: *Sorry, Wrong Number* was based on a 22-minute radio play made famous by Agnes Moorehead in 1943. Producer Hal Wallis wanted actor Lee Bowman for the role of Henry Stevenson. In September 1950, Barbara Stanwyck and Burt Lancaster reprised their roles for a *Lux Radio Theatre* broadcast of the play. In November 1954, NBC-TV's *Climax!* series presented a version starring Shelley Winters on the *series*. A 1989 TV remake starred Loni Anderson and Carl Weintraub.

Decision Before Dawn

20th Century–Fox; B&W; 120 minutes; Premiere in New York City December 21, 1951

CREDITS: Producers: Anatole Litvak, Frank McCarthy; *Director*: Anatole Litvak; *Assistant Director:* Gerd Oswald; *Screenplay:* Peter Viertel, *based on the novel* Call It Treason *by* George Howe; *Photography*: Frank Planer; *Art Director*: Ludwig Reiber; *Production Design*: Noël Howard; *Editor:* Dorothy Spencer; *Wardrobe:* Adele Flaig, Morris Harmell, Anton Daneil; *Music:* Franz Waxman; *Sound*: Alfred Bruzlin, Harry M. Leonard; *Technical Advisors:* Capt. Werner T. Michau, Major Robert Eby

CAST: Richard Basehart (Lt. Dick Rennick), Gary Merrill (Col. Devlin), Oskar Werner (Corp. Karl Maurer, also known as Happy), Hildegard Neff (Hilde), Dominique Blanchar (Monique), O.E. Hasse (Oberst von Ecker), Wilfried Seyfert (Heinz Scholtz), Hans Christian Blech (Sgt. Rudolf Barth, also known as Tiger), Helene Thimig (Paula Schneider), Robert Freytag (Sgt. Paul Richter), George Tyne (Sgt. Watkins), and the following members of the United States Armed Forces—European Command: 1st Lt. USAF C.A. Amos, S/Sgt H.L. Benedict USAF (Lt. Pete Gevers), Sgt. H.W. Briggs USA, Cpl. D.G. Devine USAF (Rennicks driver), Maj. L.E. Dixon USA, T/Sgt. B.L. Hendrickson USA, Pvt. D. Kogel USA, Pfc. S.I. Rice USA, Pfc. F. Slaman USA, and Sgt. J.E. Stratton USA, Adolph Lödel (Kurt), Arno Assmann (Corp. Ernst), Loni Heuser (Fritzi Collins), Walter Janssen (Fiedl), Erik Ebert (Freddy), Ruth Brandt (Woman Driver), Liselotte Kirschbaum, Eva Marie Andres (Flak Girls), Rudolph Vogel (Volkssturmmann), Peter Struwel-Bruck (Volkssturmmann), Dr. Charles Jacquemar (Volkssturmmann), Aguste Hansen-Kleinmichel (Newspaper Woman), Martin Urtel (Soldier), Otto Friebel (Clerk), Paul Schwed (German Soldier on Bus), Almuth Bachmann, Ursula Voss

(Streetcar Conductors), Bert Brandt, Clemens Wilemrod, Erik Jelde, Max Herbst, Klaus Krause, Alex Hohenlohe (N.C.O.s), Ruth Trumpp (Woman Attendant), Egon Lippert, Gerhard Kittler (Lieutenants), Rainier Geldern (Panzer N.C.O.), Klaus Kinski (Whining Soldier), Arnulf Schroder (Old Prisoner of War), Jaspar Gertzen, Ulrich Volkmar, Hans Mohrhard, Charles Regnier, Kurt Marquardt (Prisoners of War), Ulla Best, Katja Jobs, Eva Maria Hoppe, Maria Landrock, Lieselotte Steinweg, Elizabeth Millberg, Sonja Kosta (Wehrmacht Girls), Jochen Diestelmann, Luitpold Kummer, Heinrich Berg, Dieter Wilsing (Men in Rathskeller), Elfe Gerhart (Bar Maid), Rudolf Heimann (Truck Driver), Werner Fuetterer (Von Buelow), Ernst Hoechstaetter (Man at Office Reception Desk), Harald Wolff (Hartmann), Wolfgang Kuhnemann (Clerk in Schleissheim), Walter Ladengast (Sergeant Deserter), Gerhard Steinberg (Sgt. Klinger), Peter Luhr (V. Schirmeck), Maria Wimmer (Woman in Street), Til Kiwe (Runner), Heinz Bruening (Piano Player), Meta Weber, Henriette Speidel, Ingeborg Luther, Von Schmiedel, Harald von Troschke-Tronye, Reinhardt Neudörffer, Willy Niklaus, Uli Steigberg, Wolft Petersen, Harald Benesch, Fritz Sellwig, Kai Seefeld, Ralph Romberg, Nils Klott, Johannes Mühlstedt, Cornel von Gossow, Anselm Heyer, Herbert Lehnert, Emil Matoussek, Peter Lombard, Werner J. A. Holzhey, Reinhard Lentz, Jürgen Scheller, Bert Ude, Roland Rösler, Geza Esterhazy

PLOT: The end of the war is near and Allied troops are preparing for the invasion of German soil. Lt. Rennick has been posted to the headquarters of a mysterious Army group which uses German prisoners of war, disillusioned with Hitlerism, to work behind the Nazi lines to bring the war to a quicker end. Col. Devlin combs the P.O.W. camps for volunteers who not only risk being shot by their own countrymen in Germany but being killed by their fellow prisoners of war. Such a volunteer is Tiger, a tough German ex-jailbird who does the job for money, and Happy, an idealistic young medical corporal attached to the Luftwaffe. With them Rennick goes on a mission on which Happy has a separate destination with the object of finding out the disposition of the 1st Panzer Division. All there are thoroughly briefed and given German identity cards, uniforms, and personal effects. Once in Germany, Happy is befriended by Scholtz of the S.S., who finally suspects him. He is warned by Hild, a woman of easy virtue, that Scholtz has set her to spy on him. He manages to leave town the following morning with the headquarters of the 1st Panzer Division as his destination. But Scholtz has circulated his description and Happy knows he is hunted. The van in which he rides with Hilde and other soldiers is stopped by the Panzer Division commander and the soldiers are taken off for emergency replacements. As a medical orderly, Happy is attached for temporary duty to Oberst von Ecker, the commander, who suffers from heart disease. In von Ecker's room he gets a glance at a map showing the disposition of the Panzer Division. During the night von Ecker has a heart attack, Happy gives him an injection which saves his life and as a reward von Ecker grants his request to join his unit the following morning. But the S.S. agent who travelled with him in the van is still waiting. During an Allied air raid, Happy kills his pursuer. With the S.S. after him, Happy gets rid of his identity card and other papers. His only hope now is to find Rennick and Tiger in Munich. Arriving at the address, he finds the house badly bombed and another air raid in progress. When they move on to Tiger's relatives, the boy of the house hears them plotting and warns the S.S. After an exciting chase through the bomb-scarred buildings, the three men reach the river and try to swim for it. Tiger won't follow them; he scrambles up the bank and is shot by Rennick. Rennick and Happy reach an island in the middle of the river where

Happy courageously gives himself up to the Germans so that Rennick can swim to the farther shore with the required information.

REVIEWS:

"The picture itself is a masterpiece of suspense."—*Saturday Review*, December 14, 1951

"True, there's nothing morally elaborate or conclusive about *Decision Before Dawn*. But it packs some impulsive excitement and it plants a seed of understanding in the mind."—*New York Times*, December 22, 1951

"[A] drama that is different, interesting and impressive."—*Harrison's Reports*, December 22, 1951

REVIEWS FOR ANATOLE LITVAK:

"Director Litvak has done an excellent job of establishing the part-grim, part-picturesque atmosphere of Germany's debated cities."—*N.Y. Herald Tribune*, October 22, 1951

"And then there is Anatole Litvak directing scene after scene so as to form a string of dramatic diamonds in sequences.... Litvak's skill in telling a huge personal story within frames brings *Decision Before Dawn* rare dramatic fluency."—*Hollywood Reporter*, December 19, 1951

"[Litvak] has given the picture a strong feeling of reality through a semi-documentary treatment, the use of mostly unknown faces, and by location lensing entirely in Germany.... However, he also has made it a lengthy and methodical presentation of the use of Nazi prisoners of war for behind-the-lines spy work."—*Variety*, December 19, 1951

ADDITIONAL REVIEWS AND ARTICLES:

New York Times December 25, 1949; *Hollywood Reporter* February 28, 1950; *Hollywood Reporter* July 24, 1950; *Variety* August 9, 1950; *Hollywood Reporter* September 18, 1950; *Hollywood Reporter* October 2, 1950; *Hollywood Reporter* October 4, 1950; *Hollywood Reporter* November 2, 1950; *Hollywood Reporter* November 6, 1950; *Variety* November 22, 1950; *Hollywood Reporter* December 4, 1950; *New York Times* December 10, 1950; *Hollywood Reporter* December 15, 1950; *Variety* December 27, 1950; *Hollywood Reporter* March 29, 1951; *Hollywood Reporter* May 7, 1951; *Los Angeles Times* June 17, 1951; *Hollywood Citizen-News* June 25, 1951; *Today's Cinema* August 9, 1951; *Monthly Film Bulletin* September 1951; *Chicago Sunday Tribune* September 30, 1951; *Sight & Sound* October 1951; *Catholic World* November 1951; *Look* November 6, 1951; *The Compass* December 16, 1951; *Life* December 17, 1951; *Hollywood Reporter* December 17, 1951; *Motion Picture Daily* December 19, 1951; *Film Daily* December 19, 1951; *Motion Picture Herald Product Digest* December 22, 1951; *Los Angeles Times* December 22, 1951; *Box Office* December 22, 1951; *New York Times* December 23, 1951; *Time* December 24, 1951; *Saturday Review* December 29, 1951; *Newsweek* December 31, 1951; *Films in Review* January 1952; *Library Journal* January 1, 1952; *New Yorker* January 5, 1952; *Commonweal* January 11, 1952; *New York Times* January 13, 1952; *New Republic* January 14, 1952; *Christian Century* January 30, 1952; *American Cinematographer* February 1, 1952; *New York Times* July 25, 1965

AWARDS AND HONORS:

National Board of Review, USA 1951; Winner: Top Ten Films; Golden Globe, USA 1952; *Nominated*: Best Cinematography Black and White; Academy Awards, USA 1952; *Nominated*: Best Picture Best Editing: Dorothy Spencer; Directors Guild of America, USA 1952; Nominated: Outstanding Directorial Achievement in Motion Picture: Anatole Litvak; Parent's Magazine: USA 1952; Medal Plaque to 20th Century–Fox for *Decision Before Dawn*

NOTES: The working titles were *Legion of the Damned* and *Call It Treason*.

Act of Love

Benagoss Productions; A United Artists Release; B&W; 108 minutes; Released in New York on December 17, 1953

CREDITS: *Producer-Director*: Anatole Litvak; *Associate Producer*: Georges Maurer; *Screenplay*: Irwin Shaw; *Based on the novel* The Girl on the Via Flaminia *by* Alfred Hayes; *Production Managers*: Pierre Laurent, Gordon Griffith; *Photography*: Armand Thirard; *Set Designer*: Alexandre Trauner; *Editors*: William Hornbeck, Leonide Azar; *Sound*: Joseph de Bretagne; *Makeup:* Roger Chanteau; *Music*: Michel Emer, Joe Hajos; *Songs*: Michel Emer; *Assistant Directors*: Michel Boisrond, Serge Vallin

CAST: Kirk Douglas (Robert Teller), Dany Robin (Lise Marie Elisabeth Greifonnet), Barbara Laage (Nina), Gabrielle Dorziat (Adele La Caux), Fernand Ledoux (Fernand La Caux), Robert Strauss Blackwood), Marthe Mercadier (Young woman), George Mathews (Henderson), Richard Benedict (Pete), Leslie Dwyer (English Sergeant), Brigitte Bardot (Mimi), Serge Reggiani (Claude La Caux), Gregoire Aslan (Commissaire), Gilberte Geniat (Ethel Henderson), Jean-Pierre Cassell (Dancer), Sydney Chaplin

PLOT: Although Robert Teller had never before been to Villefranche, a picturesque fishing village on the French Riviera, he knew exactly where the Belle Rive Hotel was situated, and he knew to the smallest detail the room which he wanted: the room where Lisa had once been happy and where, maybe, he would once again find comfort in his loneliness. Teller first meets Lisa in 1944 in Paris where he is engaged on clerical duties with the Allied Liberation Army at a military replacement center. Tense, at odds with his colleagues, utterly frustrated, he logs for something personal and particular in his soldier's world of coarse banter, drinking and fighting. Nina, a casual acquaintance, understands his yearnings and introduces him to Lisa. Lisa is the daughter of respectable country folk from whom she has become separated by the war and, like Robert, she is emotionally and spiritually lost. But she is also hungry and homeless. Desperate, she accepts Robert's offer of food and shelter, although it means sharing his room at the Café des Deux Anges. The proprietors accept them as a married couple. At first, Lisa's sensitivity and shame over the situation expresses itself in anger and tears when she is at last alone with Robert in the intimacy of their room. But Robert understands her distress and gains her grudging respect and faith when he seeks only to comfort her. During their early days together, she makes many attempts to find work but fails because she refuses to become the plaything of unscrupulous men in exchange for a meal ticket. Deciding to sell a gold locket, her only possession of any value, she wanders unknowingly into the black market area and is caught up in a police raid. When she cannot produce proper identity papers, she is warned by the police to get them up to date. She realizes bitterly that this is no easy task since she is living illegally as Mrs. Robert Teller without a marriage certificate or identity card in that name. Slowly, even painfully, Robert and Lisa fall in love with each other, and it is only then that he fully understands what torments she must have suffered when hunger and despair drove her to such lengths to secure shelter and food. Nor does he fully appreciate the depth of his love for her until her second brush with the police: She is again asked to produce correct papers and since she cannot comply, she is arrested and registered by the police. Robert now asserts his love for Lisa and vows to marry her as soon as he obtains permission from his commanding officer Capt. Henderson. But even when Henderson refuses the permit, Robert promises to meet Lisa the next day with the necessary document. Tomorrow comes, and Robert is enraged when he discovers that Henderson is transferring him to Rheims. Robert persuades his closest friend, Blackwoood, to get a blank permit and meet him with it. While racing for his rendezvous with Blackwood, Robert is arrested by military police and taken to a guardhouse. Lisa is waiting at the café. As he clock passes the hour for their meeting, her heart falters. And when she learns from a garbled telephone message from one of Robert's guards that he will not be coming at all, it breaks. She departs, grief-stricken, into the wintry evening... Robert's memories, as he sat on the sunny terrace waiting for Lisa's room to be prepared for him, were interrupted by the arrival of a stranger whom he soon realizes was the wartime officer who refused to issue his marriage permit. Henderson, now a civilian, congratulated himself on saving Robert from a disastrous marriage. "By the way, what happened to the girl?" he asked. "They found her in the river," Robert replied quietly, "a long time ago." And he rose and walked into the hotel and up to the room where he and Lisa were to have started a lifetime of happiness.

REVIEWS:
"*Act of Love* is a powerful, tragic love story highlighted buy a brilliant performance on the part of Kirk Douglas."—*Hollywood Reporter,* December 15, 1953

"[T]here is much about the picture that is interesting, fascinating and impressive, particularly with regard to the character portrayals and the graphic depiction of the sordidness and low moral standards into which people sink under the influences of war."—*Harrison's Reports,* December 19, 1953

"[*Act of Love*] is a fine and strongly moving, but eventually irksome tracing of a plain romance."—*New York Times,* February 12, 1954

REVIEWS FOR ANATOLE LITVAK:
"Anatole Litvak's production is a class job that captures the ribald backgrounds with apparent authenticity but never compromises with good taste."—*Variety,* December 16, 1953

"Here Irwin Shaw's adaptation and Anatole Litvak's direction spread out a biting, sardonic picture of humanity with the jitters, with Paris a small house in which too many guests have been war-bound too long."—*New York Herald Tribune,* December 12, 1954

"The pace of M. Litvak's film is dangerously slow, but he enriches it with many little character sketches, and there is some excellent photography."—*The Times,* April 19, 1954

OTHER REVIEWS AND ARTICLES
Los Angeles Times January 8, 1949; *Daily Variety* July 20, 1949; *Daily Variety* December 6, 1949; *Daily Variety* October 26, 1951; *Daily Variety* February 5, 1952; *Daily Variety* November 5, 1952; *Cinémonde* January 16, 1953; *Hollywood Reporter* January 23, 1953; *New York Times* March 15, 1953; *Hollywood Reporter* May 5, 1953; *Los Angeles Times* May 28, 1953; *Daily Variety* June 10, 1953; *Variety* June 17, 1953; *Herald Tribune* June 20, 1953; *Daily Variety* August 12, 1953; *Film Daily* December 17, 1953; *Motion Picture Herald* December 19, 1953; *Los Angeles Times* December 25, 1953; *Los Angeles Examiner* December 25, 1953; *Films in Review* January 1954; *Box Office* January 2, 1954; *Time* January 4, 1954; *Newsweek* January 4, 1954; *Hollywood Reporter* January 8, 1954; *New York*

Times January 10, 1954; *Catholic World* February 1954; *Hollywood Reporter* February 12, 1954; *Saturday Review* February 13, 1954; *Library Journal*, February 15, 1954; *Daily Variety* February 17, 1954; *New Yorker* February 20, 1954; *New York Times* February 21, 1954; *Commonweal* March 5, 1954; *Farm Journal* March 1954; *National Parent-Teacher* April 1954; *Today's Cinema* April 2, 1954; *Kinematograph Weekly* April 8, 1954; *Monthly Film Bulletin* May 1954; *Picturegoer* May 8, 1954; *Mon Film* April 27, 1955

NOTES: This film's working titles were *The Girl on the Via Flaminia* and *Somewhere in the World*. British actress Jean Simmons and Italian Pier Angeli were both considered as possible leading ladies. The film was shot in both English and French versions sharing cast and crew. French author Joseph Kessel wrote the scenario for the French version, which was released as *Quelque part dans le monde* (other sources list the title as *Un acte d'amour*).

The Deep Blue Sea

20th Century–Fox; London Films; An Anatole Litvak Production; Eastman Color; CinemaScope; 99 minutes; World premiere in London August 25, 1955

CREDITS: *Producers*: Anatole Litvak, Alexander Korda; *Associate Producer:* Hugh Perceval; *Director:* Anatole Litvak; *Assistant Director*: Adrian Pryce-Jones; *Screenplay:* Terence Rattigan, *based on his play; Dialogue Director*: Paul Dickson; *Photography*: Jack Hildyard; *Camera Operator*: Peter Newbrook; *Production Designer*: Vincent Korda; *Assistant Art Directors:* J. Bato, W.E. Hutchinson; *Editor:* A.S. Bates; *Costumes:* Anna Duse; *Vivien Leigh's Dresses*: Pierre Balmain, Paris; *Music:* Malcolm Arnold; *Conductor*: Muir Mathieson; *Sound:* John Cox, Bert Ross, Red Law; *Makeup:* Tony Sforzini, George Frost; *Hairdresser:* Barbara Barnard; *Production Manager:* John Palmer

CAST: Vivien Leigh (Hester Collyer), Kenneth More (Freddie Page), Eric Portman (Miller), Emlyn Williams (Sir William Collyer), Moira Lister (Dawn Maxwell), Arthur Hill (Jackie Jackson), Dandy Nichols (Mrs. Elton), Jimmy Hanley (Dicer Durston), Miriam Karlin (Barmaid), Heather Thatcher (Lady Dawson), Bill Shine (Golfer), Brian Oulton (Drunk), Sidney James (Man in Street), Alec McCowen (Ken Thompson), Gibb McLaughlin (Collyer's Clerk), Brian Worth (First Skier), Peter Williams (Guide), Theodore Wilhelm (Swiss Tourist), Richard Warner (Man in Ski Lift), Frederick Schiller (Swiss Porter), Michael Ritterman (Swiss Conductor), Harold Goodwin, George Woodbridge (Singers in Three Tuns Pub), Deering Wells (Flitton), John Warren (Three Tuns bartender), John Warner (Elegant Young Man), Russell Waters (Mickie—Golf Club Steward), Beatrice Varley (Elderly Woman), Priscilla Morgan (Dot), Helen Misener (Mrs. Abrahams), Mike McKenzie (Nightclub Singer), Auric Lorand (Mr. Mohammed), Harold Kasket (Commissionaire), Gerald Campion (Commissionaire), John Boxer (Usher), Arnold Bell (Air Marshal), Raymond Francis (Chief Test Pilot), Patricia Hayes (Woman Prisoner), Alan Webb (Second Judge), Marjorie Hume (Tea Shop Proprietress)

PLOT: The door of Hester Page's room in a very ordinary London boarding house is locked. Behind that locked door, Hester lies unconscious from gas fumes and an overdose of sleeping tablets. Freddie Page is away for the weekend playing golf and it is an American corporal, Ken Thompson, who asks Mrs. Elton, the landlady, to open the door. He calls Miller, a doctor and psychiatrist, who has been struck off the Medical Register, to give her assistance. Miller revives Hester and it is agreed not to notify the police. Thompson and Dawn Maxwell, a showgirl boarder, find out from Mrs. Elton, who keeps her tenants' secrets well, that the Pages are not married. They learn that Hester is the wife of a distinguished judge, Sir William Collyer, and Dawn telephones Sir William. Sir William arrives to see Hester but she will not allow him to help her. Hester's tragic story is that of her mad infatuation for Freddie Page. A year before she was the rich, admired wife of a famous man. If she were not completely happy, at least she was as content as money and the love of a good man could make a woman. One day Sir William introduces her to Freddie, an ex-R.A.F. pilot with a fine record. Hester recognizes that Freddie is frivolous and unstable, but in spite of this she is attracted by his air of a sulky schoolboy when in trouble: his gaiety and obvious admiration please her. Freddie follows Sir William and Hester to Switzerland where she falls deeply and illogically in love with Freddie. Her love become an obsession and, on their return to London, she finally leaves her husband, home and safety to live with Freddie who, jobless and feckless, finds it quite impossible to respond on the same plane to her overwhelming feeling for him. Freddie and Hester are unhappy together but neither has the strength to break away from the unsatisfactory relationship. Hester feels that she is at fault and her attempt at suicide is made to set Freddie free in what appears to her the only way possible. When Freddie accidentally finds the letter Hester has left for him after the suicide attempt has failed, he realizes that he must get away. He tries and Hester follows him from club to club across London. When Sir William finds her, he takes her to his home to try to persuade her to return to him. Hester refuses and goes back to the boarding house where Miller takes a hand. He explains to Hester that Freddie will never be strong enough to leave her for good. He will always come back, not necessarily because he loves her but because of his inherent weakness. Miller tells her that she is the stronger of the two and that if either is to make any kind of life at all, it is up to her. He is right: Freddie comes back to fetch his luggage, expecting Hester to make another scene and that he will stay. Hester surprises him and herself by finding the strength to send him away.

REVIEWS:

"[T]here is much about this British-made romantic triangle drama that is effective and intriguing, but since the motivations of the characters are curiously foggy the overall result is a dramatic entertainment that is not wholly satisfying."—*Harrison's Reports*, October 1, 1955

"[T]he picture is so handsomely produced in CinemaScope and color and so magnificently played.... Everything is top-drawer in this picture—especially the exquisite Miss Leigh—everything except the penetration of Mr. Rattigan."—*New York Times*, October 13, 1955

"[It] is sensitively acted and beautifully directed and photographed. Nevertheless, the average spectator, even in these days of do it yourself psychiatry, will find it hard to comprehend, and sympathize with, some very murky emotions indeed."—*Films in Review*, November 1955

REVIEWS FOR ANATOLE LITVAK:

"Although the basic plot calls for exceptional use of interiors Litvak has employed his CinemaScope cameras to advantage, introducing fascinating shots of the embankment."—*Variety*, August 31, 1955

"The film has been given top production and direction by Anatole Litvak...."—*Hollywood Reporter*, September 26, 1955

"The choice of Anatole Litvak as director seems curious, as his earlier films have revealed a fondness for swift, journalistic observation and a mobile camera style. There are few opportunities for either in this instance, and the alien theatrical 'pull' of the material has resulted in some uncommonly prosaic handling."—*Monthly Film Bulletin*, October 1955

OTHER REVIEWS AND ARTICLES

Theatre Arts July 1953; *Hollywood Reporter* October 5, 1954; *Daily Variety* October 5, 1954; *Hollywood Reporter* January 7, 1955; *Hollywood Reporter* March 3, 1955; *New York Times* March 13, 1955; *Picture Show* June 11, 1955; *Pix* July 9, 1955; *Today's Cinema* August 24, 1955; *Hollywood Reporter* August 25, 1955; *Motion Picture Herald Product Digest* September 24, 1955; *Hollywood Reporter* September 28, 1955; *Sight & Sound* Autumn 1955; *Box Office* October 1, 1955; *Film Daily* October 6, 1955; *Hollywood Reporter* October 6, 1955; *NY Herald Tribune* October 13, 1955; *America* October 22, 1955; *New York Times* October 23, 1955; *Nation* October 29, 1955; *New Yorker* October 29, 1955; *Time* October 31, 1955; *Catholic World* November 1955; *Commonweal* November 4, 1955; *Film Culture* Winter 1955; *Picturegoer* November 26, 1955; *Nation Parent-Teacher* December 1955; *Los Angeles Times* December 9, 1955; *Los Angeles Examiner* January 9, 1956; *Mon Film* March 7, 1956; *New Republic* November 23, 1956

AWARDS AND HONORS:

Venice Film Festival, Italy 1955; *Winner:* Volpi Cup Best Actor: Kenneth More *Nominated:* Golden Lion, Anatole Litvak; Bafta Film Award, U.K. 1956; *Nominated:* Best British Actor: Kenneth More *Nominated:* Best British Screenplay: Terence Rattigan

NOTES: Marlene Dietrich was considered by producer Alexander Korda for the part of Hester Collyer. A British television version of *The Deep Blue Sea* starring Googie Withers appeared on TV before the film version was produced. A remake directed by Terence Davies and starring Rachel Weisz was released in 2011.

Anastasia

20th Century–Fox; De Luxe Color; CinemaScope; 105 minutes; World premiere in New York on December 13, 1956

CREW: *Producer:* Buddy Adler; *Associate Producer:* Bob Snody; *Director:* Anatole Litvak; *Assistant Director:* Gerry O'Hara; *Screenplay:* Arthur Laurents, *from the play* Anastasia *by* Marcelle Maurette *as adapted by* Guy Bolton; *Dialogue Assistant:* Paul Dickson; *Photography:* Jack Hildyard; *Art Directors:* Andrei Andrejew, Bill Andrews; *Editor:* Bert Bates; *Set Decorator:* Andrew Low; *Costumes:* Renè Hubert; *Music:* Alfred Newman; *Russian Music Arrangements:* Michel Michelet; *Sound:* Gerry Turner, Harry M. Leonard, Ralph Hickey, Jim Leppert, Eddie Rossi; *Makeup:* Dave Aylott; *Hairdresser:* Johnnie Johnson

CAST: Ingrid Bergman (Anastasia aka Anna Koreff/Anna Anderson), Yul Brynner (Gen. Sergei Pavlovich Bounine), Helen Hayes (Dowager Empress Maria Feodorovna), Akim Tamiroff (Boris Adreivich Chernov), Martita Hunt (Baroness Elena von Livenbaum), Felix Aylmer (Russian Chamberlain), Sacha Pitoeff (Piotr Ivanovich Petrovin), Ivan Desny (Prince Paul von Haraldberg), Natalie Shafer (Irina Lissemskaia), Gregoire Gromoff (Stepan), Karel Stepanek (Viados), Ina de la Haye (Marusia), Katherine Kath (Maxime), Hy Hazell (Blonde Lady), Olga Valery (Countess Baranova), Tamara Shayne (Xenia), Peter Sallis (Grischa), Polycarpe Pavlov (Schischkin), Olaf Pooley (Zhadanov), Andre Mickhelson (Older Man), Eric Pohlman (Von Drivnitz), Alexis Bobrinskoy (Bechmetieff), Edward Forsyth (Footman), Stanley Zevick (Empress' Cossack), Tutte

Lemkow, Anatole Smirnoff (Kasbek Dancers), Alan Cuthbertson (Blonde Man), Henry Vidon (Prince Bolkonoski), Norah Nicholson, Natalie Tchermoeff (Ladies-in-Waiting), Gerik Schjelderup (Train Official), Frederick Schiller (Second Taxi Driver), Paula Catton (Jean), Marguerite Brennan (Marguerite), John Dunbar (Hotel Clerk)

PLOT: Paris 1928: A group of exiled White Russians, led by Gen. Bounine, claim to have found Anastasia, the youngest daughter of the Czar; it had been presumed that she had died with the rest of her Imperial family but rumor has it that she escaped the assassination. Bounine proposes the Russian Royalists in Paris should float a limited company to aid Anastasia's claim to the £10,000,000 inheritance deposited by the czar in the Bank of England. The claimant—a destitute amnesiac—is schooled by Bounine in royal history and deportment; and so thoroughly absorbs Anastasia's identity that she convinces member of the old Russian court that she is the grand duchess. Bounine arranges a meeting in Paris with Prince Paul, Anastasia's cousin, who at once accepts and falls in love with the claimant. The aged Dowager Empress Maria Feodorovna—Anastasia's grandmother—at first refuses to see Bounine and his protégée; but they eventually meet, and the empress accepts the girl's claim. On the eve of the engagement to Prince Paul, Anastasia admits to the Empress that it is really Bounine she loves, and the Empress advises to follow her heart. When the time for the presentation ceremony arrives, neither Bounine nor Anastasia can be found.

REVIEWS:
"Tender, cruel, passionate and tantalizing, Buddy Adler's *Anastasia* has all the shimmering majesty of imperial Russia in an original and unusual love story that is yet so basic that it will reach out to everyone."—*Hollywood Reporter,* December 14, 1956

"It's a tedious movie, Arthur Laurents' script is banal and Litvak has directed it at a sluggish pace. The picture never rises to any peak of excitement, even in the famous 'recognition scene,' and it ebbs away into an ending that is hardly worthy of daytime radio."—*New York Herald Tribune,* December 14, 1956

"*Anastasia* is basically a costume romance designed for the popular box-office; that it frequently soars above that level is due to the fine acting by the principals and the smooth (sometimes a little too slick) direction of Anatole Litvak."—*Films & Filming,* March 1957

REVIEWS FOR ANATOLE LITVAK:
"Anatole Litvak has smartly staged it for a fine projection of its human ironies.... [He] is no stranger to the emotional torments of fading royalty. It was his memorable French film *Mayerling,* the poignant drama of Marie Vetsera [sic] and her Habsburg prince, that set the mark for royal romance in the movies and brought Mr. Litvak to Hollywood."—*New York Times,* December 14, 1956

"[The film was made] under the sensitive and imaginative direction of Anatole Litvak here also doing his best work in years.... Litvak has wisely concentrated on Miss Bergman and he knows how to balance his picture to keep it from becoming over-dramatic."—*Variety,* December 19, 1956

"Anatole Litvak's direction—here more satisfactorily employed than in *The Deep Blue Sea*-retains the theatrical emphasis of the original to distinct advantage."—*Monthly Film Bulletin,* February 1957

OTHER REVIEWS AND ARTICLES
Daily Variety September 10, 1953; *Hollywood Reporter* January 9, 1956; *Daily Variety* 15 January 1956; *Theatre Arts* May 1956; *Hollywood Reporter* June 1, 1956; *Hollywood*

168   FILMOGRAPHY (AS DIRECTOR)

Reporter July 11, 1956; *Hollywood Reporter* July 18, 1956; *Hollywood Reporter* July 24, 1956; *Hollywood Reporter* July 31, 1956; *New York Times* August 5, 1956; *Hollywood Reporter* August 15, 1956; *Paris Match* August 18, 1956; *New York Times* August 30, 1956; *New York Times Magazine* September 9, 1956; *Hollywood Reporter* September 14, 1956; *American Cinematographer* November 1956; *Hollywood Reporter* November 9, 1956; *Life* November 26, 1956; *Coronet* December 1956; *Saturday Review* December 8, 1956; *Newsweek* December 10, 1956; *Hollywood Reporter* December 13, 1956; *New York Times* December 13, 1956; *Film Daily* December 14, 1956; *Motion Picture Herald Product Digest* December 15, 1956; *Time* December 17, 1956; *New Yorker* December 22, 1956; *Box Office* December 29, 1956; *America* December 29, 1956; *Library Journal* January 1, 1957; *Kinematograph Weekly* January 17, 1957; *Films in Review* January 1957; *Today's Cinema* January 11, 1957; *Daily Film Renter* January 11, 1957; *Commonweal* January 11, 1957; *Catholic World* February 1957; *New Republic* February 4, 1957; *Sight & Sound* Spring 1957; *Positif* March 1957; *Sipario* April 1957; *Image et Son* April 1957; *Mon Film* May 1, 1957; *Cinéma* May 1957; *La Rivista del Cinematografo* April 1957; *Image et Son* January 1958; *Variety* January 6, 1960; *New York Times* April 29, 1972; *Films in Review* April 1980

AWARDS AND HONORS:
National Board of Review, USA 1956; *Winner:* Top Ten Films; *Winner*: Best Actor: Yul Brynner; New York Film Critics Circle Awards, USA 1956; Winner: Best Actress: Ingrid Bergman; 2nd place Best Actor: Yul Brynner; Golden Globe, USA 1957; *Nominated*: Best Motion Picture Actress—Drama: Helen Hayes; *Winner*: Best Motion Picture Actress—Drama: Ingrid Bergman; Academy Awards, USA 1957; *Winner*: Best Actress in a Leading Role: Ingrid Bergman; *Nominated*: Best Music, Scoring of a Dramatic or Comedy Picture: Alfred Newman; David di Donatello Awards, Italy 1957; *Winner:* Best Actress: Ingrid Bergman; Golden Ribbon Award, U.K. 1957; Best Musical soundtrack

NOTES: *Anastasia* cost $3,500,000 to produce.

The Journey

Metro-Goldwyn-Mayer Alby Production; Metrocolor; 126 minutes; Released in New York on February 19, 1959

CREW: *Producer-Director*: Anatole Litvak; *Assistant Producer:* Carl Szokoll; *Assistant Director*: Gerald O'Hara; *Second Unit Director*: Noel Howard; *Screenplay*: George Tabori, *loosely based on the short story "Boule de Suif" by* Guy de Maupassant; *Additional Writer:* Peter Viertel; *Photography*: Jack Hildyard, John Kotze; *Camera Operator*: Gerald Fisher; *Still Photographer*: Hermann Meroth; *Art Director*s: Werner Schlighting, Isabella Schlighting; *Editor:* Dorothy Spencer; *Costumes*: Rene Hubert*; Music*: Georges Auric; *Music Advisor and Incidental Music*: Michel Michelet; *Sound:* Kurt Schwarz, John Cox; *Makeup:* David Aylott, Eric Allwright; *Hair Styles*: Gordon Bond; *Technical Advisors*: Moura Budberg, George Daniloff, Tibor Zimanyi

CAST: Deborah Kerr (Lady Diana Ashmore), Yul Brynner (Major Surov), And introducing Jason Robards, Jr. (Paul Kedes aka Henry Flemming), Robert Morley (Hugh Deverill), E.G. Marshall (Harold Rhinelander), Anne Jackson (Margie Rhinelander), Ronny Howard (Billy Rhinelander), Flip Mark (Flip Rhinelander), Kurt Kasznar (Csepege), David Kossoff (Simon Avron), Gérard Oury (Teklel Hafouli), Marie Daems (Françoise Hafouli), Anouk Aimée (Eva), Barbara von Nady (Borbala), Maurice Sarfati

(Jacques Fabbry), Siegfried Schürenberg (Von Rachlitz), Maria Urban (Gisela von Rachlitz), Jerry Fujikawa (Mitzu), Erica Vaal (Donatella Calucci), Dimitry Fedotoff (Lt. Tulpin), Leonid Pylajew (Capt. Dembinski), Wolf Neuber (Patko), Michael Szekely (Bowler Hat), Charles Regnier (Capt. Ornikidze), Ivan Petrovich (Szabó Bácsi), Ernst Konstantin (Major Ilyashev), Senta Berger (Serving Girl in Black Scarf), Michael Janish (Russian Officer), Fred Roby (Rosso)

PLOT: A group of travellers is stranded in Budapest early in November 1956, at the very end of the unsuccessful Hungarian revolt. They are all passengers on a flight to Vienna, one of the last planes leaving the strife-torn Hungarian capital. Their ultimate destinations are as varied as their nationalities. There is a Japanese businessman bound for Amsterdam, an American oil engineer and his family returning home after years spent in the Middle East, a Swiss student, a TV correspondent, and others—14 passengers in all. Outstanding among them is Lady Diana Ashmore, a beautiful Englishwoman who seems to be travelling in the company of a mysterious gentleman named Flemming. Flemming is the holder of a British passport, but his true nationality and identity is almost immediately in doubt. The Soviet Air Force takes over the airfield, forcing the civilian passengers to take a bus chartered by the airline and start from Vienna by road. Worried and frightened, they began their journey through the revolt-ravaged countryside. However, soon all of their attentions and suspicions are focused on Lady Ashmore and Flemming. The English lady and the gentleman are obviously connected by more than a casual bond, and as the story progresses, the other members of the party begin to sense that if the truth were known about these two, it might well jeopardize the safety of the whole party. As the bus approaches the frontier and freedom, it is stopped outside a small town by a Russian roadblock and confronted by the commander of the Red Army tank patrolling the area. Major Surov informs them that their travel permit is not in order and that they will have to wait at a local inn for their clearances. He warns them that this may take a day or two. In growing uneasiness, the travellers settle down at the Hotel Red Star. Major Surov is a handsome and intelligent man, torn by inner contradictions which the Hungarian revolt and his country's intervention have accentuated. He is driven by an overwhelming need to find out the truth, and in this atmosphere of rumors, lies and chaos, it is the enemy's truth that he craves. It soon becomes evident that the main reason for delaying the travellers is not official business, but his own burning curiosity. This duel between captors and captives climaxes with the discovery that Flemming is in fact a Hungarian travelling with false papers and trying with the help of Lady Ashmore to escape the consequences of his part in the revolt. Some of the passengers feel that Flemming's presence is highly compromising. Furthermore, they realize that the situation is further complicated by the attraction that has developed between the Russian and Lady Ashmore. Some are sympathetic to Flemming; others would prefer to turn the fugitive over to the Russians and thus ensure their own safety. A drama explodes when Flemming and Lady Ashmore make an attempt to escape across a lake into Austria. They are betrayed and caught. Although Flemming's true identity has not been exposed, Surov is still unwilling, for reasons of his own, to call in his superiors. He is caught in a dilemma of duty versus conscience. But it is only after a virulent outbreak and a clash with Lady Ashmore that he finds a solution. Before he does, he exposes everything, his doubts as well as his hidden desires. Despite sharing a passionate kiss with Surov, Lady Ashmore departs. Early the next morning, the group, minus Flemming, returns to the bus. A few miles away, as the relieved passengers disembark at a small bridge leading to

Austria, Surov drives up in a Jeep with Flemming. Lady Ashmore rushes to thank Surov, but he assures her that he has acted only to clear his conscience. Moments after Lady Ashmore and Flemming are welcomed to Austria by the border guards, shots ring out as Surov is killed by a freedom fighter.

REVIEWS:

"*The Journey* has promising box-office potential due to the fact that it co-stars Deborah Kerr and Yul Brynner in a romantic melodrama shot on picturesque locations in Austria."—*Hollywood Reporter,* February 2, 1959

"*The Journey* is a powerful and provocative film.... Tabori's screen play is an honest work, and his insight into his various nationalities is especially perceptive."—*Variety,* February 4, 1959

"*The Journey* is in some ways a good picture, even very good, though it ends on an artificial note."—*New York Herald Tribune,* February 20, 1959

REVIEWS FOR ANATOLE LITVAK:

"As producer as well as director, [Litvak] has made his picture near Vienna so he could get the general look of the country and the quality of authentic types. And he has used these to build a strong foundation of pictorial atmosphere and a tangible feeling of the violent ferment that was in Hungary in 1956."—*New York Times,* February 20, 1959

"Litvak directs with an inventive freshness that brings the best from his artists. There are several fine moments."—*Films & Filming,* March 1959

"Anatole Litvak's direction is quite anonymous, and several scenes ... are unintentionally comic."—*Monthly Film Bulletin,* May 1959

ADDITIONAL REVIEWS AND ARTICLES:

Hollywood Reporter January 10, 1957; *Hollywood Reporter* February 27, 1957; *Los Angeles Times* February 27, 1957; *Los Angeles Times* April 9, 1957; *Los Angeles Times* August 14, 1957; *Hollywood Reporter* February 24, 1958; *Hollywood Reporter* March 14, 1958; *Daily Variety* March 19, 1958; *Newsweek* May 19, 1958; *Hollywood Reporter* June 27, 1958; *Daily Variety* April 14, 1958; *Morning Telegraph* June 4, 1958; *New York Journal-American* July 3, 1958; *Sunday News* August 10, 1958; *Census-Journal* January 15, 1959; *Saturday Review* January 17, 1959; *New Republic* January 19, 1959; *The Saturday Evening Post* January 21, 1959; *Catholic World* February 1959; *Film Daily* February 2, 1959; *Motion Picture Herald* February 7, 1959; *Box Office* February 9, 1959; *Time* February 9, 1959; *Commonweal* February 13, 1959; *Variety* February 18, 1959; *Los Angeles Times* February 19, 1959; *Daily News* February 20, 1959; *Cue* February 21, 1959; *New York Herald Tribune* February 22, 1959; *Newsweek* February 23, 1959; *New Yorker* February 28, 1959; *ABC Film Review* March 1959; *Films in Review* March 1959; *New York Times* March 1, 1959; *America* March 14, 1959; *The Daily Cinema* March 18, 1959; *Reporter* March 19, 1959; *Nation* March 28, 1959; *Filmkritik* May 1959; *ABC Film Review* July 1959; *Image et Son* December 1959

NOTES: First Anna Magnani and later Ingrid Bergman were slated to play *The Journey*'s leading role. *The Journey* marked the screen debut of Jason Robards, Jr.

Goodbye Again

(*Aimez-vous Brahms?*)

Argus Productions; Mercury Productions; An Anatole Litvak Production; United Artists; B&W; 120 minutes; Released in New York June 29, 1961

Filmography (As Director)

CREDITS: *Producer-Director:* Anatole Litvak; *Second Unit Director:* André Smagghe; *Assistant Director:* Paul Feyder; *Screenplay:* Samuel Taylor; *Based on the novel* Aimez-Vous Brahms? *by* Françoise Sagan; *Script Supervisor:* Lucy Lichtig; *Music:* George Auric; *Lyrics:* Dory Langdon; *Music Editor:* Leon Birnbaum; *Photography:* Armand Thirard; *Operators:* Louis Nee, Robert Florent; *Art Directors:* Alexandre Trauner, A. Capelier; *Editor:* Bert Bates; *Gowns:* Christian Dior; *Sound:* Jacques Carrère; *Makeup:* John O'Gorman, Georges Bouban; *Hair Styles:* Joan Johnstone, Marc Blanchard; *Set Dressing:* Maurice Barnathan; *Production Manager:* Julien Derode

CAST: Ingrid Bergman (Paula Tessier), Yves Montand (Roger Demarest), Anthony Perkins (Philip Van der Besh), Jessie Royce Landis (Mrs. Van der Besh), Jackie Lane (Maisie I), Pierre Dux (Maitre Fleury), Jean Clarke (Maisie II), Peter Bull (Client), Michèle Mercier (Maisie III), Uta Taeger (Gaby), André Randall (Monsieur Steiner), David Horne (Queen's Counsel), Lee Patrick (Madame Fleury), Colin Mann (Assistant Lawyer), Diahann Carroll (Nightclub Singer), Annie Duperoux (Madeline Fleury), Raymond Gérôme (Jimmy), Jean Hebey (Monsieur Cherel), Michel Garland (Young Man in Nightclub), Paul Uny (Waiter), Alison Leggatt

PLOT: Paula Tessier, a Paris interior decorator, closes her shop earlier than usual one evening and rushes home. It is the fifth anniversary of her meeting with Roger Demarest. She asks her maid Gaby to draw her bath. Roger phones; not only is he unaware of tonight's occasion, but he cancels their date pleading a sudden, important "business appointment." On their next date, Roger is apologetic, friendly, attentive. But he says good night at the downstairs door. Before leaving, however, he tells her that he has recommended her as a decorator to a rich American woman, Mrs. Van der Besh. Late the next morning, Paula calls on her rich client and is greeted by her son Philip. When Paula comes outside after a brief meeting with Mrs. Van der Besh, Philip is waiting for her. He rattles on about his mother and her eccentricities. She asks his age and he tells her 25. Then he counters by asking her age. Somehow startled, she blurts out the truth: She's 40. At a Paris law office where Philip is tolerated as an apprentice because his mother is one of the wealthiest clients, Philip confides in one of the secretaries that he is in love. He doesn't know anything about Paula—not even her name. That evening, Paula and Roger are at a nightclub, when Philip turns up at their table, very drunk. His uninhibited admiration for Paula annoys Roger, but Paula is not displeased. Philip passes out, and she and Roger take the young man home. Her tenderness for Philip arouses anger in Roger. That night, for the first time in a long time, when he takes Paula home, he invites himself in for a drink. The next day, Philip turns up at Paula's shop to apologize for the previous evening and talks her into having lunch with him. Somehow he manages to get the conversation around to "her husband"—and learns that Paula doesn't have a husband. Philip pursues her all around Paris. When Roger breaks a weekend date with Paula—pleading business, but actually going off with a sexy young starlet—Philip persuades her to go to a Brahms concert with him. Philip openly declares his love for her and Paula finds herself more upset by the effect he is having on her. She rushes away during the intermission and goes home. Shortly afterwards, Roger turns up at her apartment—his interlude with the starlet over, for the moment. He finds Paula in a state of distress. She tells him about Philip and tries to explain her growing confusion and panic. She's in love with a man who says he loves her, but who is around less and less. It's getting to the point where she doesn't know what to believe about herself and Roger. Roger tries to convince her that he really does love her. He almost succeeds. Then an inadvertent slip betrays the fact that he lied about the weekend. Despite Paula's resistance, Philip keeps declaring his love for her at every opportunity. After Rogers becomes angry, she rushes out to the Orly airport to intercept him before his departure on an authentic business trip. Frightened by her feelings for Philip, she begs Roger to take her along with him, but he can't. She returns to Paris and tries to avoid Philip's calls, but after seeing him standing in the rain wet and coatless, she falls into his arms and takes him to her home. Roger returns from his business trip genuinely anxious to see Paula. When he hears she is having an affair with Philip, he reacts with harshness. Paula, rejected by the man she loves, goes back to the youth who loves her. While Roger tries to forget Paula with different women, she tries to believe that Philip will succeed in helping her to forget Roger, but it simply doesn't work. One day, after an inadvertent meeting at a nightclub, Roger visits Paula at her shop. He blurts out that he loves her and cannot live without her. Paula falls happily into his arms. That evening she breaks the news to Philip. Overwrought and inconsolable, he rushes out of her apartment and out of her life. Not long afterwards, Roger and Paula are married. One night while dressing for a date with Roger, he calls and pleads an unexpected and important "business engagement." Paula nods and hangs up.

REVIEWS:
"Subtly and sensitively acted, *Goodbye Again* is a wry, worldly-wise look at life—sex life, that is—as sketched by Sagan and urbanely expanded by a knowing director."—*Hollywood Reporter,* June 30, 1961

"Altogether, the picture suffers from anemia of story that no amount of emotional acting on the part of Miss Bergman or soothing speech from Montand can cure."—*New York Herald Tribune,* June 30, 1961

REVIEWS FOR ANATOLE LITVAK:
"Mr. Litvak's direction, while attentive to the matter of rapidly changing moods and the electrifying atmosphere of Paris, has no distinctive and agitating style. In several important places, it permits tenuous action to sag."—*New York Times,* June 30, 1961

"High style ... is the keynote to Litvak's meticulous, handsomely photographed production made entirely in Paris."—*Variety,* July 5, 1961

"The trouble with the film is that Mr. Litvak's direction is altogether too smooth and predictable."—*The Times* August 21, 1961

ADDITIONAL REVIEWS AND ARTICLES:
New York Post September 11, 1960; *Los Angeles Times* September 23, 1960; *Woman's Day* February 1961; *Il Giornale d'Italia* March 28, 1961; *New York Post,* April 9, 1961; *Cinéma* June 1961; *Theatre Arts* June 1961; *Movie Spotlight* June 7, 1961; *La Cinématographie Française* June 10, 1961; *Le Film Français* June 23, 1961; *New York Post,* June 30, 1961; *The Film Daily* June 30, 1961; *Motion Picture Herald* July 1, 1961; *Harrison's Reports* July 8, 1961; *The Daily Cinema* August 4, 1961; *Kine Weekly* August 3, 1961; *Monthly Film Bulletin* September 1961; *Films and Filming* September 1961; *Image et Son* December 1961; *Il Paese* October 26, 1961; *Cinémonde* November 26, 1963; *Newark Evening News* September 4, 1964

AWARDS AND HONORS:
XIV Cannes Film Festival, France 1961 *Winner*: Palme d'Or, Best Actor: Anthony Perkins; *Nominated*: Palme d'Or, Best Director: Anatole Litvak; David di Donatello Awards, Italy 1962 *Winner*: Best Foreign Actor: Anthony Perkins; Grosse Otto Award, Germany 1962; *Winner*: Best International Actor: Anthony Perkins; Grand Prix, Bel-

gium 1962 *Winner*: Best International Actor: Anthony Perkins; Victoire du Cinéma Français, France 1963 *Winner*: Best Actor: Anthony Perkins

NOTES: *Goodbye Again* opened in Paris in May 1961 after having been shown at the 14th Cannes Film Festival.

Five Miles to Midnight

(*Le couteau dans la plaie* aka *La troisième dimension*)

Mercury Productions; An Anatole Litvak Production; Dear Film; United Artists; B&W; 110 minutes; Released in Paris on December 12, 1962

CREW: *Producer-Director*: Anatole Litvak; *Associate Producer*: André Smagghe; *Assistant Director*: Paul Feyder; *Screenplay*: Peter Viertel, Hugh Wheeler; *Dialogue*: Maurice Druon; *Adaptation*: Peter Viertel; *Original Idea*: André Versini; *Script Supervisor*: Alice Ziller; *Photography:* Henri Alekan; *Camera*: André Domage; *Art Directors*: Alexandre Trauner, A. Capelier; *Set Dressing:* Maurice Barnathan; *Editors*: Bert Bates, Ginou Dodard; *Costumes:* Guy Laroche; *Costume Supervisor:* Sophie Litvak; *Music*: Mikis Theodorakis; *Additional Music*: Jacques Loussier; *Sound:* Jacques Carrère, Edward Mason; *Production Manager*: Louis Wipf, *Makeup:* Jill Carpenter, Giuseppe Annunziata; *Hair Styles*: Maria Angelini, Marc Blanchard

CAST: Sophia Loren (Lisa Macklin), Anthony Perkins (Robert Macklin), Gig Young (David Barnes), Jean-Pierre Aumont (Alan Stewart), Yolande Turner (Barbara Ford), Thomas Norden (Johnny), Mathilde Casadesus (Madame Duval, the Concierge), Billy Kearns (Capt. Wade), Barbara Nicot (Mrs Wade), Louis Falavigna (Pharmacist), Elina Labourdette (Madame Lafont), Régine (Régine), Pascale Roberts (Streetwalker), Sophie Réal (Housemaid), Jean Ozenne (Monsieur Bagasse), Clément Harari (Monsieur Schmidt), Nicolas Vogel (Eric Ostrum), Giselle Preville (Mrs. Harrington), Jean Hebey (Nikandros), Yves Brainville (Monsieur Dompier), Guy Laroche (Guy Laroche), Albert Rémy (Inspector), Nina Grégoire (Shop Clerk), Ghislane (Fashion Model), R.K. Cunningham (Vice-Cousul), Jacques Marin, Jacqueline Porel

PLOT: The marriage of Lisa Macklin, a lovely Italian girl, and Robert, an American, has come to an unhappy impasse. Ill-tempered and immature, Robert finds his wife dancing the twist in a nightclub, slaps her face and walks out on her. Later that evening he tries to shrug off the incident, but she refuses to accept his apology. The following day when he has to fly from Paris—where they are living—to Casablanca on business, she accompanies him to the airport and there tells him that she does not want to see him again. Lisa is with newspaper correspondent Alan Stewart that evening when she learns that her husband's plane crashed with all aboard presumed dead. Lisa is filled with remorse and grief. After the funeral, her friend Barbara puts her to bed with a sedative. In the darkness of the early morning, Lisa wakes alone in the apartment to see the door open and Robert enter. He is dirty, hurt and in pain. He tells Lisa that he had been seated beside the escape hatch and thrown clear. As Lisa bandages his wounds, he tells her of his plan to collect the $120,000 insurance he had taken out just before takeoff. Lisa will be his accessory, collecting the money. Lisa wants to turn to Alan for advice, but he has been called back to America. His apartment is now occupied by correspondent David Barnes, who makes a play for her and is rebuffed. Mixing cajolery and charm, Robert persuades Lisa to go along with his scheme, hinting that once he has the money, she will be rid of him. She inquires at the insurance company and learns that collecting the money will not be difficult, although there are a number of formalities including signing an affidavit that her husband is dead. Hiding out in their apartment, Robert is seen through a window by a boy, Johnny. When Johnny gets into the Macklin apartment, Robert must make friends with him. Robert scares Johnny and the boy almost falls the roof. Meanwhile, Lisa and Barnes are falling in love. Barnes begins to suspect that Robert is alive. The police question Lisa about a raincoat which they believe may have been Robert's, found near the wreckage. At last Lisa collects the check from the insurance company and cashes it. Then she meets Robert. As they drive to the Belgian border in their car, he tells her that she must stay with him always or he will turn her over to the police for insurance fraud. Desperate, she tricks him into getting out of the car and then runs him down. Shattered and driven out of her mind by the experience, she returns to Barnes, who telephones the authorities.

REVIEWS:

"*Five Miles to Midnight* is a psychological crime melodrama, ambitious in its design to give depth and stature to a sordid story, but unsuccessful on several accounts."—*Hollywood Reporter,* February 20, 1963

"It's all a bit fraudulent and tedious."—*New York Times,* March 21, 1963

"It is the immediate descendant of the slick, cynical French thrillers which occupy a permanent place on Gallic movie production schedules, and, until it grinds down to a clanking mock tragedy in the last reel, it is a well-ordered exercise in mechanical suspense."—*Show,* April 1963

REVIEWS FOR ANATOLE LITVAK:

"Litvak handles the tale in a pro manner but his direction cannot gloss over the lack of true character portrayal or the contrived scripting. It is technically good."—*Variety,* January 16, 1963

"Anatole Litvak, maker of films standing somewhere between serious but difficult artistic attempts and the big commercial entertainments, has here applied all of his technical know-how."—*New York Post,* March 21, 1963

"Litvak tangles the skein of fate with finesse."—*Time,* March 12, 1963

ADDITIONAL REVIEWS AND ARTICLES:

New York Times February 25, 1962; *Los Angeles Times* March 11, 1962; *New York Post* March 11, 1962; *La Production Cinématographique Française* April 1962; *Cinémonde* December 4, 1962; *Filmkritik* January 1963; *La Cinématographie Française* January 5, 1963; *Film-Echo/Filmwoche* January 5, 1963; *Le Film Français* 18 January 1963; *Evening Standard* April 11, 1963; *Sunday Express* April 14, 1963; *Films in Review* February 1963; *Image et Son* February 1963; *The Film Daily* February 21, 1963; *Commonweal* March 1, 1963; *Motion Picture Herald* March 6, 1963; *Newsweek* March 11, 1963; *Sunday Review* March 16, 1963; *The Daily Cinema* April 10, 1963; *Kine Weekly* April 11, 1963; *Time* April 12, 1963; *America* April 20, 1963; *Monthly Film Bulletin* May 1963; *Film & Filming* June 1963; *Image et Son* December 1963; *Film Dope* September 1986; *Télérama* August 14, 1996

NOTES: The original title was *All the Gold in the World*. It was later changed to *The Third Dimension*, then *The Fourth Dimension* and finally *Five Miles to Midnight*. Jeanne Moreau was originally announced for the part of Lisa Macklin.

The Night of the Generals

Columbia Pictures; Horizon Pictures; Filmsonor S. A.; Technicolor; 148 minutes; World Premiere in London on January 29, 1967

Filmography (As Director) 175

CREDITS: *Producer*s Sam Spiegel, Anatole Litvak; *Director:* Anatole Litvak; *Screenplay*: Joseph Kessel, Paul Dehn; *Based on the novel* The Wary Transgressor *by* James Hadley Chase *and the Novel* Die Nacht der Generale *by* Hans Hellmut Kirst; *Photography:* Henri Decaë; *Camera Operator*: Charles-Henry Montel; *Production Designer:* Alexander Trauner; *Art Director*: Auguste Capelier; *Editors:* Alan Osbiston, Willy Kemplen, Ginou Billo; *Set Dresser*: Maurice Barnathan; *Costumers:* Rosine Delamare, J. Claude Philippe, Jean Zay; *Music Composer and Conductor:* Maurice Jarre; *Sound Recorders*: William Sivel, Jacques Carrère; *Dubbing Editor*: Ted Mason; *Music Cutter*: Dominique Amy; *Hair Styles*: Marc Blanchard, A. G. Scott; *Production Manager*: Louis Wipf; *Unit Manager*: Lucien Lippens; *Continuity:* Alice Ziller; *Polish Location Assistant:* Zjednoczone Zespoly; *Casting*: Maude Spector, Margot Capelier; *Title Sequences Design:* Robert Brownjohn

CAST: Peter O'Toole (Gen. Tanz), Omar Sharif (Major Grau), Tom Courtenay (Corporal Hartmann), Donald Pleasence (Gen. Kahlenberge), Joanna Pettet (Ulrike von Seidlitz-Gabler), Philippe Noiret (Inspector Morand), Charles Gray (Gen. von Seidlitz-Gabler), Coral Browne (Eleanore von Seidlitz-Gabler), John Gregson (Colonel Sandauer), Nigel Stock (Otto), Christopher Plummer (Field Marshal Rommel), Juliette Gréco (Juliette), Yves Brainville (Liesowski), Sacha Pitoëff (Doctor), Charles Millot (Wionczek), Raymond Gérôme (Colonel in War Room), Véronique Vendell (Monique), Pierre Mondy (Kopatski), Eléonore Hirt (Melanie), Nicole Courcel (Raymonde), Jenny Orléans (Otto's Wife), Gérard Buhr (Von Stauffenberg), Michael Goodliffe (Hauser), Gordon Jackson (Capt. Engel), Patrick Allen (Colonel Mannheim), Harry Andrews (Stupnagel), Bogusz Bilewski, Janusz Bukowski (German Soldiers), Jackie Blanchot, Paul Pavel (Hamburg Suspects), Guy Bonnafoux (German Officer at Hitler's Headquarters), Philippe Castelli (French Forensic Physician), Adrien Cayla-Legrand, Donald O'Brien, Claude Salez, François Valorbe, Nicolas Vogel (Plotting German Officers), Jacques Chevalier (Barman at Paradis Bar), Georges Claisse (Rommel's Orderly), Henri Coutet (Café Waiter), Damian Damiecki, Stefan Friedmann (Polish Partisans), Maciej Damiecki (Fugitive Prisoner), Valentine Dyall (Voice of German Radio Announcer), Robert Favart (Airport Employee), Martine Ferrière (The Polish Woman), Wolf Frees (German Officer at Raymonde's Apartment), Jan Kociniak (Gen. Tanz's Orderly), Roger Lumont (Wine Butler), Gaston Meunier (Man at the 25th Anniversary), Hans Meyer (Wehrmacht Adjutant), Józef Nalberczak (Polish Policeman), Jean Ozenn (Gen. Dietrich), Raymond Pierson (German Officer), Maciej Rayzacher (Fidgeting Prisoner), Mac Ronay (Tanz's Driver), Jacques Seiler (Maître d'hôtel), Mieczyslaw Stoor (German Reporter of "Wochenschau"), Sabine Sun (Hamburg Prostitute), Maurice Teynac (A General), Pierre Tornade (Orderly), César Torres (Spanish Laborer), Hans Verner (German Officer), Howard Vernon (Suspect in Erica Muller's Murder), Andrzej Zaorski (German Radiotelegraphist),

PLOT: In the winter of 1942, German-occupied Warsaw lies partially devastated; the buildings not bombed to rubble are being systematically blown up to flush out the remaining Polish snipers and partisans. The mutilated body of a prostitute is discovered in a seedy tenement. In a time of war the crime would normally attract little attention, but in this case is singular, both for its bestiality and the fact that all evidence points to the murderer being one of three German generals: von Seidlitz-Gabler, a wife-dominated stuffed shirt; Kahlenberge, a cynical, evasive conniver; and Tanz, a steely-eyed, ruthless Nazi robot who lives for war. Von Seidlitz-Gabler's pretty daughter Ulrike is entangled in a love affair with a sensitive young German corporal, Hartmann, and this adds further undercurrents to the explosive situation. Due to the incredible devotion to justice of Major Grau of German Military Intelligence, the murder investigation continues through the Nazi occupation of Paris where, two years later, a similar crime is committed (again with the three suspected generals in the city). Years later, after his imprisonment as a war criminal, Tanz arrives in Hamburg for a neo–Nazi rally. There he is confronted by Inspector Morand of the French police who, during the war, helped Grau with his investigation. Morand produces Hartmann, who identifies Tanz as the murderer of the Parisian prostitute. Faced with disgrace and humiliation, Tanz kills himself.

REVIEWS:

"The picture is efficiently constructed and played.... All the business of action and intrigue is done with theatrical style.... For those who like vivid melodrama, there is plenty of it here."—*New York Times,* February 3, 1967

"To stress the simpler, mystery-novel aspects of the story, as the movie does, is inevitably to cheapen it. But it need not have destroyed the film entirely, since the important material is still present, if de-emphasized."—*Life,* February 17, 1967

"*The Night of the Generals* is another dubious and superfluous statement about moral and war. If Hans Hellmut Kirst's novel had anything relevant to tell a guilt-ridden German public after the holocaust, it has been lost in this puffed-up, big screen rendition."—*Cinema,* Summer 1967

REVIEWS FOR ANATOLE LITVAK:

"Anatole Litvak brings to the glossy production much helming competence, but he cannot fill out those middle reaches where the story loses its way in a side alley."—*Variety,* February 1, 1967

"Producer [Sam] Spiegel and director Litvak are adept with the magic that inveigles audiences into the suspension of disbelief, and the Spiegel-Litvak wizardry here on display is fascinating to watch."—*Films in Review,* February 1967

"Anatole Litvak's direction is occasionally flamboyant ... but mostly flat."—*Monthly Film Bulletin,* March 1967

OTHER REVIEWS AND ARTICLES:

New York Times June 22, 1965; *The Daily Cinema* December 31, 1965; *New York Times* May 8, 1966; *Kine Weekly* January 28, 1967; *Hollywood Reporter* January 30, 1967; *The Daily Cinema* February 1, 1967; *The Film Daily* February 3, 1967; *Time* February 10, 1967; *Motion Picture Herald* February 15, 1967; *Los Angeles Times,* February 19, 1967; *Film & Filming* March 1967; *Monthly Film Bulletin* July 1967; *Image et Son* September 1967; *Sight and Sound* February 1994; *Télérama* April 30, 1997

AWARDS AND HONORS:

David di Donatello Awards, Italy 1967 *Winner*: Best Foreign Actor: Peter O'Toole

NOTES: Dirk Bogarde was originally cast as Major Grau, but producer Sam Spiegel preferred Omar Sharif. Singer Marianne Faithfull was screen-tested for the role of Ulrike. Gore Vidal and Irwin Shaw re-wrote some of the dialogue in a few scenes.

The Lady in the Car with Glasses and a Gun

(*La dame dans l'auto avec des lunettes et un fusil*)

Columbia Pictures; Lira Films; An Anatole Litvak Production Eastmancolor; 105 minutes ;Released in Paris on October 22, 1970

Filmography (As Director)

CREDITS: *Producers*: Raymond Danon, Anatole Litvak; *Director:* Anatole Litvak; *Assistant Directors*: Francis Pernet, Richard Overstreet, Bernard Stora; *Screenplay*: Sébastien Japrisot, Anatole Litvak; *Based on the novel* La dame dans l'auto avec des lunettes et un fusil *by* Sébastien Japrisot; *English Dialogue*: Richard Harris, Eleanor Perry; *French Dialogue*: Sébastien Japrisot, Anatole Litvak; *Photography* Claude Renoir; *Camera:* Philippe Brun; *Assistant Camera:* Roger Tellier, René Chabal; *Art Director:* Willy Holt; *Assistant Art Directors:* Gérard Viard, Georges Richard; *Editor*: Peter Thornton; *Assistant Editor*: Geneviève Billo; *Dresses*: Christian Dior; *Wardrobe*: Jean Zay; *Music Composer-Conductor*: Michel Legrand; *Sound Editor*: Barry McCormick; *Sound Recording*: William Sivel; *Makeup*: Michel Deruelle; *Hair Styles*: Simone Knapp; *Production Manager*s: Marc Maurette, Claude Ganz; *Unit Manager*: René Fargeas; *Continuity:* Alice Ziller; *Casting:* Margot Capelier; *Dialogue Coach:* Frawley Becker; *Main Titles*: Jean Fouchet.

CAST: Samantha Eggar (Dany Lang), Oliver Reed (Michael Caldwell), John McEnery (Philippe), Stéphane Audran (Anita Caldwell), Billie Dixon (Secretary), Bernard Fresson (Jean), Philippe Nicaud (Highway Policeman), Marcel Bozzufi (Manuel), Jacques Fabbri (Doctor), Yves Pignot (Baptistin), Jacques Legras (Policeman), Maria Mériko (Madame Pacaud), André Oumansky (Bernard Thorr), Martine Kelly (Kiki), Robert Déac (Boy in Cassis), Monique Mélinand (Barmaid), Claude Vernier (Psychiatrist), Lisa Jouvet, Fred Fisher (Danish Tourists), Raoul Delfosse, Louise Rioton (American Tourists), Jacqueline Porel (Second secretary), Paule Noelle (Third Secretary), Henry Czarniak (Garage Proprietor), Edmond Ardisson (Garage Night Man), Gilberte Géniat (Village Storekeeper), Roger Lumont (Hotel Clerk)

PLOT: Dany, an English secretary employed by an international advertising agency, suddenly finds herself in the middle of an adventure which gradually turns into a nightmare full of mystery and danger. One Friday evening at the start of a long weekend, Michael Caldwell, who runs the firm's English branch, asks her to type out a report which he has to take with him to an important meeting in Geneva the next day. He knows that Dany does not plan to leave Paris for the holiday: Could she come to his home that evening and have the report ready for him the next morning? At Michael's home, Dany is welcomed by his wife Anita, whom Dany knew in the old days, when she was a secretary. Dany settles into an office with adjoining bedroom where she can rest while the Caldwells go out for the evening. Dany types for a good part of the night and gets a few hours' rest. Michael comes in the next morning just as she is finishing and asks if she will accompany him and Anita to Orly Airport, then return the car—a large American convertible—to their home. Dany agrees. After leaving Orly, Dany is alone in the big car when she decides to take advantage of the long weekend and go wherever this marvelous car happens to take her. Mysterious events cast a shadow over her plans: Several people (a pump attendant, a café waitress, a speed cop and so on) "recognize" her and claim to have seen her on this road the previous evening, going in the opposite direction. After Dany is nearly murdered by a stranger in a gas station washroom, there are moments when she doubts her own sanity. She has a brief idyll with Philippe, a young hitch-hiker; after they stop at the Pont du Gard for a cozy lunch, Philippe takes Dany off into the hills on a romantic stroll. There he gives her the slip and steals the car. She hitches a lift with a coach-load of tourists and gets off at the first stop. She remembers that at lunch Philippe made a telephone call. She calls the restaurant at the Pont du Gard and learns that Philippe spoke to a garage owner at Cassis. Arriving there by taxi, she learns that the garage specializes in second-hand American cars—and that Philipe has not been there. Dany wanders among the holiday crowds on the promenade. The mystery suddenly turns into a murder story and everything points to her as the murderer: It seems that she has killed a stranger who betrayed her. Bravely overcoming her fear, she sets out to track down the culprit, not knowing whether she is the murderer or the next victim.

REVIEWS:

"[The film] explodes with plethoras of plot, photography, French geography, stars and assorted talents, like the foregoing extended title.... What's missing is the lure that pulls you into the action. It's just too remote, farfetched and lacking in clues."—*New York Post,* December 26, 1970

"Unfortunately, the plot alone will not provide adequate nourishment for the most starved mystery lovers. It is an altogether mechanical affair, proceeding on mystification alone for most of the film, and resolved finally in a manner more comical than satisfying."—*The Village Voice,* January 7, 1971

"A thriller of rather piled and fragmented puzzles, with one apparently central mystery ... created without much style or real tension...."—*Monthly Film Bulletin,* October 1971

REVIEWS FOR ANATOLE LITVAK:

"Litvak gives this okay production flair if sometimes not punchy enough in building the scenes of persecution and despair of the hapless girl."—*Variety,* November 11, 1970

"Litvak's method, which consists of piling on the production values, not only lacks the tension required of a good thriller, but it feels like the work of a man completely out of touch with audiences' expectations."—*Hollywood Reporter,* December 24, 1970

"Given the possibilities of his plot, Mr. Litvak has emphasized local effect and psychological thrills at the expenses of malevolent logic that is supposed to trap his heroine."—*New York Times,* December 26, 1970

OTHER REVIEWS AND ARTICLES:

Los Angeles Times March 5, 1969; *Le Film Française* July 11, 1969; *Hollywood Reporter* September 26, 1969; *Le Monde* October 27, 1970; *Le Film Française* November 20, 1970; *Morning Telegraph* December 26, 1970; *Christian Science Monitor* January 18, 1971; *Time* January 25, 1971; *Motion Picture Herald* January 27, 1971; *Boston After Dark* February 9, 1971; *Today's Cinema* 27 August 1971; *Kinematograph Weekly* August 28, 1971; *Daily Express* August 24, 1971; *Daily Mirror* (U.K.) August 27, 1971; *The Sunday Telegraph* August 29, 1971; *Image et Son* September 1961

NOTES: The picture was shot at Pinewood Studios in England and in the South of France in July 1969. Peeter Urbia remade it in Estonia in 1992 as *Daam autos* (*The Lady in the Car*).

Television Films

Mayerling

Showcase Productions NBC-TV; Color; 90 minutes; Aired on February 4, 1957

CREDITS: *Producer-Director:* Anatole Litvak, *Associate Producers*: Andrew McCullough, Leo Davis; *Executive Producer*: Mort Abrahams; *Screenwriter*: Michael Dyne; *Based on the Novel* La Fin d'une Idylle *by* Claude Anet; *Set Designer*: Otis Riggs; *Costumes*:

Dorothy Jeakins; *Music Composer-Conductor*: George Bassman; *Casting Director:* Joan MacDonald, *Makeup:* Dick Smith; *Program Assistant:* Edith Hamlin; *Production Stage Manager*: George Lawrence; *Choreography*: Marc Breaux; *Audio:* Fred Christie; *Lighting Director:* Jack Fitzpatrick; *Technical Director*: Jack Coffey; *Film Technical Director*: Ed Hoffmeister; *Graphic Arts*: Bill Orgill; *Editor*: Herman Kitchen; *Associate Director*: Dean Whitmore; *Unit Manager*: Warren Burmeister; *Production Supervisor*: Shelley Hull; *Production Executive*: Alvin Cooperman; *Camera Director*: Kirk Browning

CAST: Audrey Hepburn (Maria Vetsera), Mel Ferrer (Prince Rudolph), Eaymond Massey (Taafe, the Prime Minister), Diana Wynyard (The Empress), Basil Sydney (Emperor Franz Josef), Judith Evelyn (Countess Larische), Isobel Elsom (Baroness Vetsera), Lorne Greene (The Emperor's Aide), Nancy Marchand (Princess Stephanie), David Opatoshu (Police Officer), Nehemiah Persoff (Police Officer), Ian Wolfe (Loschek), Pippa Scott (Hanna Vetsera), Michael Evans (Hoyos), Monique Van Vooren (Marinika), John McGovern (Szeps), David Atkinson (Philip de Cobourg), Berry Kroeger (Headwaiter), Francis Compton (Prater Waiter), Anne Dere (Nurse), Nat Norbert (Puppets)

PLOT: See *Mayerling* (1936) in Anatole Litvak filmography.

REVIEWS:

"[A] triumph for Anatole Litvak, Audrey Hepburn, Mel Ferrer and the future of color television."—*New York Evening Journal,* February 5, 1957

"*Mayerling* proved that television needs only a good story and a good cast to provide entertainment equal to any other medium."—*Los Angeles Times,* February 6, 1957

"It was an almost totally meritless production. I had hoped that the ratings would be disastrous, not to salve my personal pride in the American people."—*Saturday Review,* March 2, 1957

REVIEWS FOR ANATOLE LITVAK:

"Anatole Litvak, who made his reputation with the original film version, produced and staged the televersion, apparently not departing much from the style of the original. In today's market, however, this rather old-fashioned treatment is too heavy-handed and there were some obvious directorial devices that added jarring notes above and beyond those sounded by erratic performances."—*Variety,* February 5, 1957

"Mr. Litvak clearly undertook to compress CinemaScope into twenty-one inches: he demonstrated that TV can achieve more sweeping effects that the medium had thought. But one must be questioned whether a tender and intimate tragedy involving two people calls for the DeMille approach."—*New York Times,* February 5, 1957

"I was impressed by the way Litvak's direction gave you the feeling on live television of a crowded imperial city.... Litvak may have squandered a lot of money, but he sure as hell got his money's worth out of those costume extras whose muscles must be aching still."—*New York Herald Tribune,* February 8, 1957

OTHER REVIEWS AND ARTICLES

Variety October 17, 1956; *Variety* January 16, 1957; *New York Times Sunday Magazine* January 27, 1957; *New Yorker* February 2, 1957; *Mirror* February 3, 1957; *Life* February 4, 1957; *People* April 12, 1976

NOTES: *Mayerling* had a $620,000 budget, a cast of 107 actors, 30 indoor sets and lavish costumes. The broadcast reached the largest audience of any *Producer's Showcase* program since 1955. It was theatrically released as a film in Europe.

Documentaries

During World War II, Anatole Litvak was part of the 834th Photo Signal Detachment which, under the supervision of Frank Capra, produced seven information films for the servicemen. The series was titled *Why We Fight*. In 1943, this series won the New York Critics Circle Awards and in 2000 it was put on the National Film Registry by the National Preservation Board. Lt. Col. Litvak was involved in six of these films.

Why We Fight: Prelude to War

Special Service Division Information, Film #1 The War Department, Army Service Forces in cooperation with the Signal Corps; B&W; 53 minutes; May 27, 1942

CREDITS: *Producer*: Lt. Col. Frank Capra, *Associate Producer:* Lt. Col. Anatole Litvak; *Directors*: Lt. Col. Frank Capra, Lt. Col. Anatole Litvak; *Writers*: Capt. Anthony Veiller, Maj. Eric Knight, Robert Heller; *Editor*: Maj. William Hornbeck, Sgt. Rex McAdam; *Music*: Alfred Newman, Leigh Harline, David Raksin, Arthur Lange, Cyril J. Mockridge, Hugo Friedhofer; *Sound*: Clem Portman; *Animation*: Walt Disney Productions, *Narrator*: Walter Huston

PLOT: *Prelude to War* presents a general picture of two worlds, the slave and the free, and the rise of totalitarian militarism from Japan's conquest of Manchuria to Mussolini's conquest of Ethiopia. (from F. Capra, *The Name Above the Title*, see Bibliography)

REVIEWS AND ARTICLES:

PM Journal November 23, 1942; *Hollywood Reporter* April 6, 1943; *Hollywood Reporter* April 26, 1943; *Film Daily* April 27, 1943; *Motion Picture Herald* May 1, 1943; *Motion Picture Herald Product Digest* May 1, 1943; *Variety* May 12, 1943; *New York Times* May 14, 1943; *Box Office* May 15, 1943; *Hollywood Reporter* May 17, 1943; *New Yorker* May 22, 1943; *Hollywood Reporter* May 28, 1943; *Time* May 31, 1943; *New Republic* May 31, 1943; *American Cinematographer* June 1943; *Nation* June 12, 1943; *This Week* July 18, 1943; *New York Herald Tribune* November 15, 1943; *Nation* December 25, 1943

NOTE: The film was subtitled *Project 6,000 Information Film #1*. Some sources claim that Litvak was not involved in this project, but further investigation confirmed his participation.

AWARDS AND HONORS:

National Board of Review, USA 1943 Winner: *Best Documentary;* Academy Awards, USA 1943 Won: *Best Documentary*

Why We Fight: The Nazi Strike

Special Service Division Information, Film #2 The War Department, Special Service Division S.O.S. with cooperation of the Signal Corps; B&W; 42 minutes; May 4, 1943

CREDITS: *Producer*: Lt. Col. Frank Capra, *Associate Producer:* Lt. Col. Anatole Litvak; *Directors*: Lt. Col. Frank Capra, Lt. Col. Anatole Litvak; *Writers*: Capt. Anthony Veiller, Eric Knight; *Editor*: Maj. William Hornbeck, *Music Supervisors*: Dimitri Tiomkin, Morris Stoloff; *Music*: Alfred Newman, Roy Webb, John Leipold, Sidney Cutner, Leigh Harline, Anthony Collins; *Sound*: Clem Portman; *Animation:* Walt Disney Productions; *Narrators*: Walter Huston, Capt. Anthony Veiller

PLOT: Hitler rises. Imposes Nazi dictatorship on Germany. Goose-steps into

Rhineland and Austria. Threatens war unless given Czechoslovakia. Hitler invades Poland. Curtain rises on the tragedy of the century—World War II. (from F. Capra, *The Name Above the Title*, see Bibliography)
REVIEWS AND ARTICLES:
Film Daily April 27, 1943; *The New Statesman and Nation* January 29, 1944
NOTES: This film was subtitled *Project 6001*. The production cost $54,728. Charles Boyer recorded narration for a French version in the spring of 1943. Columbia Pictures provided services and materials necessary for cutting sound effects, scoring and dubbing the film. Litvak shot footage at 20th Century–Fox. The first public showing took place on May 4, 1943, at the inaugural meeting of the Cinema Lodge of B'nai B'rith in New York.

Why We Fight: Divide and Conquer

Special Service Division Information, Film #3 The War Department, Special Service Division-Army Service Forces with cooperation of the Signal Corps; B&W; 58 minutes; 1943

CREDITS: *Directors:* Lt. Col. Frank Capra, Lt. Col. Anatole Litvak; *Producers:* Lt. Col. Frank Capra, Gordon Hollingshead; *Writer*: Roger Q. Denny; *Editor*: Doug Gould, Maj. William Hornbeck, *Art Director:* Hugh Reticker; *Photography*: Arthur Todd; *Sound*: Charles David Forrest; *Music*: Alfred Newman, Dimitri Tiomkin; *Narrators*: Walter Huston, Anthony Veiller.

PLOT: Hitler occupies Denmark and Norway, outflanks Maginot Lines, drives British Army into North Sea, forces surrender of France. (from F. Capra, *The Name Above the Title*, see Bibliography)
REVIEWS AND ARTICLES:
Monthly Film Bulletin April 27, 1943
NOTES: This film was subtitled *Project 6002*. Its working title was *The Nazis Turn West*. According to government documents at NARS, work began on the scenario on July 23, 1942, and an answer print was submitted on March 18, 1943. The film contained newsreel footage, Hollywood studio stock shots, captured German, Italian and Japanese film, footage from the French Signal Corps, film shot by Consolidated Film Industries, and film shot for a number of Fox feature films including *A Yank in the RAF* (1941] and *The Pied Piper* (1942].

Why We Fight: The Battle of Russia

Special Service Division, Film #5 The War Department, Special Service Division-Army Service Forces with the cooperation of the Signal Corps; B&W; 83 minutes; November 13, 1943

CREDITS: *Director:* Lt. Col. Anatole Litvak, *Producers:* Lt. Col. Frank Capra, Lt. Col. Anatole Litvak; *Supervisor:* Lt. Col. Frank Capra; *Writers*: Lt. Col. Anatole Litvak, Capt. Anthony Veiller, Robert Heller; *Editor*: Maj. William Hornbeck, *Sound*: William Montague; *Music*: The Army Air Forces Orchestra, Dimitri Tiomkin; *Animation*: Walt Disney Productions; *Narrators*: Capt. Anthony Veiller, Walter Huston

PLOT: History of Russia: people, size, resources, wars. Death struggle against Nazi armies at gates of Moscow and Leningrad, At Stalingrad, Nazi put through meat grinder. (from F. Capra, *The Name Above the Title*, see Bibliography)

REVIEWS:

"It is a striking tribute to the excellent conception and technical work of the Special Services Division of the Army Services Forces. For here is a film as fascinating as it is educationally valuable."—*New York Post,* September 25, 1943

"[A] powerful, stimulating document...."—*The Morning Telegraph-New York,* September 29, 1943

"It is a film which everyone ought to see for his soul's good, not least because it presents us with the complete image of the wicked folly which has raged throughout the world in the last decade."—*Monthly Film Bulletin,* May 31, 1944

REVIEWS FOR ANATOLE LITVAK:

"*Battle for Russia* is a powerful yet simple drama vividly depicting the greatest military achievement of all time.... It also stands as a tribute to Lt. Col. Anatole Litvak, who produced the film under Capra's supervision."—*Variety,* October 13, 1943

"The job of assembling this picture was directed by Lieut. Col. Anatole Litvak and the continuity and commentary were written by Capt. Anthony Veiller, both former Hollywood men. Together they have made a brilliantly instructive and inspiring film, in which the visual image, the word and the music are blended magnificently."—*New York Times,* November 15, 1943

ADDITIONAL REVIEWS AND ARTICLES:

Daily Variety September 29, 1943; *Hollywood Reporter* September 29, 1943; *Hollywood Reporter* October 25, 1943; *Nation* October 30, 1943; *Motion Picture Herald* November 6, 1943; *Times-Herald* (Washington, D.C.) November 11, 1943; *Los Angeles Examiner* November 13, 1943; *Los Angeles Times* November 13, 1943; *New Yorker* November 20, 1943; *The Washington Post* November 25, 1943; *Time* November 29, 1943; *Nation* December 25, 1943; *Sight and Sound* January 1944; *Independent Film Journal* March 4, 1944; *Today Cinema* May 23, 1944; *Kinematograph Weekly* May 25, 1944; *The Film User* May 1952

AWARDS AND HONORS:

National Board of Review, USA 1943 Winner: *Best Documentary;* Academy Awards, USA 1944 Nominated: *Best Documentary, Features*

NOTES: This film was subtitled *Project 6004.* Its working title was *Know Your Ally: Russia, War in the East.* Work began on the scenario on April 1, 1942, and an answer print was submitted for approval on July 9, 1943. There were three versions of the film in lengths of six, nine and ten reels. The film was released in two parts, the first half covering events through 1941, the second tracing the war since then on the eastern front. For a French version, Charles Boyer recited Andre David's translation of the narration.

Why We Fight: The Battle of China

Morale Service Division Film #6 War Department, Signal Corps Army Service Forces for the Morale Services Division; B&W; 63 minutes; 1944

CREDITS: *Producer-Director:* Lt. Col. Frank Capra, Lt. Col. Anatole Litvak; *Production Supervisor*: Joseph Sistrom; *Writers*: Capt. Anthony Veiller, James Hilton, John Gunther, Joseph Sistrom; *Editor*: Maj. William Hornbeck; *Sound*: Tom McAdoo; *Music*: The Army Air Forces Orchestra, Dimitri Tiomkin; *Animation*: Walt Disney Productions; *Narrators*: Capt. Anthony Veiller, Walter Huston

PLOT: Japan's warlords commit total effort to conquest of China. Once conquered,

Filmography (Documentaries) 183

Japan would use China's manpower for the conquest of all Asia. (from F. Capra, *The Name Above the Title*, see Bibliography)
REVIEWS AND ARTICLES:
Daily Variety May 15, 1944; *Hollywood Reporter* May 15, 1944, *Motion Picture Herald Product Digest* May 20, 1944
NOTES: This film was subtitled *Project 6005 Information Film #6*. Its working title was *War in the East*, the same working title *The Battle of Russia* had. According to government documents at NARS, the first scenario was dated January 30, 1943, and the film was completed by April 20, 1944. A Chinese-language version was produced but in June 1945, orders were given to suspend production of the French, Spanish and Portuguese versions. Beset by political problems, *The Battle of China* was quickly withdrawn from distribution to the armed forces. It was never released to the general public.

Why We Fight: War Comes to America

War Department, Army Pictorial Service for the Information and Education Division Film #7; B&W; 70 minutes; 1945
CREDITS: *Producer*: Lt. Col. Frank Capra; *Directors*: Lt. Col. Frank Capra, Lt. Col. Anatole Litvak; *Writers*: Capt. Anthony Veiller, Lt. Col. Anatole Litvak, Sgt. Irving Wallace; *Editor*: Capt. Merrill G. White, Maj. William Hornbeck; *Music*: Army Air Forces Orchestra, Dimitri Tiomkin; *Narrator:* Walter Huston; *Animation:* Walt Disney Productions
PLOT: Dealt with who, what, where, why and how we came to be the U.S.A.—the oldest major democratic republic still living under its original constitution. But the heart of the film dealt with the depth and variety of emotions with which Americans reacted to the traumatic events in Europe and Asia. How our convictions slowly changed from total non-involvement to total commitment as we realized that loss of freedom anywhere increased the danger to our own freedom. This last film of the series was, still is one of the most graphic visual histories of the United States ever made. (from F. Capra, *The Name Above the Title*, see Bibliography*)*
REVIEWS AND ARTICLES:
Motion Picture Herald June 9, 1945; *Journal of Popular Film and Television* Summer 1994
NOTES: The film was subtitled *Project 6006 Information Film #7*. According to government documents at NARS, its working title was *America Goes to War*. Originally it was going to be produced in two parts, *War Comes to America* and *War Comes to America, Part II*. In addition to newsreel and government footage, captured enemy newsreels and films, Allied films and stock shots from Hollywood studio libraries, footage from a number of well-known films is included in the picture. The music score includes compositions taken from previous films in the *Why We Fight* series. *War Comes to America* was released by RKO in 1945 and later copyrighted and re-released in 1948.

Substitution and Conversion (*Project 6021*)

U.S. War Department; B&W; September 1943
CREDITS: *Producer*: Lt. David Miller; *Supervisors*: Lt. Col. Frank Capra, Lt. Col. Anatole Litvak; *Editor*: Harold Minter; *Assistant Editors*: Corp. Maurice Vaccanino, Sgt. Jack Woelz; *Music*: Dimitri Tiomkin, Charles Previn; *Composer*: Robert Crawford;

Animation: Walt Disney Productions; *Narrators*: Lester Cohen, Robert Lees, Fred Rinaldo

PLOT: This Army orientation film describes the Pentagon's program of substitution and conversion of resources during wartime, and the necessity for ingenuity in dealing with the lack of critical materials,

NOTES: The film was subtitled *Project 6021*. According to government documents at NARS, work started on the scenario on September 23, 1942, and the first answer print was submitted for approval on May 15, 1943. The production's cost was $39,095. The film was released to the Armed Forces in the U.S. in September 1943 in a long and short version, and an additional short version was prepared for overseas distribution. The film included footage shot by the Capra Unit and Consolidated Film Industries, in addition to footage obtained from the Office for Emergency Management, the Signal Corps, the U.S. Marine Corps, the Canadian National Film Board, American newsreels, stock footage from Hollywood studios, and captured German film. (American Film Institute source)

Operation Titanic

U.S. War Department Army Pictorial Service Signal Corps in cooperation with Army Air Forces; B&W; 37 minutes; 1944

CREDITS: *Director*: Lt. Col. Anatole Litvak; *Music*: Dimitri Tiomkin; *Animation*: Walt Disney Productions; *Text:* Carl Foreman

PLOT: A propaganda film showing the success of the cooperation between the Allies and the use by the American Air Force of bases in the Soviet Union.

D-Day: The Normandy Invasion

U.S. War Department Army Pictorial Service Signal Corps in cooperation with U.S. Navy and Army Air Forces; B&W; 20 minutes; 1945

CREDITS: *Director*: Anatole Litvak; *Photography*: U.S. Coast Guard Cameramen.

PLOT: June 6, 1944, has gone down in history as D-Day, the beginning of the end of World War II. Code-named Operation Overlord, the Normandy Invasion took the German Army by surprise as Allied soldiers from all over the world stormed the beaches of France and began the liberation of Europe. The picture examines the operation in a strategic context and also focuses on many smaller-scale stories of courage and heroism: the wonderful welcome given by the newly liberated French the brave rangers at Pointe du Hoc and the desperate battle for Omaha beach.

NOTE: Part of the original footage shot by Litvak was destroyed by enemy action and the project was downgraded to a shorter documentary.

Mission to No-Man's Land

BBC-TV; B&W; 30 minutes; Aired on January 13, 1960

CREDITS: *Producer*: Stanley Wright; *Production Supervisor:* Anatole Litvak; *Director:* Georges Pessis; *Writer:* Stanley Wright; *Narrator*: Yul Brynner.

A short documentary reporting on refugee children in Eastern European camps. Made in collaboration with BBC for the United Nations High Commissioner for Refugees.

Other Work as Screenwriter

Samiy Yuniy Pioner
(*The Youngest Pioneer* aka *A Very Young Pioneer*)
Kino-Server; B&W; 27 minutes; silent film; Released in 1925
CREDITS: *Director:* Konstantin Derzhavin; *Screenplay:* Anatole Litvak, Konstantin Derzhavin; *Photography*: Albert Kyun; *Production Designer*: I. Brif.
CAST: Galochka Levina, V. Chernetskii, P. Zhukov, A. Ivanov, M. Zubov.
PLOT: The adventures of a 13-year-old activist girl at the White Army's rear in the days of the Russian Civil War.

Other Works as Producer

10:30 p.m. Summer
Jorilie Productions; Argos Films; United Artists; Technicolor; 85 minutes; Released in New York on October 24, 1966
CREDITS: *Producers*: Jules Dassin, Anatole Litvak (uncredited); *Director:* Jules Dassin; *Screenplay:* Jules Dassin, Marguerite Duras; *Based on the novel* Dix heures et demie du soir en été *by* Marguerite Duras; *Photography:* Gabor Pogany; *Art Director*: Enrique Alarcón; *Editor:* Roger Dwyre; *Music:* Cristóbal Halffter, Dimitri Kritzas; *Sound*: Jean Labussière; *Makeup:* Julian Rutz
CAST: Melina Mercouri (Maria), Romy Schneider (Claire), Peter Finch (Paul), Julián Mateos (Rodrigo Palestra), Isabel María Pérez (Judith), Beatriz Savon (Rodrigo's Wife)
PLOT: During a violent thunderstorm in a Spanish village, a young peasant murders his unfaithful wife and her lover. At the same time, foreign travelers drive into the overcrowded town: 40-year-old Englishman Paul, his alcoholic Greek wife Maria, their small daughter Judith, and their friend Claire. Because the only hotel has no available rooms, the four are obliged to spend the night in a corridor. Maria, believing that Paul want to forsake her for the beautiful Claire, drinks to dull despair. But sleep does not come and, in the middle of the night, she goes out on a balcony and sees Paul and Claire embracing on another balcony. Then during a flash of lightning, she also sees the fugitive peasant crouched on the next roof. In her alcoholic haze, Maria somehow identifies with this stranger's violent crime of honor and she helps him escape by driving him to an isolated spot in a nearby field. After assuring him that she will return in the morning, she goes back to the hotel. At first Paul doubts her wild story but eventually he accompanies her to the field, where the peasant lies dead in a pool of blood. That afternoon Maria sits in the sunlight, sipping wine and imagining that Paul and Claire are making passionate love. By evening she has slipped even further from reality and tells Paul that she no longer loves him. Later, while Paul, Claire and Maria are at a cafe, Maria suddenly disappears. Paul and Claire set out to search for her, roaming the narrow streets and shouting her name into the silence.
REVIEWS:
"*10:30 p.m. Summer* is only 85 minutes long but seems longer.... It's just a dull film."—*Variety,* October 19, 1966

"[It's] is a romantic melodrama drenched in symbolism and mysticism. Jules Dassin's film is really a small thing for major talents, It is trivial despite the life-and-death involvements of the principals."—*Hollywood Reporter,* October 19, 1966

"A preposterous melodrama ... all hope of subtlety or emotional truth is lost."—*Film & Filming,* May 1967

NOTES: Litvak and Jules Dassin originally asked Joseph Losey to direct the film since it was a project Losey had long been interested in. It was co-produced by Dassin and Litvak, but Litvak's name does not appear in the on-screen credits.

Other Works as Director

The Roaring Twenties
Warner Bros., 1939
Raoul Walsh replaced Litvak after only two days of work because Litvak had differences of opinion with the producers.

'Til We Meet Again
Warner Bros., 1940
When director Edmund Goulding fell ill for a week with pneumonia, Litvak replaced him.

New Orleans
Majestic Productions, 1947
Litvak was briefly committed to the film and then withdrew in favor of Arthur Lubin.

Projects with Litvak's Name Attached

Sahara, 1936, starring Charles Boyer and Madeleine Carroll; unrealized
The Phantom of the Opera, 1936; unrealized
Wuthering Heights, 1936
Joan of Arc, 1936, based on the life of the French heroine starring Claudette Colbert; unrealized
Saturday's Children, 1939, Warner Bros., directed in 1940 by Vincent Sherman
Villa on the Hill, 1939, based on Somerset Maugham's novel; unrealized
Footsteps in the Dark, 1939, Warner Bros.; announced as a vehicle for Edward G. Robinson; it was directed in 1941, without Robinson, by Lloyd Bacon
The Sea Wolf, 1941, Warner Bros., first assigned to Litvak and later given to Michael Curtiz
One Foot in Heaven, 1941, Warner Bros.; Litvak was the first director assigned to the picture, but the studio decided to pull him from the project and entrust it to Irving Rapper
Coup de grâce, 1946, Enterprise Production, based on a novel by Joseph Kessel. The novel was later filmed as *Sirocco* (1951) by Curtis Bernhardt.

Montserrat, 1949; Litvak bought the rights of the play written by Emmanuel Robles, planning to make a film starring Gregory Peck, but the project was never realized.

Freud, 1950; Litvak was assigned to direct the film by 20th Century–Fox; it was unrealized. In 1962 Universal produced *Freud* directed by John Huston and starring Montgomery Clift

Take Care of My Little Girl, 1950; Litvak was attached to the project; when the film made a year later, Jean Negulesco was director.

The Steeper Cliff, 1951; based on a novel by David Davinson, this picture (intended as a sequel to *Decision Before Dawn*) was unrealized.

Time of the Cuckoo, 1953, based on a play in two acts by Arthur Laurents. Litvak was offered the chance to direct a screen adaptation. When it was made in 1955 under the title *Summertime,* the director was David Lean.

Désirée, 1954; Fox wanted Litvak to direct it. He turned it down and the picture was made by Henry Koster starring Marlon Brando and Jean Simmons.

Two Different Worlds, 1958; this unrealized picture was scheduled to be filmed in Paris and Istanbul starring Yul Brynner. Litvak was supposed to produce and direct.

The Mad King, 1959; based on the life of Paul of Russia, son of Catherine the Great. Litvak announced that he would write, direct and produce it in collaboration with Yul Brynner. United Artists was supposed to finance and release the film

A Shot in the Dark, 1964; Litvak was attached to the original project starring Sophia Loren. After the Italian actress turned the part down, he withdrew from the project and was replaced by Blake Edwards. Many sources claim incorrectly he started shooting the film.

The Deputy, 1964; Litvak was reportedly interested in making a film of Rolf Hochhuth's controversial play *The Deputy,* an indictment of the alleged silence of Pope Pius XII (God's "Deputy" on Earth) over the Nazi persecution of the Jews during World War II. Marlon Brando was supposed to star in it. The film was never made.

The Ski Bum, 1967 In April 1967, Embassy Pictures producer Joseph E. Levine announced that Litvak would direct *The Ski Bum* starring Peter O'Toole and Katharine Ross. Because of scripting difficulties, O'Toole and others were reassigned to another production. Litvak decided to withdraw and the film was directed in 1971 by Bruce Clark. In February 1968, Embassy sued Litvak for breach of contract..

As Assistant Director

Le Chant de l'amour triomphant

Société des Film Albatros; B&W; 79 minutes; silent film; Released in Paris on September 21, 1923

CREDITS: *Producers:* André Pironet, Constantin Geftman; *Director:* Vyacheslav (aka Viktor) Tourjansky; *Assistant Director:* Anatole Litvak; *Screenplay:* Vyacheslav (aka Viktor) Tourjansky, Vassili Choukhaeff, *based on a short story by* Ivan Tourgenev; *Photography*: Joseph-Louis Mundwiller, Fédote Bourgassoff, Nicolas Toporkoff; *Art Director*: Vassili Choukhaeff, César Lacca; *Costumes:* Vassili Choukhaeff

CAST: Nathalie Kovanko (Valeria), Jean Angelo (Muzio), Rolla Norman (Fabio), Nicolas Koline (Antonio le majordome), Jean d' Yd (Le serviteur hindou), Basile Kourotchkine (Brahma), Nathalie Kovanko (Valeria), Joe Alex

PLOT: In sixteenth-century Ferrara, Italy, rich young friends Muzio and Fabio, a musician and a painter, fall in love with striking beauty Valeria, daughter of an impoverished widowed noblewoman. To preserve their friendship, Muzio and Fabio make an oath: the loser in the competition for her love will accept her choice without complaint. Advised by her mother, Valeria marries Fabio. Devastated, Muzio goes overseas, returning four years later. His new practices make him very mysterious and attractive to Valeria, who starts to fall in love with him.

NOTES: Litvak was very close-mouthed about his Soviet period; only one Russian source (*Sovetskie hudožestvennye fil'my*, Moscow, 1961) indicates his participation as assistant director in Tourjansky's film.

Die Freudlose Gasse

(In the U.S. and in the U.K., *The Joyless Street* aka *Street of Sorrow*)
Sofar Film-Produktion GmbH; B&W; 151 minutes; silent film; Released in Berlin on May 18, 1925
CREDITS: *Producers:* Michael Salkin, Romain Pinès, G.W. Pabst; *Director:* G.W. Pabst; *Assistant Directors*: Mark Sorkin, Anatole Litvak; *Screenplay:* Willy Haas; *Based on the Novel by* Hugo Bettauer; *Photography*: Guido Seeber, Curt Oertel, Walter Robert Lach; *Art Directors:* Hans Sohnle, Otto Erdmann; *Editors:* Mark Sorkin, G.W. Pabst
CAST: Greta Garbo (Grete Rumfort), Asta Nielsen (Maria Lechner), Loni Nest (Mariandl Rumfort), Max Kohlhase (Vater Lechner), Jaro Fürth (Josef Rumfort), Sylvia Torf (Mrs. Lechner), Karl Etlinger (Director General Rosenow), Ilka Grüning (Mrs Rosenow), Countess Agnes Esterhazy (Regina Rosenow), Alexander Mursky (Dr Leid), Tamara Tolstoi (Lia Leid), Henry Stuart (Egon Stirner), Robert Garrison (Don Alfonso Ganez), Einar Hanson (Lieutenant Davy, USA), Mario Cusmich (Colonel Irving, USA), Valeska Gert (Frau Greifer), Countess Tolstoi (Miss Henriette), Edna Markstein (Mrs. Merkl), Werner Krauss (Josef Gieringer, the butcher), Hertha von Walther (Else), Otto Reinwald (Else's Husband), Gregory Chmara (Waiter at Hotel Merkl), M. Raskatoff (Trebitsch), Kraft Rasching (American Soldier), Marlene Dietrich (Woman in Butcher's Queue).
PLOT: In post–World War I Vienna, Franz Rumfort is the head of a very poor family. Grete, one of his two daughters, loses her office job after spurning the advances of her employer, and her father loses all his money when the price of the shares which he bought with his redundancy money fall sharply when there are rumors of a miners' strike. Those false rumors were circulated by a group of rich businessmen in order to buy up shares cheaply and make a profit. Wealthy Secretary Egon finds himself accused of the murder of a lawyer's wife with whom he had an affair. The accuser is a former girlfriend, Maria, who saw him with the woman; in a fit of jealousy and despair, Maria strangled her. Almost mad with guilt and remorse, and seriously ill, she confesses to the police. Grete's family take in a lodger, but the money disappears on paying her father's debts and the lodger, who liked Greta, subsequently leaves when her father is angered at accusations that his youngest daughter stole some tins of food. Desperate for money to feed the family, Grete is lured to Frau Greifer's establishment, frequented by wealthy men and prostitutes, but she cannot bring herself to prostitute herself or appear in a semi-pornographic show. While the show is going on, people gather outside and angrily stone Frau Greifer's. The young lodger who was at the show is at first angry with Grete, until

he realizes the truth of the situation and what led her to that position. A starving woman, desperate for food for her child and family, begs from the villainous local butcher to whom she once prostituted herself for a piece of meat. He spurns her and she violently attacks and kills him with a meat cleaver. She sets on fire the attic room in which she, her husband and their child live, but at the last moment the child is saved when the husband lowers it out of the window to the crowd below.

NOTES: Released versions of the film vary radically in running length and editing sequence according to each country, from a maximum of 151 minutes to a minimum of 94 minutes. A dubbed version was released in the U.S. in 1937 as *Street of Sorrow*.

Napoleon

Consortium Wengeroff-Stinnes; Société Général de Films; B&W (tinted and toned); 331 minutes; silent film; Released in Paris on April 7, 1927
CREDITS: *Producers:* Willaim Delafontaine, Louis Osmont (production managers), Noé Bloch, Edouard De Bersaucourt (financial administrators); *Director:* Abel Gance; *Assistant Director*s: Henri Andréani, Pierre Danis, Henry Krauss, Mario Napas, Viacheslav Tourjansky, Alexander Volkoff, Anatole Litvak; *Screenplay:* Abel Gance; *Photography:* Jules Kruger, Fédor Bourgassoff, Paul Briquet, Léonce-Henri Burel, Eyvinge, Roger Hubert, Emile Pierre, Jean-Paul Mundviller; *Art Directors:* Alexander Benois, Pierre Schildknecht, Lochakoff, Georges Jacouty, Vladimir Meinhardt, Serge Piménoff; *Editor:* Marguerite Beaugé
CAST: Gina Manès (Joséphine de Beauharnais), Albert Dieudonné (Napoléon Bonaparte), Eugénie Buffett (Letizia Bonaparte), Annabella (Violine Fleuri), Vladimir Roudenko (Young Bonaparte), Robert de Ansorena (Desaix), Antonin Artaud (Marat), Pierre Batcheff (Général Lazare Hoche), Edmond Van Daële (Maximilien Robespierre), Daniel Buiret (Agustine Robespierre), Alexandre Koubitizky (Danton), Abel Gance (Louis Saint-Just), Max Maxudian (Barras), Acho Chakatouny (Pozzo di Borgo), Nicolas Korine (Tristan Fleuri), Georges Lampin; (Joseph Bonaparte), Roger Blum (Talma), Alex Bernard (Dogummier), Robert Vidalin (Camille Desmoulins), Jack Rye (Gen. O'Hara), Suzanne Bianchetti (Marie-Antoinette), Georges Cahuzac (Vicomte Beuaharnais), Guy Favière (Fouché), Louis Vonelly (Couthon), Harry Krimer (Rouget de Lisle), Genica Missirio (Joachim Murat), Sylvio Cavicchia (Lucien Bonaparte), Yvette Dieudonné (Elisa Bonaparte), Marguerite Gance (Charlotte Corday), Simone Genevois (Pauline Bonaparte), Jean d'Yd (La Bussière), Damia (La Marseillaise), Louis Sance (Louis XVI), Janine Pen (Hortense de Beauharnais), Francine Mussey (Lucile Desmoulins), Pierre de Canolle (Capt. August Marmont), Léon Courtois (Gen. Carteaux), Gilbert Dacheux (Gen. du Teil), Jean Henry (Sergeant Andoche Junot), Jean Gaudrey (Jean-Lambert Tallien), Serge Freddy-Karl (Marcellin Fleuri), Pierre Danis (Colonel Muiron), Lomon (Hérault de Séchelles), Florence Talma (Louise Gely), Suzy Vernon (Madame Recamier), Carrie Carvalho (Madameoiselle Lenormant), Roblin (Picot de Peccaduc), Boris de Fast (L'Oeil-Vert)
PLOT: Youthful Napoléon attends military school where he manages a snowball fight like a military campaign, yet he suffers the insults of other boys. Ten years later, on his home island of Corsica, politics shift against him and put him in mortal danger. He flees, taking his family to France. Serving as an artillery officer in the Siege of Toulon, his leadership is rewarded with a promotion to brigadier general. Jealous revolutionaries

imprison Napoléon but then the political tide turns against the Revolution's own leaders. Napoléon leaves prison, forming plans to invade Italy. He falls in love with the beautiful Joséphine de Beauharnais. The emergency government charges him with the task of protecting the National Assembly. Succeeding in this, he is promoted to commander-in-chief of the Army of the Interior, and he marries Joséphine. He takes control of the army, which protects the French–Italian border, and propels it to victory in an invasion of Italy.

NOTES: *Napoleon* New York City premiere was on February 11, 1929. At least 19 versions of the film exist and all vary in running length, from 330 minutes to a mutilated cut of only 75 minutes. The project had been initially conceived as a massive six-part work, which was to include the whole of Napoleon's life, but director Abel Gance was unable to find funds for the other five. Litvak was one of seven assistant directors Gance had over a three-year-period.

Casanova

(In the U.S., *The Loves of Casanova* aka *Prince of Adventurers*)
Ciné-Alliance; Universum Film A.G. (UFA); B&W; 132 minutes; silent film; Released in Germany in 1927

CREDITS: *Producers:* Noé Bloch, Gregor Rabinovitch; *Director*: Alexander Volkoff; *Assistant Director*: Anatole Litvak; *Screenplay*: Norbert Falk, Ivan Mozzhukhin, Alexander Volkoff; *Photography*: Léonce-Henri Burel, Nicolas Toporkoff, Fedor Bourgassoff; *Art Directors:* Alexander Lofchakoff; Noé Bloch; *Costumes:* Boris Bilinsky

CAST: Ivan Mosjoukine (Casanova), Suzanne Bianchetti (Catherine II), Diana Karenne (Maria, Duchess de Landi), Jenny Hugo (Thérèse), Rina De Liguoro (Corticelli), Nina Koshetz (Countess Vorontzoff), Raymond Bouamerane (Djimmy), Olga Day (Lady Stanhope), Albert Docoeur (Duc de Bayreuth), Dimitri Dimitriev Lord Stanhope), Paul Guidé (Gregory Orloff), Rudolf Klein-Rogge (Tsar Peter III), Michel Simon (Sbire), Carlo Tedeschi (Menucci), Maria Ivogün (Soprano).

PLOT: Young Casanova travels from Venice to Russia and back again on a variety of "secret missions." This doesn't prevent the amorous hero from enjoying the favors of many charming ladies. Even Russia's Czarina Catherine the Great briefly falls under his spell. But eventually, it is the lovely Thérèse who captures the protagonist's heart. Highlights include a spectacular hand-tinted sequence set during the Carnival of Venice along with magnificent scenes within the palace walls of Catherine II.

NOTE: When the film ran into some curious censorship troubles in the U.S., it was retitled *Prince of Adventurers*, with the main character rechristened Roberto Ferrara. Swiss actor Michel Simon, who plays a small part, later became one of France's outstanding character actors, doing unforgettable work for director Jean Renoir, Jean Vigo and Marcel Carné.

Geheimnisse des Orients

(aka *Sheherazade*) (In the U.S. and in the U.K., *Secrets of the Orient* aka *Secrets of the East*)
Universum Film A.G. (UFA); B&W; 103 minutes; silent film; Released in Berlin on October 19, 1930

CREDITS: *Producers:* Noé Bloch, Gregor Rabinovitch; *Director:* Alexander Volkoff; *Assistant Director:* Anatole Litvak; *Screenplay:* Norbert Falk, Robert Liebmann, Alexander Volkoff; *Photography:* Curt Courant Nicolas Toporkoff, Fedor Bourgassoff; *Art Director:* Alexander Lochakoff; *Costumes:* Boris Bilinsky

CAST: Nikolai Kolin (Ali), Ivan Petrovich (Prince Achmed), Dimitri Dimitriev (Sultan Schariah), Gaston Modot (Prince Hussein), Julius Falkestein (Sultan's Astrologer), Hermann Picha (Sultan's Court Jester), Aleksandr Vertinsky (Vizier), Marcella Albani (Sobeide—Sultan's Favorite), Agnes Petersen (Princess Gylnare), Nina Koshetz (Fatime—Ali's Wife), Dita Parlo (Slave of the Princess)

PLOT: In ancient Bagdad, Ali, a cobbler, dreamed he had become the grand vizier. Ali's master, the Sultan awaits suitors for the hand of his daughter Princess Gylnare and anticipating their rich gifts. Prince Hussein plans to be her suitor helped by Sobeide, the Sultan's favorite, who also plots to win Prince Achmed, the princess' true love. Every night Achmed sits disconsolately at the foot of the wall of the harem garden which separates him from his beloved, waiting for her to appear. The official suitors began to arrive, first a prince from India appearing on a magnificent elephant laden with treasure. That night Achmed risks his life infiltrating the harem garden to find Princess Gylnare. Meanwhile the richest of the suitors, the emperor of China, is about to arrive to Bagdad by sea, confident that none will be able to match his gifts. Later that night a handmaid to the princess hears a noise in the garden and discovers Prince Hussein about to abduct the princess. The servant struggles with him and is threatened with death. Achmed hears the princess' call for help, but Hussein's guards stop him and take him to a dungeon. The plot of Hussein and Sobeide progresses, while the ship of the emperor of China bursts in flame within sight of land. Ship, emperor and treasure are lost. Ali the grand vizier reveals Hussein's plot and Achmed's devotion to the sultan. Hussein is arrested and Princess Gylnare is rescued and able to marry Achmed. Ali, caught dallying in the harem pool, is saved from capital punishment by suddenly waking from his dream.

NOTE: The American premiere of *Secrets of the Orient* was held in New York City on December 30, 1931. It was released nationwide in January 1932.

Der Weisse Teufel

(In the U.S., *The White Devil*)
Universum Film A.G. (UFA); B&W; 110 minutes; silent film with added sound; Released in Berlin on January 29, 1930

CREDITS: *Producers:* Noé Bloch, Gregor Rabinovitch; *Director:* Alexander Volkoff (as Alexander Wolkoff); *Assistant Director-Production Manager:* Anatole Litvak; *Screenplay:* Michael Linsky, Alexander Volkoff (as Alexander Wolkoff), *Based on the Novel* Hadji *Murad by* Leo Tolstoy; *Photography:* Curt Courant, Nicolas Toporkoff; *Art Directors:* Alexander Lofchakoff, W. Meinhard; *Costumes:* Boris Bilinsky, *Sound:* Walter Ruhland, Fritz Seidel

CAST: Ivan Mosjoukin (Hadji Murad), Lil Dagover (Nelidowa), Betty Amann (Saira), Fritz Alberti (Czar Nicolai I), Georg Seroff (Rjaboff), Acho Chakatouny (Schamil), Alexander Murski (Woronzoff), Kenneth Rive (Jussuff, Murad's Son), Alexei Bondireff (Sado), Eduardowa-Ballett (Dancers)

PLOT: Caught in a violent struggle between Europeanized Russia and Muslim Chechnya, Hadji Murad, a valiant and chivalrous Avar, leads the mountain people's revolt against ruthless leader Imam Shamil. Murad's actions catch the attention of Czar Nicolai I, who hopes to use him as a go-between in his plans to conquer the Caucasus mountaineers. Nevertheless the Russian ruler finds that the hero is not so easily manipulated. Murad unveils the plans of the despotic ruler leading a populist revolt against him. He also rescues the beautiful Saira from the czar's clutches.

NOTE: *The White Devil* was originally produced as a silent film but sound and musical score were later added. Several filmographies mistakenly list actor Peter Lorre as an extra, possibly confusing *Der Weisse Teufel* with *Der Weisse Dämon* (The White Demon) in which he appeared in 1932.

As Co-Author

Meet Me at Dawn

20th Century–Fox; B&W; 99 minutes; Released in London on January 6, 1947

CREDITS: *Producer*: Marcel Hellman; *Director*: Thornton Freeland; *Screenplay*: Lesly Storm, James Seymour; *Based on the Story "Le Tueur" by* Marchel Achard *and* Anatole Litvak; *Dialogue*: Peter Creswell, Maurice Cowan; *Photography*: Gunther Krampf; *Cameraman*: Bunny Francke; *Assistant Director*: Mickey Delamar; *Music*: Mischa Spoliansky; *Lyrics*: Robert Musel; *Sound*: John C. Cook; *Editor*: Edward B. Jarvis; *Costumes*: Gower Parks, H. Nathan; *Art Director*: Norman G. Arnold; *Makeup*: George Claff

CAST: William Eythe (Charles Morton), Stanley Holloway (Emile), Hazel Court (Gabrielle Vermorel), George Thorpe (Senator Philippe Renault), Irene Brown (Madame Renault), Beatrice Campbell (Margot), Basil Sydney (Georges Vermorel), Margaret Rutherford (Mme. Vermorel), Ada Reeve (Concierge), Greame Muir (Count de Brissac), James Harcourt (Butler), Wilfred Hyde-White (Garin—News Editor), Charles Victor, John Salew (Clients), Percy Walsh (Shooting Gallery Man), Hy Hazell, Diana Decker (Girls in Restaurant), Katie Johnson (Mme Vermorel's Housekeeper), O.B. Clarence (Ambassador), Aubrey Mallalieu (Prefect of Police)

PLOT: In Paris in the early 1900s, Charles Morton takes his work as a professional duelist light-heartedly. We meet him as he begins another day by incapacitating—temporarily—yet another opponent. The fees are collected by the faithful Emile. One of Charles' bigger commissions comes along: He is to "insult" and challenge Senator Philippe Renault, whose political adversaries wants him to retire for a few months. The meeting between Charles and the Senator is planned, but Charles also meets the lovely girl who is to be used as a pretext for the challenge. Charles is captivated and the two enjoy the fun of the fair together until an accident on the scenic railway leaves the girl with a sprained ankle. Anxious to avoid publicity, she slips away with Charles. When she faints, Charles takes her to his apartment, binds the ankle and gives her his bed. When he goes to waken her the following morning, she has gone, leaving a note signed "Gabrielle." Gabrielle is in reality the daughter of a fiery newspaper editor, Georges Vermorel, who sees the news of the Senator's duel over a woman as a fine opportunity to ruin the man politically. Unaware that the woman is his daughter Gabrielle, he dubs her "Madame X" and splashes his columns with news of the search for her. Charles is more concerned over Gabrielle's disappearance than over his forthcoming duel. When they reunite, he refuses her plea to cancel the duel. Senator Renault is no mean adversary and both duelists are wounded. The two men become good friends and Renault guesses that Charles is a professional duelist. Unknown to the two men, Gabrielle overhears Charles' admission that this is so. She is angered by the revelation, believing as she had that Charles was quixotically dueling for her honor. As Vermorel's search for Madame X becomes more intense, Charles begs him to stop. A chance meeting with Gabrielle makes Charles realize the identity of Madame X. Charles next meets the Vermorels at a ball given by Senator Renault. Their situation is embarrassing from the start, but far more so when the gossip spreads that Gabrielle is Madame X. Charles spends more time handing his card to future opponents than in dancing. Gabrielle leaves home and goes to stay with her grandmother. Believing that she has gone to Charles, Vermorel insults the young duelist, who is forced to accept his challenge. Charles allows the editor to wound him and the affair of Madame × comes to an end. Months later, Charles is still using the foils professionally, the difference being that his profession is now on the right side of the law. With Gabrielle as his wife, he earns an honest living as a fencing instructor.

REVIEWS:

"All this international personnel has created is an embarrassing little piece of facetiousness...."—*Sunday Express* (U.K.), January 12, 1947

"General level of acting is good, and production has a nice quality, particularly in dueling scenes, which also owe something to the music of Spoliansky."—*Variety,* January 15, 1947

"*Meet Me at Dawn* ... is something less than choice either as comedy or romance. In truth, it is plain boring...."—*New York Times,* May 18, 1948

ADDITIONAL REVIEWS AND ARTICLES:

Kinematograph Weekly January 9, 1947; *The Star (UK)* January 10, 1947; *Daily Herald (UK)* January 10, 1947; *Daily Mail (UK)* January 10, 1947; *Motion Picture Herald* January 25, 1947; *Variety* March 17, 1948; *New York Herald Tribune* May 18, 1948; *Today's Cinema* March 6, 1953; *Kinematograph Weekly* March 12, 1953

NOTES: *The Gay Duellist* was the film's working title. *Meet Me at Dawn* opened in London in January 1946 and in New York City on May 17, 1948. For American distribution the print was cut from 99 minutes to 89.

Radio Programs and Personal Appearances

Broadcast adaptations based on Anatole Litvak's films:
Lux Radio Theatre, CBS
"Mayerling" September 1, 1939; "Tovarich" May 5, 1939; "The Sisters" Sept. 10, 1939; "All This, and Heaven Too" Dec. 15, 1941; "City for Conquest" Sept. 2, 1942; "This Above All" Sept. 14, 1942; "Sorry, Wrong Number" Sept. 1, 1950; "The Snake Pit" Oct. 4, 1950
NOTE: *Film Dope* magazine (London, September 1986) incorrectly indicated that Litvak directed the *Screen Director's Playhouse* radio episode "Back Street" (NBC, May 24, 1951). That show was directed by Robert Stevenson.

Litvak appeared as an uncredited extra in two scenes of his film *Aimez-vous Brahms* (*Goodbye Again*, 1961): dancing in a nightclub and walking a street in Paris.

Show-Business at War

Volume IX Number 10 of *The March of Time*; 20th Century–Fox; B&W; 17 minutes; 1943
CREDITS: *Director*: Louis deRochement
CAST: Eddie "Rochester" Anderson, Louis Armstrong, Jack Benny, Joe E. Brown, James Cagney, Bing Crosby, Michael Curtiz, Linda Darnell, Bette Davis, Olivia de Havilland, Marlene Dietrich, Walt Disney, Irene Dunne, W.C. Fields, Errol Flynn, John Ford, Clark Gable, John Garfield, Bert Glennon, Rita Hayworth, Bob Hope, Al Jolson, Brenda Joyce, Kay Kyser, Hedy Lamarr, Dorothy Lamour, Carole Landis, Anatole Litvak, Carole Lombard, Myrna Loy, Fred MacMurray, Victor Mature, the Mills Brothers, Tyrone Power, the Ritz Brothers, Mickey Rooney, Frank Sinatra, Darryl F. Zanuck and many others (Themselves)
NOTE: Litvak appears approximately five minutes into this documentary.

X Venice Film Festival

Istituto Luce; B&W; 1 minute; Released in September 1949
This Italian newsreel shows international stars and filmmakers attending the 10th Venice Film Festival. Litvak appears briefly, being in the competition with *The Snake Pit*. Other celebrities featured are Cécile Aubry, Vittorio Gassman and Josephine Baker.

Geneva Conference on Indochine

British Pathé; B&W; 4 minutes; May 10, 1954

A newsreel with footage of Litvak and actress Barbara Laage on a visit to the Palace of United Nations in Geneva, Switzerland

XV Venice Film Festival

Istituto Luce; B&W; 1 minute; Released in September 1954

In this Italian newsreel, international stars and filmmakers attend the 15th Venice Film Festival. Litvak appears briefly, being in the competition with *The Deep Blue Sea*. Other celebrities featured are Marcel Carné, Rock Hudson and Gloria Swanson.

Film Profile of Anatole Litvak

BBC; B&W; 30 minutes; September 13, 1955
Presenter: Alan Sleath

Litvak is interviewed by Peter Haigh and introduces scenes from some of his films, including *Sorry, Wrong Number*, *The Snake Pit*, *Decision Before Dawn* and *The Deep Blue Sea*.

Behind the Screen

20th Century–Fox; 1956
CREDITS: *Producer-Director*: Michael Forster; *Narrator*: Derek Bond

A brief documentary on the making of *Anastasia*.

Cinépanorama

B&W; 30 minutes
Presenter: François Chalais.

In the February 21, 1959, episode of this French TV series, Litvak talks about *The Journey*. In the November 19, 1960, episode, he appears along with Ingrid Bergman, Henri Fabian, Henri Decoin, Léa Garcia, Henri Crolla and Lourdes de Oliveira.

The World of Sophia Loren

NBC; B&W; 50 minutes; Aired on February 27, 1962

CREDITS: *Executive Producer*: Donald B. Hyatt; *Producer*: Eugene S. Jones; *Associate Producer*: James L. Reina; *Assistant Producer*: Shirley A. Chabot; *Research Supervisor*: Charles Grinker; *Writer*: Joseph Liss; *Music*: Robert Emmett Dolan; *Narrator*: Sophia Loren.

CAST: Sophia Loren, Art Buchwald, Vittorio De Sica, Anatole Litvak, Anthony Perkins, Carlo Ponti (Themselves)

This 1962 special examines the life and the artistry of Italian film actress Sophia Loren. Litvak is seen playing puzzle games with Loren and Anthony Perkins on the *Five Miles to Midnight* set. Loren comments on the filmmaking process. Litvak, Perkins, Vittorio De Sica and Art Buchwald also comment about Loren as a person and as an actress.

I Don Giovanni della Costa Azzurra

(Released in the U.S. as *Beach Casanova*)
Glomer Film; Technicolor; 98 minutes; Released in Rome on December 22, 1962

CREDITS: *Producer*: Enzo Merolle; *Director*: Vittorio Sala; *Screenplay*: Adriano Baracco, Ennio De Concini, Vittorio Sala; *Story*: Fabio Rinaudo, Vittorio Sala; *Photography*: Fausto Zuccoli; *Editor*: Renato Cinquini; *Music*: Roberto Nicolosi; *Production Designers-Costumers*: Giorgina Baldoni, Ugo Pericoli, George Petitot; *Art Directors*: Ugo Pericoli, Gerorges Petitot; *Production Managers*: Armando Grottini, Alex Maineri, Sergio

Merolle; *Sound*: Manlio Magar, Fiorenzo Magli; *Assistant Director*: Romana Fortini; *Secretaries to Producer*: Primo D'Amici, Raymond Millery

CAST: Curd Jürgens (Mr. Edmond), Annette Stroyberg (Gloria), Martine Carol (Nadine Leblanc), Gabriele Ferzetti (Avvocato Leblanc), Daniela Rocca (Assuntina Greco/ Geneviève), Paolo Ferrari (Michele), Eleonora Rossi Drago (Jasmine), Riccardo Garrone (Assuntina's Pimp), Ingrid Schoeller (Denise), Alberto Farnese (Commendatore milanese), Agnès Spaak (Nicole), Tiberio Murgia (Melchiorre), Coccinelle (Herself), Francesco Mulé (Baldassarre Giaconia), Raffaella Carrà (Hotel Housekeeper), Adriana Facchetti (Ugly American Tourist), Giuseppe Porelli (Gloria's Father), Carlo Giustini (Yacht Captain), Mino Doro (Jasmine's Husband), Ignazio Leone (Gaspare Patanè), Pia Gemberg, Mia Gemberg, Capucine, Mylène Demongeot, Jean-Paul Belmondo, Ingrid Bergman, Danielle Darrieux, Anatole Litvak, Jean Marais, Yves Montand, Anthony Perkins (Themselves)

Premiere of Orson Welles' The Trial

Gaumont; B&W; 1 minute; Released in 1963

Newsreel showing Litvak arriving together with Anthony Perkins at the premiere of director Orson Welles' *The Trial*.

New Battle of Warsaw

Pathé; B&W; 1 minute; April 6, 1966

Newsreel showing Litvak directing *The Night of the Generals* on location.

All About Bette

Turner Network Television; Color; 48 minutes; July 17, 1994

CREDITS: *Director*: Susan F. Walker; *Producers:* Susan F. Walker, Louise M. Gallup; *Executive Producer*: Ellen M. Krass; *Writer*: David Ansen; *Music:* Steve Orich; *Host:* Jodie Foster

Jodie Foster hosts this documentary on the life of Bette Davis, with interview clips of the elderly Davis interspersed with some career highlights. Litvak appears in relation to *The Sisters* and *All This, and Heaven Too*. Celebrities appearing include George Brent, Kim Carnes, Dick Cavett, Joan Crawford, Claudette Colbert. Bette Davis, Olivia de Havilland, Arthur Farnsworth, Errol Flynn, Lillian Gish, Miriam Hopkins, Gary Merrill, Harmon Nelson, Barbara Davis Sherry, William Grant Sherry, Jack Warner, William Wyler.

Hinter der Leinwand (Behind the Screen)

German TV series ARD Channel; B&W; 30 minutes; Aired on October 18, 1970

CREDITS: *Director-Writer*: Nikolai von Michaelwsky; *Producer*: Hessischer Rundfunk

A TV program produced by Hessischer Rundfunk (Public Broadcaster for the German region Hesse) reporting on current cinema with interviews with stars and filmmakers. Litvak appears along with Ingrid Bergman, Götz Burger, Joachim Hess, Roland Klick, Michèle Mercier and Eos Schopohl.

Backstory: Anastasia

AMC Network; Color; 30 minutes; Aired on January 29, 2001

CREDITS: *Director*: Michele Farinola; *Writer:* Mimi Freedman

This behind-the-scenes look at the making of *Anastasia* includes film clips and interviews. Litvak appears in several shots taken on the film set.

Chapter Notes

Chapter 1

1. Arthur Laurents, *Original Story* (New York: Knopf, 2000), p. 107.
2. William R. Meyer, *Warner Brothers Directors* (New Rochelle, NJ: Arlington House, 1978), p. 246.
3. Michel Aubriant, "Anatole Litvak: Un film est une symphonie," *Cinémonde*, January 16, 1953, p. 11.
4. "Mr. Litvak Comes to Film Sahara," *New York Times*, February 23, 1936.
5. Helga Belach, *Dolly Haas* (Berlin: Stiftung Deutsche Kinemathek, 1983), p. 9.
6. C. Hooper Trask, "Audible Films Inspire German Producers," *The New York Times*, November 23, 1930, IX, sec.2, p. 6.
7. H. T. S., "Another German Film Farce," New York Times, July 28, 1931, p. 16.
8. Max Ophüls, *Souvenirs* (Petite Bibliothèque des Cahiers du Cinéma, Paris, 2002), p. 16.
9. *Ibid.*

Chapter 2

1. René Lucot, *Magic City (*Paris: Pierre Bordas et Fils, 1989), pp. 106–107.
2. *Ibid.*, pp. 110–111.
3. Charles Zigman, *World's Coolest Movie Star: The Complete 95 Films of Jean Gabin* (Los Angeles: Allenwood Press, 2008), p. 114.
4. Jack Edmund Nolan, "Anatole Litvak," *Films in Review*, November 1967, pp. 550–551.
5. *Variety*, March 1, 1932.
6. *The Hollywood Reporter*, February 4, 1933, p. 3.
7. *Film Weekly, August 5, 1939.*
8. Sandy Wilson, *Ivor Novello* (London: Michael Joseph, 1975), p. 103.

9. Nino Frank, "Anatole Litvak va a realizer Cette veille canaille," *Pour Vous*, June 22, 1933, p. 11.
10. Larry Swindell, *Charles Boyer: The Reluctant Lover* (London: Weidenfeld and Nicolson, 1983), pp. 53–54.
11. *Pour Vous*, February 8, 1934.
12. Jeanne Witta-Montrobert, *La lanterne magique* (Paris: Calmann Lévy, 1980), p. 56.
13. Yves Courrière, *Joseph Kessel ou sur la piste du lion* (Paris: Plon, 1985), p. 448.
14. Witta-Montrobert, p. 52.
15. Christian Gilles, *Le Cinema des Annees 30. Tome I* (Paris: L'Harmattan, 2000), p. 45.
16. Wiliam M. Drew, *At the Center of the Frame: Leading Ladies of the Twenties and Thirties* (Lanham, MD: Vestal Press, 1999), p. 122.
17. André Lang, "L'Equipage," *Pour Vous*, October 24, 1935, p. 6.
18. Swindell, *Charles Boyer*, p. 86.
19. Henry-Jean Servat, *Les Trois Glorieuses* (Paris: Pygmalion, 2008), p. 51.
20. Witta-Montrobert, pp. 59–60.
21. Swindell, *Charles Boyer*, p. 87.
22. Kate Cameron, "Ace Romance is Presented at Filmarte," *Daily News*, September 14, 1937.

Chapter 3

1. Robert C. Franklin, *Popular Arts Project: Anatole Litvak*, Oral History Research Office (New York: Columbia University, 1959), p. 10–11.
2. "Mr. Litvak Comes to Film Sahara," *New York Times*, February 23, 1936.
3. Allen Eyles and Barrie Pattison, "Litvak. A Cutter at Heart," *Film & Filming*, February 1967, p. 17.

4. Joseph Kessel, *Hollywood, Ville Mirage* (Paris: Gallimard, 1937).
5. Witta-Montrobert, p. 61.
6. Jean Negulesco, *Things I Did and Things I Think I Did* (New York: Linden Press, 1984), pp. 183–184.
7. Edwin. Schallert, "Miriam Hopkins' Latest Design for Living," *Motion Picture*, February 1937, p. 92.
8. Nino Frank, "Anatole Litvak retourne à Hollywood," *Pour Vous*, October 15, 1934, p. 11.
9. *The Hollywood Reporter*, January 18, 1937, p. 7.
10. Jerome Lawrence, *Actor: The Life and Times of Paul Muni* (New York: Putnam's, 1974), pp. 230–231.
11. Ibid.
12. George Eells, *Ginger, Loretta and Irene Who?* (New York: Putnam's 1976), p. 107.
13. Douglas W. Churchill, "Hollywood Peers into Its Magic Looking-Glass," *New York Times*, July 25, 1937.
14. Laurence J. Quirk, *Claudette Colbert: An Illustrated Biography* (New York: Crown, 1985), pp. 99–100.
15. Ibid., p. 101.

Chapter 4

1. B.R. Crisler, "Gossip of the Films," *New York Times*, December 5, 1937.
2. "Warren Low—The Amazing Dr. Clitterhouse (1982)," *American Cinemeditor*, Summer/Fall 1982, pp. 24–25.
3. Ibid., p. 25
4. Ibid.
5. Charles Higham, *Errol Flynn the Untold Story* (London: Granada 1980), p. 133.
6. Whitney Stine, *Mother Goddam: The Story and the Career of Bette Davis* (London: Hawthorn Books, New York, 1974), pp. 102–103.
7. Lawrence Quirk, *The Passionate Life of Bette Davis* (London: Robson Book, 1991), pp. 156–157.
8. Whitney Stine, *Conversations With Bette Davis* (London: Virgin Books, 1990), p. 181.
9. Michael Buckley, "Irving Rapper," *Films in Review*, August/September 1986, p. 395.
10. Bette Davis, *The Lonely Life. An Autobiography* (London: Macdonald, 1963), p. 181.
11. Gene Tierney, *Self-Portrait* (New York: Wyden Books, 1979), p. 11.
12. Ibid., p. 10.
13. Ibid., p. 12.
14. Warren Low, "Litvak a Cutter at Heart," *Films and Filming*, February 1967, p. 17.
15. Franklin, *Anatole Litvak*, pp. 10–11.
16. Hal Wallis, *Starmaker: The Autobiography of Hal Wallis* (New York: Macmillan, 1980), pp. 70–71.
17. Edward G. Robinson, *All My Yesterdays: An Autobiography* (London: W. H. Allen, 1974), p. 205.
18. Don Siegel, *A Siegel Film: An Autobiography* (London: Faber & Faber, 1994), pp. 59–60.
19. Jack Warner, *My First Hundred Years in Hollywood* (New York: Random House 1965), p. 263.
20. Michael Freedland, *The Warner Brothers* (London: Harrap, 1983), p. 117.
21. "Chaplin Called for Movie Inquiry," *New York Times*, September 14, 1941.
22. Stine, *Conversations With Bette Davis*, p. 138.
23. James Spada, *More Than a Woman: An Intimate Biography of Bette Davis* (London: Time Warner Books, 1994), p. 221.
24. Lawrence J. Quirk, *The Passionate Life of Bette Davis* (London: Robson Books, 1991), p. 179.
25. Negulesco, *Things I Did and Things I Think I Did*, pp. 184–185.
26. Nolan, *Films in Review*, p. 555.

Chapter 5

1. "Goulding, "Litvak Off to Hollywood," *New York Post*, June 1939.
2. Robert Nott, *He Ran All the Way: The Life of John Garfield* (New York: Limelight Editions, 2003) p. 118.
3. Negulesco, *Things I Did and Things I Think I Did*, pp. 188–189.
4. Swindell, *Charles Boyer*, p. 158.
5. Eells, *Ginger, Loretta and Irene Who?*, p. 110.
6. Davis, *The Lonely Life*, p. 200.
7. Boze Hadleigh, *Bette Davis Speaks* (New York: Barricade Books, 1996), p. 110.
8. Quirk, *The Passionate Life of Bette Davis*, pp. 213–214.
9. Swindell, *Charles Boyer*, p. 163.

10. Davis, *The Lonely Life*, p. 200.
11. Stine, *Mother Goddam*, p. 130.
12. Stine, *Conversations With Bette Davis*, p. 181.
13. Bernard F. Dick, *Hal Wallis. Producer to the Stars* (Lexington, KY, University Press of Kentucky, 2004), p. 37.
14. Swindell, *Charles Boyer*, p. 163.
15. Clifford Odets, *The Time is Ripe* (New York: Grove Press, 1988), p. 317.
16. Negulesco, *Things I Did and Things I Think I Did*, pp. 186–187.
17. Julie Gilbert, *Opposite Attraction: The Lives of Erich Maria Remarque and Paulette Goddard* (New York: Pantheon Books, 1995), p. 270.

Chapter 6

1. James R. Parish and Don E. Stanke, *The Forties Gals* (Westport, CT: Arlington House, 1980), p. 278.
2. John McCabe, *Cagney* (New York: Knopf, 1997), p. 194.
3. Elia Kazan, *A Life* (New York: Knopf, 1988), p. 185.
4. *Ibid*.
5. Eyles and Pattison, "Litvak. A Cutter at Heart," p. 17.
6. *Ibid*. p. 186.
7. James Cagney, *Cagney by Cagney* (New York: Pocket Books, 1987), p. 110.
8. Richard Schickel, *James Cagney: A Celebration* (London: Pavilion, 1985), p. 124.
9. "Cagney and Litvak Score Triumph," *Hollywood Reporter*, September 10, 1940, p. 3.
10. William Donati, *Ida Lupino: A Biography* (Lexington: University Press of Kentucky), 1995, p. 80.
11. Kazan, *A Life*, p. 190.
12. *Ibid*. p. 188.
13. Siegel, *A Siegel Film*, pp. 64–65.
14. Ibid.
15. "Litvak Fined in Auto Case, Loses License, *Los Angeles Times*, August 23, 1941.
16. Joan Fontaine, *No Bed of Roses* (New York, Morrow: 1978), p. 151.
17. John Kobal, *People Will Talk* (London: Aurum Press, 1986), p. 437.
18. Tyrone Power, "The Role I Liked Best...," *The Saturday Evening Post*, June 27, 1946, p. 100.
19. Nolan, *Films in Review*, p. 556.

Chapter 7

1. Tex Mccrary, and Jinx Falkenburg, "New York Close-Up," *New York Herald-Tribune*, December 26, 1951.
2. Letter from Julius H. Amberg to Senator Ralph O. Brewster, April 5,1943, folder "1943 August–Sept.," box 7A, Capra Collection, Wesleyan University, Middleton, CT.
3. Frank Capra, *The Name Above the Title* (New York: Macmillan, 1971), p. 336.
4. Bosley Crowther, "'The Battle of Russia' Fifth in 'Why We Fight' Series, Now on View at the Globe, *New York Times*, November 15, 1943.
5. Mccrary, and Falkenburg, *New York Herald-Tribune*.
6. Philip K. Scheuer, "Anatole Litvak—a Movie Career on Two Continents," *L.A. Times*, February 19, 1967.
7. Edgar Snow, "The Lights Go on Again," *The Saturday Evening Post*, September 16, 1944, p. 96.
8. Michael Shnayerson, *Irwin Shaw. A Biography* (New York: Putnam, 1989), pp. 145–147.
9. Hellmuth Karasek, *Billy Wilder. Un Viennese a Hollywood* (Milano: Mondadori,1993), pp. 174–175.
10. Lucy Chase Williams, *The Complete Films of Vincent Price* (Secaucus, NJ: Citadel Press, 1995), p. 106.
11. Ibid.
12. Jack D. Grant, "Barbara Bel Geddes in Stunning Debut," *Hollywood Reporter*, May 28 1947, p. 3.
13. Bennett Cerf, *At Random: The Reminiscences of Bennett Cerf* (New York: Random House, 1977), p. 229.
14. "Shocker," *Time*, December 20 1948, p 46.
15. Anatol [sic] Litvak, "Se un'attrice vuole avere vita lunga," *Hollywood*, July 2 1949, p. 3.
16. Tony Thomas, *The Films of Olivia de Havilland* (Seacacus, NJ: Citadel Press, 1983), p. 218.
17. Arthur Laurents, *Original Story* (New York: Knopf, 2000), p. 64.
18. *Ibid.*, pp.106–107.
19. Patrick McGilligan, *Backstory 2: Interviews with Screenwriters from 1940 and 1950* (Berkley, CA: University of California Press, 1991), p. 137.
20. Sheridan Gibney, "Mailed Opinions," *New York Times*, November 14, 1948.

21. Rudy Behlmer, *Memo from Darryl F. Zanuck* (New York: Grove, 1993), p. 112.
22. John C. Tibbetts and James Welsh, *American Classic Screen Profiles*, (Latham: MD, Scarecrow Press, 2011), p. 106.
23. Thomas F. Brady, "Hollywood Briefs," *New York Times*, September 7 1947.
24. Thomas M. Pryor, "Of Litvak and the 'Pit,'" *New York Times*, November 7 1948.
25. Betsy Blair, *The Memory of All That* (New York: Knopf, 2003), p. 170.

Chapter 8

1. Allen Eyles, Barrie Pattinson, *Films & Filming*, p. 17.
2. Ella Smith, *Miss Barbara Stanwyck* (New York: Crown Publishers, 1974), p. 211.
3. Al Di Orio, *Barbara Stanwyck* (New York: Coward-McCann, 1983), pp.151–152.
4. Smith, *Miss Barbara Stanwyck*, p. 211.
5. David Fury, *The Cinema History of Burt Lancaster* (Minneapolis: Artist's Press, 1989), pp. 28–29.
6. Minty Clinch, *Burt Lancaster* (London: Arthur Barker, 1984), pp. 24–25.
7. Kate Buford, *Burt Lancaster. An American Life* (New York: Knopf, 2000), p. 91.
8. Litvak, *Hollywood*, p. 3.
9. Behlmer, *Memo from Darryl F. Zanuck*, p. 160.
10. Tachella, "Quatre 'directors' à Paris," *L'Écran Français*, June 8 1948, p. 5.
11. Peter Viertel, *Dangerous Friends* (New York: Nan A. Telese, 1992), p. 69.
12. *Ibid.*, pp. 70–71.
13. "Litvak Mops Brow After German Job," *Los Angeles Times*, June 17 1951.
14. Hildegard Knef, *The Gift Horse* (London: Andre Deutsch, 1971), pp. 237–239.
15. Witta-Montrobert, *La lanterne magique*, p. 61.
16. Brigitte Bardot, *Mi chiamano B. B.* (Milano: Bompiani, 1999), p. 100.
17. Kirk Douglas, *The Ragman's Son*, (New York: Simon & Schuster, 1988), p. 217.
18. Joseph McBride, *Kirk Douglas* (New York: Pyramid Books, 1976), p. 76.
19. "Anatole Litvak Off 20th" *Variety*, February 17 1954.
20. Kenneth More, *More or Less. An Autobiography* (London: Hodder and Stoughton, 1978,) p. 165.
21. Kenneth More, *Happy Go Lucky* (London: Robert Hale, 1959), p 150.
22. *Ibid.*, p. 151.
23. Hugo Vickers, *Vivien Leigh* (Boston: Little Brown, 1981), pp. 120–121.
24. "The Twenty Questions Everyone is asking About Vivien Leigh," *Picturegoer*, November 26 1955, p. 15.
25. Alan Dent, *Vivien Leigh. A Bouquet* (London: Hamish Hamilton, 1969), p. 82.
26 Viertel, *Dangerous Friends*, p. 153.
27. Michael Gross, *Model. The Ugly Business of Beautiful Women* (New York: Morrow, 1995), p. 138.

Chapter 9

1. Joseph Henry Steele, *Ingrid Bergman: An Intimate Portrait* (New York: David McKay, 1959), p. 321.
2. Ingrid Bergman, *Ingrid Bergman: My Story* (New York: Viking, 1980), p. 317.
3. McGillian, *Backstory 2*, p. 149.
4. Bergman, *Ingrid Bergman: My Story*, p. 318.
5. Stephen Watts, "Following Anastasia Along the Thames," *New York Times*, August 5 1956.
6. Helen Hayes, *My Life in Three Acts* (New York: Harcourt Brace Jovanovich, 1990), p. 190.
7. *Alvin Cooperman Interview. Broadcasting Collection* (New York: Oral History Library, American Jewish Committee, 1994), pp. 29–30.
8. "Scandal in Rehearsal," *Life*, February 4, 1957, p. 57.
9. Warren G. Harris, *Audrey Hepburn. A Biography* (New York: Simon & Schuster, 1994), p. 147.
10. "TV's Got More Sparkle: Litvak," *Variety*, January 16 1957.
11. *Alvin Cooperman Interview*, pp. 31–32.
12. Viertel, *Dangerous Friends*, p. 346.
13. *Ibid*.
14. Russ Bradley, "It's Never Dull With Yul," *Sunday News*, August 10, 1958, p. 77.
15. "Litvak Explains 'Friendly Russian' in The Journey," *Variety*, February 18, 1959.
16. Hal Boyle, "Stars Blind Filmland, Litvak Says," *New York World Telegram and Sun*, June 28, 1961.
17. Bergman, *Ingrid Bergman: My Story*, p. 366.

18. Irene Thirer, "Movie Spotlight," *New York Post*, June 7, 1961.
19. Bergman, *Ingrid Bergman: My Story*, p. 366.
20. *Ibid. p. 135.*
21. B. Darrach "Psycho Ii," *People,* June 13 1983, p. 61.
22. H. Alpert, "Tony Perkins on the Past, Present and Future of Love," *Woman's Day*, February 1961, p. 16.
23. Charlotte Chandler, *Ingrid. A Personal Biography* (New York: Simon & Schuster, 2007), p. 222.

Chapter 10

1. Charles Hamblett, *Anatole Litvak*, 1962.
2. Charles Hamblett, "Suspense on the Seine," *New York Times*, February 25 1962.
3. Alan Levy, *Sophia Loren. An Intimate Portrait* (London: Magnum Books, 1979), pp. 52–53.
4. David Caute, *Joseph Losey* (London: Faber & Faber 1994), pp. 216–217.
5. Joanne Stang, "Marlon Brando at 40: Acting Never Dominated His Life," *New York Times*, November 29, 1964.
6. Eyles and Pattison, "Litvak. A Cutter at Heart," p. 16.
7. Natasha Fraser-Cavassoni, *Sam Spiegel* (New York: Simon & Schuster, 2003), pp. 282–283.
8. Omar Sharif, *The Eternal Me* (London: W.H. Allen, 1977), p. 123.
9. Christopher Plummer, *In Spite of Myself* (London: JR Books, 2010), pp. 435–436.
10. Dominique Maillet, *Philippe Noiret* (Paris: Editions Henri Veyrier, 1978), p. 7.
11. Nicholas Wapshott *Peter O'Toole. A Biography* (London: New English Library, 1983), p. 141.
12. Frawley Becker, *And the Stars Spoke Back (*Laham, MD: The Scarecrow Press, 2004), pp. 68–69.
13. Philip K. Scheurer, "Anatole Litvak—a Movie Career on Two Continents," *Los Angeles Times*, February 19, 1967.
14. Thomas Quinn Curtiss, "To an American Movie, Warsaw Said OK," *New York Times*, May 8, 1966.
15. Scheurer, "Anatole Litvak—a Movie Career on Two Continents,"
16. Bob Willoughby, *The StarMakers (*London: Merrell, 2003,) p. 322.
17. Witta, *La lanterne magique,* p. 61.
18. Negulesco, *Things I Did and Things I Think I Did,* pp. 189–190.

Selected Bibliography

Bardot, Brigitte. *Mi chiamano B.B.* Milano: Bompiani, 1999.

Becker, Frawley. *And the Stars Spoke Back.* Lanham, MD: Scarecrow Press, 2004

Behlmer, Rudy. *Memo from Darryl F. Zanuck.* New York: Grove, 1993.

Bergman, Ingrid. *Ingrid Bergman: My Story.* New York: Viking, 1980.

Blair, Betsy. *The Memory of All That.* New York: Knopf, 2003.

Brook, Vincent. *Drive to Darkness: Jewish Émigré Directors and the Rise of Film Noir.* New Brunswick, NJ: Rutgers University Press, 2009.

Buford, Kate. *Burt Lancaster: An American Life.* New York: Knopf, 2000.

Cagney, James. *Cagney by Cagney.* New York: Pocket Books, 1987.

Capra, Frank. *The Name Above the Title.* New York: Macmillan, 1971.

Capua, Michelangelo. *Anthony Perkins: Prigioniero della paura.* Torino: Lindau, 2003.

_____. *Deborah Kerr: A Biography.* Jefferson, NC: McFarland, 2010.

_____. *Vivien Leigh: A Biography.* Jefferson, NC: McFarland, 2003.

_____. *Yul Brynner: A Biography.* Jefferson, NC: McFarland, 2006.

Caute, David. *Joseph Losey.* London: Faber & Faber 1994.

Cerf, Bennett. *At Random: The Reminiscences of Bennett Cerf.* New York: Random House, 1977.

Chandler, Charlotte. *Ingrid: A Personal Biography.* New York: Simon & Schuster, 2007.

Chase Williams, Lucy. *The Complete Films of Vincent Price.* Secaucus, NJ: Citadel Press, 1995.

Clinch, Minty. *Burt Lancaster.* London: Arthur Barker, 1984.

Courrière, Yves. *Joseph Kessel ou sur la piste du lion.* Paris: Plon, 1985.

Cowe, Susan and Tom Johnson. *The Films of Oliver Reed.* Jefferson, NC: McFarland, 2011.

Davis, Bette. *The Lonely Life: An Autobiography.* London: Macdonald, 1963.

Dent, Alan. *Vivien Leigh: A Bouquet.* London: Hamish Hamilton, 1969.

Di Orio, Al. *Barbara Stanwyck.* New York: Coward-McCann, 1983.

Dick, Bernard F. *Hal Wallis: Producer to the Stars.* Lexington: University Press of Kentucky, 2004.

Donati, William M. *Ida Lupino: A Biography.* Lexington: University Press of Kentucky, 1995.

Douglas, Kirk. *The Ragman's Son.* New York: Simon & Schuster, 1988.

Drew Wiliam M. *At the Center of the Frame: Leading Ladies of the Twenties and Thirties.* Lanham, MD: Vestal Press, 1999.

Eells, George. *Ginger, Loretta and Irene Who?* New York: Putnam, 1976.

Fontaine, Joan. *No Bed of Roses.* New York: Morrow, 1978.

Fraser-Cavassoni, Natasha. *Sam Spiegel.* New York: Simon & Schuster, 2003.

Freedland, Michael. *The Warner Brothers.* London: Harrap, 1983.

Fury, David. *The Cinema History of Burt Lancaster.* Minneapolis: Artist's Press, 1989.

Gilbert Julie. *Opposite Attraction: The Lives*

Selected Bibliography

of *Erich Maria Remarque and Paulette Goddard*. New York: Pantheon Books, 1995.

Gilles, Christian. *Le Cinéma des Années 30. Tome I*. Paris: L'Harmattan, 2000.

Gross, Michael. *Model: The Ugly Business of Beautiful Women*. New York: Morrow, 1995

Gussow, Mel. *Darryl F. Zanuck: Don't Say Yes until I'm Finished Talking*. London: W.H. Allen 1971.

Hayes, Helen, and Katherine Hatch. *My Life in Three Acts*. San Diego: Harcourt Brace Jovanovich, 1990.

Harris, Warren G. *Audrey Hepburn: A Biography*. New York: Simon & Schuster, 1994.

Higham, Charles. *Errol Flynn the Untold Story*. London: Granada 1980.

Karasek, Hellmuth *Billy Wilder: Un Viennese a Hollywood*. Milan: Mondadori, 1993.

Kazan, Elia. *A Life*. New York: Knopf, 1988.

Kessel, Joseph. *Hollywood, Ville Mirage*. Paris: Gallimard, 1937.

Knef, Hildegard. *The Gift Horse*. London: Andre Deutsch, 1971.

Kobal, John. *People Will Talk*. London: Aurum Press, 1986.

Laurents, Arthur. *Original Story*. New York: Knopf, 2000.

Lawrence, Jerome. *Actor: The Life and Times of Paul Muni*. New York: Putnam, 1974.

Levy, Alan. *Sophia Loren: An Intimate Portrait*. London: Magnum Books, 1979.

Lucot, René. *Magic City*. Paris: Pierre Bordas et Fils, 1989.

Maillet, Dominique. *Philippe Noiret*. Paris: Editions Henri Veyrier, 1978.

McBride, Joseph. *Kirk Douglas*. New York: Pyramid Books, 1976.

McCabe John. *Cagney*. New York: Knopf, 1997.

McGilligan, Patrick. *Backstory 2: Interviews with Screenwriters from 1940 and 1950*. Berkeley: University of California Press.

Meyer, William R. *Warner Brothers Directors*. New Rochelle, NJ: Arlington House, 1978.

More, Kenneth. *Happy Go Lucky*. London: Robert Hale, 1959.

_____. *More or Less: An Autobiography*. London: Hodder and Stoughton, 1978.

Negulesco, Jean. *Things I Did and Things I Think I Did*. New York: Linden Press, 1984.

Nott, Robert. *He Ran All the Way: The Life of John Garfield*. New York: Limelight Editions, 2003.

Odets, Clifford. *The Time Is Ripe*. New York: Grove Press, 1988.

Omar Sharif. *The Eternal Me*. London: W.H. Allen, 1977.

Ophüls, Max. *Souvenirs*. Petite Bibliothèque des Cahiers du Cinéma, Paris, 2002.

Parish, James R., and Don E. Stanke. *The Forties Gals*. Westport, CT: Arlington House, 1980.

Plummer, Christopher. *In Spite of Myself*. London: JR Books, 2010.

Quirk, Laurence J. *Claudette Colbert: An Illustrated Biography*. New York: Crown, 1985.

_____. *The Passionate Life of Bette Davis*. London: Robson Book, 1991.

Robinson Edward G. *All My Yesterdays: An Autobiography*. London: W. H. Allen, 1974.

Schickel, Richard. *James Cagney: A Celebration*. London: Pavilion, 1985.

Servat, Henry-Jean. *Les Trois Glorieuses*. Paris: Pygmalion, 2008.

Shnayerson, Michael. *Irwin Shaw: A Biography*. New York: Putnam, 1989.

Siegel, Don. *A Siegel Film: An Autobiography*. London: Faber & Faber, 1994.

Smith, Ella. *Miss Barbara Stanwyck*. New York: Crown Publishers, 1974.

Spada, James. *More Than a Woman: An Intimate Biography of Bette Davis*. London: Time Warner Books, 1994.

Steele, Joseph Henry. *Ingrid Bergman: An Intimate Portrait*. New York: David McKay, 1959.

Stine, Whitney. *Conversations with Bette Davis*. London: Virgin Books, 1990.

_____. *Mother Goddam: The Story and the Career of Bette Davis*. London: Hawthorn Books, New York, 1974.

Swindell, Larry. *Charles Boyer: The Reluctant Lover*. London: Weidenfeld and Nicolson, 1983.

Thomas, Tony. *The Films of Olivia de Havilland*. Secaucus, NJ: Citadel Press, 1983.

Tibbetts John C., and James Welsh. *American Classic Screen Profiles*. Lanham, MD: Scarecrow Press, 2011.

Tierney Gene. *Self-Portrait*. New York: Wyden Books, 1979.

Vickers, Hugo. *Vivien Leigh*. Boston: Little Brown, 1981.

Viertel, Peter. *Dangerous Friends*. New York: Nan A. Telese, 1992.

Wallis, Hal. *Starmaker: The Autobiography of Hal Wallis*. New York: Macmillan, 1980.

Wapshott, Nicholas. *Peter O'Toole: A Biography*. London: New English Library, 1983.

Warner, Jack. *My First Hundred Years in Hollywood*. New York: Random House 1965.

Willoughby, Bob. *The StarMakers*. London: Merrell, 2003.

Wilson, Sandy. *Ivor Novello*. London: Michael Joseph, 1975.

Witta-Montrobert, Jeanne. *La Lanterne magique*. Paris: Calmann Lévy, 1980.

Zigman, Charles. *World's Coolest Movie Star: The Complete 95 Films of Jean Gabin*. Los Angeles: Allenwood Press, 2008.

Index

Achard, Marcel 16, 68, 103, 128, 196
Act of Love 25, 86–88, 116, 162–164
Adler, Buddy 93, 166, 167
Aimée, Anouk 99, 168
Aimez-vous Brahms see *Goodbye Again*
All My Sons 80
All the Gold in the World see *Five Miles to Midnight*
All This, and Heaven Too 37, 38, 47–51, 141–143, 194, 196
Allister, Claude 13, 125
The Amazing Dr. Clitterhouse 34–36, 134–136
Amberg, Julius H. 65
Anastasia 1, 92, 93–96, 98, 116, 166, 195, 196
Anderson, Maxwell 47
Anderson, Robert 112
Anet, Claude 19, 129
Angels with Dirty Faces 45
Annabella 9, 17, 18, 27, 28, 61, 127, 189
Arabian Nights 6
Archard, Marcel 108
Arletty 70, 154
Ashcroft, Peggy 89
Astaire, Fred 29
Astley, Capt. Philip 14
Aumont, Jean-Pierre 17, 18, 25, 127, 173

Balcon, Michael 14, 125
Ballets Russes 6
Banton, Travis 31, 132
Barber, Maurice 9, 10, 11, 122
Bardot, Brigitte 87, 88, 162
Bartley, Tony 100
Basehart, Richard 83, 85, 86, 159
Bask, Leon 6
The Battle of China 65, 182–183
The Battle of Russia 65, 66–67, 181–182
Baur, Harry 15, 126
Baxter, Anne 7
Be Mine Tonight see *Tell Me Tonight*
Becker, Frawley 113–114, 177
Becky Sharp 25
Bel Geddes, Barbara 70, 152
Bel Geddes, Norman 70
Benim, André 15

Benois, Alexander 6, 189
Bergman, Ingrid 73, 93, 94, 95, 96, 102, 103, 104, 105, 107, 157, 166, 167, 168, 170, 171, 172, 195, 196
Bernard, Raymond 18–19
Bernard, Tristan 9, 122
Bernhardt, Curtis 59, 69, 149, 186
Berry, Jules 70, 154
Berstl, Julius 7, 120
Biberman, Herbert J. 68
The Big Trees 87
Bilinsky, Boris 6, 127, 190, 191
Binger, Dr. Carl 73
Black Legion 45
Blair, Betsy 76, 77, 155
Blanchar, Pierre 15, 19, 126
Blanke, Harry 57, 146, 148
Blatty, William Peter 109
Bloch, Noé 6, 16, 20, 119, 120, 121, 127, 189, 190, 191
Blues in the Night 55, 57, 59–60, 147–149
Bogarde, Dirk 112
Bogart, Humphrey 34–35, 36, 55, 57, 69, 134, 136, 138, 147
Boleslavsky, Richard 36
Bolivar, Simon 81
Bolton, Guy 166
Bond, Ward 35, 134, 138, 144
Bondi, Beulah 76, 136, 155
Le Bonheur 15
Bonjour Tristesse 102
Bowman, Lee 80, 159
Boy Meets Girl 23
Boyer, Charles 15, 19, 20, 21, 23, 24, 25, 27, 28, 31, 33, 47, 48, 50, 51, 61, 127, 129, 132, 133, 142, 181, 182, 186, 193
Boyer, Jean 7
Brahm, John 6
Brand, Millen 73, 74, 154, 157
Brando, Marlon 111, 187
Brasseur, Pierre 12, 124
Brent, George 47, 196
Brewster, Sen. Ralph O. 65
The Bridge on the River Kwai 112
Brinig, Myron 36, 136

INDEX

Browning, Kirk 98, 179
Brute Force 80, 110
Brynner, Yul 1, 93, 94, 95, 96, 98–99, 100, 101–102, 103, 116, 166, 168, 170, 184, 187
Buchwald, Art 107, 195
Burr, Raymond 39
Buydens, Anne 87

Cagney, James 44, 54, 55–56, 59
Cagney, William "Bill" 54, 143
Calais-Douvres 7, 8, 85, 121–122
Call It Treason 82, 159, 162
Callahan, Herbert L. 70
Capone, Al 70
Capra, Frank 64, 65, 66, 67, 180, 181, 182, 183, 184
Caravan 15
Carné, Marcel 70, 154, 190, 194
Carroll, Madeline 13–14, 24, 125, 186
Carroll, Sidney 115
Carson, Jack 59, 148
Casanova 5–6, 190
Castle on the Hudson 38, 45–47, 140–141, 149
Cerf, André 18, 127
Cerf, Bennett 64, 72, 73
Cette Vielle Canaille 14–16, 30, 126–127
La Chanson d'une nuit 12, 124
Le Chant de l'amour triomphant 4, 187
Chaplin, Charlie 52
Charell, Erik 15
Charitonoff 16
Churchill, Winston 66
City for Conquest 38, 54–57, 143–146, 194
Cliff, Laddie 13, 14, 125
Clift, Montgomery 7, 81, 86, 187
Clive, Colin 29, 131
Cluzot, George Henri 12, 124
Le Coeur see *Hearts and Dollars*
Coeur de Lilas 9–11, 122–123
Cohn, Harry 25
Colbert, Claudette 27, 30, 31, 32, 33, 132, 186, 196
Colman, Roger 34
Colman, Ronald 60, 61, 136
Confessions of a Nazi Spy 39–43, 138–140
Conquest 31
Conte, Richard 76, 157
Cooper, Gary 86
Cooperman, Alvin 97, 98, 179
Coppel, Alec 108
Les Corbeau 12
The Corn Is Green 37
Cotten, Joseph 76, 157
Coup de grâce 68
Courtney, William 70
Le Couteau dans la plaie see *Five Miles to Midnight*
The Crew 16
Les Croix de bois 18–19
Curtiz, Michael 59, 186, 194

Dagover, Lil 6, 191
Dallas 70
Darrieux, Danielle 19, 20, 21, 129, 196
Darvas, Lili 30
Dassin, Jules 110–111, 185, 186
Davidson, David 86
The Da Vinci Code 101
Davis, Barbara "Bobby" 38
Davis, Bette 30, 36–38, 43, 44, 47, 48, 50–51, 136, 137, 138, 141, 142, 194, 196
Dead End 23
de Canonge, Maurice 9
Decision Before Dawn 1, 83–86, 159, 187, 194
Deep Are the Roots 70
The Deep Blue Sea 89–91, 92, 164–166, 167, 195
Deering, John 42, 138
de Havilland, Olivia 47, 73, 75, 76, 77, 81, 155, 157, 196
De Maupassant, Guy 99, 168
The Deputy 111, 187
Derzhavin, Konstantin 5
De Sica, Vittorio 106
Desire Under the Elms 106
Désirée 88, 89, 187
Deval, Jacques 30, 132, 134
Les Diaboliques 12
Diaghilev, Sergei 6
Dieterle, William 36
Dietrich, Marlene 5, 25, 40, 89, 166, 188, 194
Disney, Walt 65, 180, 182, 183, 184, 194
Distel, Sacha 103
Divide and Conquer 65, 181
Dr. Jekyll and Mr. Hyde 25
Dolly Gets Ahead see *Dolly Macht Karriere*
Dolly Macht Karriere 6–7, 119–120
Dolly's Way to Stardom see *Dolly Macht Karriere*
Donat, Robert 61, 152
Douglas, Kirk 86, 87–88, 162, 163
Dragomir, Dimitri 10, 122
Dreyer, Carl Theodor 17
Druon, Maurice 67, 103, 173
Dubost, Pauline 16
Dunne, Irene 36, 61, 194
Duras, Marguerite 110
Dyne, Michael 96

Earhart, Amelia 29
Eason, B. Reeves 51
Eells, George 30
Eggar, Samantha 115, 116, 177
Entratter, Jack 92
Epstein, Julius 47, 136
Epstein, Philip 47
L'Équipage 16–19, 20, 27, 28, 62, 68, 127–128, 132
Escadrille see *The Woman I Love*
Esterhazy, Einar 5
Evelyn, Judith 97, 179

Index

Falconetti, Marie 17
A Farewell to Arms 31
Farnum, Dorothy 9, 122
Faulkner, William 34
Fear Strikes Out 104
Feldman, Charles 31, 61, 92
Fernandel 9, 10, 122
Ferrer, Mel 96, 97–98, 130, 179
Field, Alice 15, 16, 126
Field, Betty 59, 148
Field, Rachel 47, 142, 143
Finch, Peter 110, 11, 185
Five Miles to Midnight 106–109, 110, 173–174, 195
Fletcher, Lucille 78, 89, 157, 158, 159
Flight into Darkness see *L'Équipage*
Flynn, Errol 36–37, 38, 136, 194, 196
Fog Over London 34
Fonda, Henry 70, 71, 152
Fontaine, Joan 61–62, 73, 150
Ford, Eileen 92
Ford, John 55
Ford, Wallace 59, 148
The Fourth Dimension see *Five Miles to Midnight*
Francis, Kay 30
Frank, Nino 14
Freeland, Thornton 68, 192
Fresnay, Pierre 19
Freud, Sigmund 81, 187
Die Freudlose Gasse 5, 188
Frings, Kurt 97
Fujikawa, Jerry 99, 169

Gabin, Jean 9, 11, 16, 70, 122, 154
Gable, Clark 28, 194
Gance, Abel 5, 9, 189, 190
Garbo, Greta 5, 31, 47, 89, 143, 188
The Garden of Allah 25
Garfield, John 36, 45, 46, 57, 58–59, 140, 141, 146, 149, 194
Garland, Judy 105
Gary, Romain 115
Gauthier, Marthe 19
The Gay Duellist see *Meet Me at Dawn*
Geheimnisse des Orients 5, 6, 190
Genn, Leo 75, 76, 155, 157
The Gentle People see *Out of the Fog*
Gibney, Sheridan 75
Gilbert, Edwin 59, 148
Gilbert, John 29
Goddard, Paulette 49, 52–53, 68
Goebbels, Joseph 42
Gone with the Wind 52, 68
Goodbye Again 102–105, 170–173, 194
Goodin, Peggy 81
Gorss, Sal 41–42
Goulding, Edmund 47, 186
Green, Richard 61, 152
Greene, Lorne 97, 179
Greenwillow 102

Grive, Harold 30
Gross, Michael 92
Guinness, Alec 92
Gwenn, Edmund 12, 125

Haas, Dolly 6–7, 120
Hadji Murat 6, 191
Hahn, Bill 79
Hakim, Raymond 69, 152
Hakim, Robert 69, 152
Hale, Sonnie 12, 125
Halop, Billy 59, 148
Hammond, Kay 12, 125
Hannold, Douglas 30
Hardwicke, Cedric 34
Harriman, W. Averell 53, 66
Harvey, Laurence 102
Harvey, Lilian 8–9, 120
Haskin, Byron 32, 60, 132, 140, 142, 143
Havelock-Allan, Anthony 98, 99
Hayes, Alfred 86
Hayes, Helen 47, 93, 94, 95, 96, 143, 166, 168
Hayward, Leland 86
Hayward, Louis 28, 57, 131, 147
Hayward, Susan 136, 138
Hearts and Dollars 4–5, 119
Heller, Robert 65, 180, 181
Hellman, Lillian 81
Hepburn, Audrey 96, 97–98, 130, 179
Hepburn, Katharine 27
Here Is Germany 67
High Sierra 57
Hilde 86
Hildyard, Jack 95, 164, 166, 168
Hiroshima Mon Amour 110
Hirsch, Charles Henry 9, 122
Hirschfeld, Al 6
Hitchcock, Alfred 7, 70, 102, 106
Hochhuth, Rolf 111, 187
Hollingshead, Gordon 39
Holloway, Stanley 13, 125, 192
Honegger, Arthur 27, 127, 129, 131, 132
Hoover, J. Edgar 39, 40
Hopkins, George 32
Hopkins, Michael 30, 44
Hopkins, Miriam 23, 25–26, 28–30, 32, 33, 41, 43–44, 47, 64, 65, 131, 143, 196
Hornbeck, William 65, 162, 180, 181, 182, 183
Horsting, Olga 87
Hot Nocturne see *Blues in the Night*
How Green Was My Valley 57
Howard, Ron 101, 168
Howe, George 82, 159
Hulswit, Jean 9, 122
The Hunchback of Notre Dame 34
Hunter, Ian 38, 136
The Hustler 57
Huston, John 34–35, 77, 81, 82, 87, 134, 187
Huston, Walter 66, 180, 181, 182, 183

I Confess 7
I Live with You 14
I Walk Alone 80
L'Idiote 108
Ironside 39

Jackson, Anne 99, 168
Jackson, Gordon 113, 175
Jaffe, Henry 96–97
Jaffe, Saul 96–97
Japrisot, Sébastien 116, 177
Jezebel 31, 36
Joachimson, Felix 6
Johnny Belinda 81
Johnson, Celia 89
Joseph, Albrecht 12, 123, 124, 125
Le Jour se lève 70, 71, 154
The Journey 98–101, 168–170
Joyless Street see *Die Freudlose Gasse*

Kane, Robert 61
Kaufman, Charles 81
Kaufmann, Dr. Ralph 73
Kazan, Elia 55–56, 59, 60, 143, 145, 148
Kelly, Gene 77
Kennedy, Arthur 54, 115, 143, 145
Kerr, Deborah 1, 89, 99–101, 117, 168, 170
Kessel, George 23
Kessell, Joseph 16–17, 19, 23, 24–25, 27, 68, 86, 99, 127, 128, 129, 130, 164, 175, 186
Kiepura, Jan 12, 123, 124, 125
The Killers 80
The King and I 99
Knight, Eric 61, 62, 65, 152, 180
Know Your Ally 67
Know Your Enemy 67
Kohner, Paul 52
Koline, Nicholas 6, 187, 191
Koòin, Nikolai see Koline, Nicholas
Korda, Alexander 27, 89, 90, 91, 164, 166
Krasna, Norma 108
Krims, Milton 40, 136, 138
Kurnitz, Harry 108

Laage, Barbara 88, 162, 194
The Lady in the Car with Glasses and a Gun 115, 116, 176–178
Laemmle, Carl, Jr. 34
Lancaster, Burt 80–81, 157, 158
Lane, Priscilla 59, 148
Lang, André 18
Lang, Charles 31, 32, 132
Lanza, Mario 13
Laroche, Guy 107, 173
Lassie, Come Home 61
Laurents, Arthur 73–74, 93, 154, 166, 167, 187
Lawes, Lewis E. 45, 140
Lawrence of Arabia 112
Lederer, Francis 40, 138
Legion of the Damned see *Decision Before Dawn*

Leigh, Vivien 1, 89–91, 164
Levina, Galochka 5
Levine, Joseph E. 115, 187
Levy, Jules 68
Lewis, Albert 28, 61, 130
Lewis, David 47, 50, 51, 136, 143
L'Herbier, Marcel 15
Das Lied einer Nacht 12, 123–124
Lilac see *Coeur de Lilas*
Lilith 57
Lindstrom, Peter 93
Lister, Moira 90, 164
Litvak, Sophie 92, 105, 107, 108, 117, 173
Livingston Potter, Phyllis 29
Lochakoff, Ivan 6, 189, 191
Loewenberg, Wilhelm 20–21
Logan, Josh 67
The Long Night 69–71, 152–154
Look Homeward Angel 102
Lord, Robert 30, 32, 34, 132, 134, 136, 138, 139
Loren, Sophia 106–108, 109, 110, 173, 187, 195
Losey, Joseph 110–111, 186
Lotti, Mariella 77
Low, Warren 35, 134, 136, 142, 146, 157
Lubin, Arthur 68, 186
Lubitsch, Ernst 25
Luceford, Jimmy 59, 148
Lucot, René 10–11
Luguet, André 9, 122
Lukas, Paul 40, 138
Lupino, Ida 57, 58, 146
Lyndon, Barré 34, 134, 135

Macauley, Robert 57
Macbeth 70
The Mad King 101–102, 187
Mademoiselle Docteur 15–16
Mademoiselle Mozart 20
Magnani, Anna 98, 99, 170
Malgat Steur Simone see Litvak, Sophie
The Maltese Falcon 34
March, Fredric 36
March of the Time 42
Marshall, Gen. George C. 65, 82
Martin, Mary 98
Massey, Raymond 97, 179
Matthau, Walter 108, 110, 187
Maugham, Somerset 47, 186
Maurette, Marcelle 93, 166
Mayerling 16, 19–22, 23, 25, 27, 49, 86, 128–130, 194
Mayerling (1957) 96–98, 130, 178
McCarthy, Frank 82, 83
McEnery, John 115, 177
McHugh, Frank 56, 143
McNight, Judge William 44
Meet Me at Dawn 68, 192–193
Mendoza, John 92
Mercouri, Melina 110, 11, 185
Meredith, Burgess 46, 140, 141

Index

Merrill, Gary 83, 159, 196
Meyerhold, Vsevolod 4
Mildred Pierce 74
Milestone, Lewis 61
Miller, Charlie 70
Miller, Yvonne 29
Miracle on 34th Street 12
Mirisch, Harold 108
Mirisch, Marvin 108
Mirisch, Walter 108
Mission to No-Man's Land 102, 184
Montand, Yves 102, 103, 105, 171, 172
Montel, Blanche 25
Montserrat 81, 187
Moorehead, Agnes 78, 159
More, Kenneth 89–90, 91, 164, 166
Moreau, Jeanne 106, 174
Morley, Robert 99, 168
Mosjoukin, Ivan 5, 6, 190, 191
Moulin Rouge 87
Muni, Paul 28, 29, 34, 131
Murat, Jean 17, 127
Murder on the Telephone 78
Le Mystère de la chambre jaune 23

The Naked City 110
Napoleon 5, 9, 189
Natan, Émile 20
Nazi Spies in America 40
The Nazi Strike 65, 180–181
Nébenzahl, Seymour 20, 128
Neff, Hildegard 83–84, 86, 159
Negulesco, Jean 2, 26, 44, 46–47, 52–53, 55, 81, 117, 145, 187
Never Love Again see *Nie wieder Liebe!*
New Orleans Blues 68, 186
Newman, Alfred 96, 150, 154, 157, 166, 168, 180, 181
Nichols, Richard 51, 142
Nie wieder Liebe! 7–8, 85, 120–121, 122
Nielsen, Asta 5, 188
The Night of the Generals 111–115, 174–176, 196
Nocturnes Blues 59
Noiret, Philippe 112, 113, 175
Nolan, Lloyd 59, 148
The Normandy Invasion 67, 184
Novello, Ivor 13, 14, 125
Now, Voyager 37
Nozièr, Fernand 14, 126

Oberon, Merle 47
Odets, Clifford 52
The Old Maid 43
The Old Rogue see *Cette Vielle Canaille*
Old San Francisco 38
Olivier, Laurence 61, 152
One Foot in Heaven 59, 186
Operation Titanic 67, 184
Ophüls, Marcel 8
Ophüls, Max 8

Orry-Kelly 48, 136, 142
Orton, John 12, 123, 125
Osborne, Will 59, 148
O'Toole, Peter 112, 113, 114, 115, 175
Out of the Fog 57–59, 146–147

Pabst, Georg Wilhelm 5, 16, 188
Le Parfum de la dame en noir 23
Parsons, Louella 56
Partos, Frank 73, 74, 154, 157
The Passion of Joan of Arc 17
Patton, Gen. George S. 64
Peck, Gregory 81, 187
Perkins, Anthony 1, 102, 103–105, 106, 107, 108, 109, 110, 171, 172, 173, 195, 196
Perkins, Osgood 105
Perry Mason 39
Peter Pan 98
Peterson, Edgar 65
Petrov, Nikolai 4, 119
The Phantom of the Opera 27, 186
Pier Angeli, Annamaria 87, 88, 164
The Pink Panther 109
Planner, Frank 85, 120, 121, 159
Pleasence, Donald 112, 175
Plummer, Christopher 112–113, 175
Poliakoff, Volodia 17
Polito, Sol 81, 138, 143, 145, 152, 157
Ponti, Carlo 108, 195
Power, Tyrone 54, 61–62, 150, 194
Prelude to War 65, 180
Preminger, Otto 102
Prévert, Jacques 70
Price, Vincent 70, 71, 152
Producer's Showcase 96–97, 98, 130, 178, 179
Psycho 102, 104, 106
Pudovkin, Vsevolod 66

Quinn, Anthony 54, 56, 143

Rabinovitch, Gregor 6, 119, 120, 121, 123, 124, 125, 190, 191
Raft, George 45, 54, 57
Rapper, Irving 36, 37, 38, 59, 136, 138, 141, 143
Rathbone, Basil 33, 132
Rattigan, Terence 89, 90, 164, 165, 166
Raum, Judge Arnold 89
Rebecca 61
Reed, Oliver 116, 177
Renoir, Jean 190
Renoir, Pierre 16
Richardson, Ralph 34
Ridgell, Pinckney 67
Riefenstahl, Leni 42, 65
Rififi 110
The Roaring Twenties 44, 186
Robards, Jason 99, 168, 170
Robin, Dany 87, 88, 162
Robinson, Edward G. 34, 35–36, 40, 41, 42, 60, 135, 135, 136, 138, 140, 186
Roblès, Emmanuel 81, 187

Rogers, Ginger 54, 145
Romée, Marcelle 9, 10, 122
Romero, Cesar 54
Roosevelt, Eleanor 21
Roosevelt, Pres. Frank Delano 38, 40, 53
Ross, Katharine 115
Rossellini, Roberto 93
Rossen, Robert 45, 54, 57, 59, 143, 146, 148
Rubistein, Arthur 108
Rush 101
Rust, Henri 19, 31, 123, 125, 126, 127, 129, 131, 132

Sagan, Françoise 102, 103, 105, 171, 172
Sahara 24–25, 186
Samiy Yuniy Pioner 5, 185
Sanders, George 40, 138
Saturday's Children 47, 186
Schickel, Richard 2
Schiffer, Marcellus 6
Schiffrin, Simon 16, 17, 126
Schneider, Magda 12, 123, 124, 125
Schneider, Romy 12, 110, 185
Schulz, Fritz 12, 123
The Sea Wolf 59, 186
Selepegno, Ann 73
Sellers, Peter 109
Selznick, David O. 25, 61, 75
Selznick, Irene 74
Sharif, Omar 111, 112, 113, 175, 176
Shaw, Irwin 57, 67, 86, 117, 146, 162, 163, 176
Sheherezade see *Geheimnisse des Orients*
Sheridan, Ann 45–47, 54–55, 56, 57, 140, 143, 147
Sherwood, Robert E. 30, 132
Shnayerson, Michael 66
A Shot in the Dark 108
Sidney, Sylvia 27, 54
Siegel, Don 41, 59–60, 148
Signoret, Simone 110
Simpson, Wallis 28
Sirocco 69, 186
The Sisters 36–39, 43, 45, 49, 76, 136–138
Skouras, Spyros 81, 93, 94
The Sky Bum 115, 187
Sleeping Car 13–14, 125–126
The Snake Pit 1, 67, 71–77, 78, 81, 82, 154, 194, 195
Snow, Edgar 66
Sokoloff, Vladimir 21, 129, 134
Somewhere in the World see *Act of Love*
Sorry, Wrong Number 1, 78–81, 82, 89, 157, 194, 195
Spewack, Bella 23
Spiegel, Sam 52, 11, 112, 113–114, 175, 176
Spiegelgass, Leonard 65
Stagecoach 99
Stanislavski, Constantin 4
Stanwyck, Barbara 57, 78–80, 81, 157, 159
The Steeper Cliff 86, 187
Steur Sophie see Litvak, Sophie

Stevens, Mark 76, 155, 157
Stevenson, Maj. Edgar 67
Stewart, James 47
Storm Over America see *Confessions of a Nazi Spy*
The Street of Sorrow see *Die Freudlose Gasse*
Substitution and Conversion 67, 183–184
Sullivan, Ed 96
Suspicion 61
Sydney, Basil 97, 179

Tabori, George 99, 168, 170
Take Care of My Little Girl 81, 187
Tallichet, Margaret "Talli" 69
Tamarin, Dr. Sidney Loseef 73
Tamiroff, Akim 94, 166
Tatiana 4–5, 119
Tea and Sympathy 95
The Teahouse of the August Moon 99
Tell Me Tonight 12, 13, 124–125
10.30 P.M. Summer 110–111
Thalberg, Irving 23
That Certain Smile 102
That Old Bum see *Cette Vielle Canaille*
They Drive by Night 57
They Made Me a Criminal 45
Thirard, Armand 86
The Third Dimension see *Five Miles to Midnight*
This Above All 61–63, 64, 72, 150–152, 194
Tierney, Butch 39
Tierney, Gene 38–39, 73
'Til We Meet Again 47, 186
A Time to Kill see *The Long Night*
The Tin Star 104
Tiomkin, Dimitri 66, 152, 180, 181, 182, 183, 184
Tolstoy, Leo 6, 191
Tone, Franchot 57
Tonight Is Ours 32, 33
Tonight's Our Night see *Tovarich*
Tourgenev, Ivan 4, 187
Tourjansky, Vyacheslav (aka Viktor) 4, 17, 188
Tourneur, Maurice 16, 128
Toutain, Roland 23
Tovarich 27, 30–33, 34, 49, 132–134, 193
Tover, Leo 75, 154
Tozere, Fred 41, 138
Tracy, Spencer 45, 141
Tragödie im House Habsburg 19, 130
Trauner, Alexander 114, 162, 171, 173, 175
The Treasure of Sierra Mother 77
Trevor, Claire 35, 134
Triumph of Will 42, 65
Trouble in Paradise 25
Truman Pres. Harry S. 67
Turrou, Leon G. 39, 40, 138
20,000 Years in Sing Sing 45, 140
Two Different Worlds 101–102, 187
Two Women 106

Up to the Villa 47, 186

Vakhtangov, Yevgeny 4
Vanel, Charles 17, 18, 127
Van Parys, George 16, 126
Van Voorhis, Westbrook 42
Veber, Serge 15, 122, 124, 126, 127
Veiller, Anthony 29, 65, 66, 180, 181, 182, 183
Versini, André-Michel 106, 173
Vertigo 70
Very Young Pioneer see *Samiy Yuniy Pioner*
Die Vetsera see *Das Schicksal derer von Habsburg*
Vidal, Gore 112, 176
Viertel, Peter 82, 92, 99–100, 106, 117, 159, 168, 173
Villa on the Hill 47, 186
Volkoff, Alexander 5, 6, 189, 190, 191
Von Cube, Irma 7, 12, 16–17, 19, 119, 120, 121, 123, 124, 125, 128

Wagner, Fritz Arno 12, 119, 123, 124, 125
Wallis, Hal 35, 39, 40, 42, 44, 50, 51, 58, 59–60, 78, 80, 132, 134, 136, 138, 139, 141, 143, 146, 148, 157, 159
Walsh, Raoul 44, 54, 55, 186
Wanger, Walter 24–25, 27
War Comes to America 65, 183
Ward, Mary Jane 71, 72, 154
Warner, Anne 42
Warner, Harry 39, 43
Warner, Jack 25, 27, 28, 33, 35, 36, 39, 42, 44, 50, 54, 55, 57, 58, 141, 196
Der Weisse Teufel see *The White Devil*

Welles, Orson 92, 196
Werner, Oskar 83, 86, 159
Wessel, Kai 86
Wexley, John 34, 54, 134, 138, 143, 152
Weyl, Carl Jules 48, 57, 134, 136, 138, 142, 146
Wheeler, Hugh 106, 173
When Tomorrow Comes 46
The White Devil 5, 6, 191–192
Whorf, Richard 59, 148
Why We Fight 65–67, 180, 181, 182, 183
Wilder, Billy 52, 68, 82
Willems, Jeroen 86
Williams, Emlyn 91, 164
Willoughby, Bob 116
Withers, Googie 89
Witta, Jean 16–17, 20–21, 25, 86, 116
The Woman I Love 19, 28–29, 30, 130–132
Wonder Bar 32
Wong Howe, George 143, 145, 146
The World of Sophia Loren 107, 195
Wuthering Heights 26, 186
Wyler, William 49, 52, 68, 69, 196
Wyman, Jane 81, 93
Wynward, Diana 97, 179

Years Without Days see *Castle on the Huston*
Youngest Pioneer see *Samiy Yuniy Pioner*

Zanuck, Darryl 61, 62, 65, 72–73, 74, 75, 77, 81, 82, 86, 89, 92, 93, 150, 154, 194
Zizler, Wolfgang 41
Zuckmeier, Carl 85

www.ingramcontent.com/pod-product-compliance
Ingram Content Group UK Ltd.
Pitfield, Milton Keynes, MK11 3LW, UK
UKHW041959140426
5217IPUK00015B/878